CASTES IN INDIA : A HISTORICAL PERSPECTIVES

CASTES IN INDIA : A HISTORICAL PERSPECTIVES

S.K.PANIGRAHI

CYBER TECH PUBLICATIONS
4264/3, Ansari Road, Daryaganj, New Delhi-110002 (India)
Ph.: 011-23244078, 011-43559448 Fax: 011-23280028
E-Mail: cyberpublicationsdelhi@yahoo.com
Website: www.cybertechpublications.com

CASTES IN INDIA : A HISTORICAL PERSPECTIVES

S.K.PANIGRAHI

First Edition 2011

Published by :

G.S. Rawat for Cyber Tech Publications
4264/3, Ansari Road, Daryaganj, New Delhi-110002 (India)
Ph.: 011-23244078, 011-43559448 Fax: 011-23280028
E-Mail: cyberpublicationsdelhi@yahoo.com
Website: www.cybertechpublications.com

Printed at: Asian Offset Printers, Delhi-53

PREFACE

There are different theories about the establishment of the caste system. There are religious-mystical theories. There are biological theories. And there are socio-historical theories.

The religious theories explain how the four Varnas were founded, but they do not explain how the Jats in each Varna or the untouchables were founded. According the Rig Veda, the ancient Hindu book, the primal man-Purush-destroyed himself to create a human society. The different Varnas were created from different parts of his body. The Brahmans were created from his head; the Kshatriyas from his hands; the Vaishyas from his thighs and the Sudras from his feet. The Varna hierarchy is determined by the descending order of the different organs from which the Varnas were created. Other religious theory claims that the Varnas were created from the body organs of Brahma, who is the creator of the world.

The biological theory claims that all existing things, animated and inanimated, inherent three qualities in different apportionment. Sattva qualities include wisdom, intelligence, honesty, goodness and other positive qualities. Rajas include qualities like passion, pride, valour and other passionate qualities. Tamas qualities include dullness, stupidity, lack of creativity and other negative qualities. People with different doses of these inherent qualities adopted different types of occupation.

According to this theory the Brahmans inherent Sattva qualities. Kshatriyas and Vaishyas inherent Rajas qualities. And the Sudras inherent Tamas qualities.

Like human beings, food also inherents different dosage of these qualities and it affects its eater's intelligence. The Brahmans and the Vaishyas have Sattvic diet which includes fruits, milk, honey, roots and vegetables. Most of the meats are considered to have Tamasic qualities. Many Sudra communities eat different kinds of meat (but not beef) and other Tamasic food. But the Kshatriyas who had Rajasic diet eat some kinds of meat like deer meat which is considered to have Rajasic qualities. Many Marathas who claim to be Kshatriyas eat mutton. The drawback of this theory is that in different parts of India the same food was sometimes qualified to have different dosage of inherent qualities. For example there were Brahmans who eat meat which is considered Tamasic food.

The social historical theory explains the creation of the Varnas, Jats and of the untouchables. According to this theory, the caste system begaen with the arrival of the Aryans in India. The Aryans arrived in India around 1500 BC. The fair skinned Aryans arrived in India from south Europe and north Asia. Before the Aryans there were other communities in India of other origins. Among them Negrito, Mongoloid, Austroloid and Dravidian. The Negrito have physical features similar to people of Africa. The Mongoloid have Chinese features. The Austroloids have features similar the aboriginals of Australia. The Dravidians originate from the Mediterranean and they were the largest community in India. When the Aryans arrived in India their main contact was with the Dravidians and the Austroloids. The Aryans disregarded the local cultures. They began conquering and taking control over regions in north India and at the same time pushed the local people southwards or towards the jungles and mountains in north India.

—Author

CONTENTS

1

HISTORY OF THE INDIAN CASTES

INTRODUCTION

Some researchers believe that the caste system began with the Indo-Aryan migration to India. The early Indo-Aryans organized among themselves in groups that later led to the caste system. A 2001 study, led by Michael Bamshad of the University of Utah, revealed that Indians belonging to higher castes are genetically closer to Europeans than are individuals from lower castes, whose genetic profiles are closer to those of Asians. The researchers believe their results support the theory that Europeans who migrated into India may have merged with or imposed their social structure on the native northern Indians and placed themselves into the highest castes.

However, the theory of Indo-Aryan migration itself is a highly disputed topic. The critics claim that it was formulated to undermine the historical significance of India, and was exploited by the British to show that they had the right to invade India, as the Indians supposedly themselves were invaders. A 2006 genetic study by India's National Institute of Biologicals supported the idea that Indians have acquired few genes from Europeans, thus disputing the Aryan Invasion Theory.

Megasthenes, the Greek ambassador to Chandragupta Maurya's court in India classified people of India into seven classes: philosophers, peasants, herdsmen, craftsmen and traders, soldiers, government officials and councillors.

Hindu Scriptures: Although the Hindu scriptures contain some passages that can be interpreted to sanction the caste system, they also contain indications that the caste system is not an essential part of the Hindu religion, and both sides in the debate are able to find sections in scriptures that support their views.

The most ancient scriptures-the Shruti texts, or Vedas, place very little importance on the caste system, mentioning caste only rarely and in a cursory manner. A hymn from the Rig Veda seems to indicate that one's caste is not necessarily determined by that of one's family:

I am a bard, my father is a physician, my mother's job is to grind the corn. Rig Veda 9.112.3

In the Vedic period, there also seems to no discrimination against the Shudras (which later became an ensemble of the so-called low-castes) on the issue of hearing the sacred words of the Vedas and fully participating in all religious rights, something which became totally banned in the later times.

Later scriptures such as Bhagavad Gita and Manusmriti state that the four varnas are created by God. However, at the same time, the Gita says that one's varna is to be understood from one's personal qualities and one's karma (work), not one's birth. Some scholars believe that, in its initial period, the caste system was flexible and it was merit and job based. One could migrate from one caste to other caste by changing one's profession. This view is supported by records of sages who became Brahmans. For example, the sage Vishvamitra belonged to a Kshatriya caste, and only later became recognized as a great Brahmin sage, indicating that his caste was not determined by birth. Similarly, Valmiki, once a low-caste robber, became a great sage. Veda Vyasa, another sage, was the son of a fisherwoman. Vashishtha was a shudra and he became sage later.

Manusmriti, dated between 200 BC and 100 AD, contains some laws that codified the caste system. Varna is mentioned as caste equivalent in Manusmriti. However, the Puranas use the term in the context of skin colour too. Manusmriti and some other shastras mention four varnas: The Brahmins (teachers, scholars and priests), the Kshatriyas (kings and warriors), the Vaishyas (traders, landowners and some artisan groups), and Shudras (agriculturists, service providers, and some artisan groups). Another group of untouchables excluded from the main society was called Parjanya or Antyaja. A varna can be viewed as a group of castes or a social division that consists of various sub-castes called jatis.

Passages in Manusmriti and other scriptures suggest that the Indian caste system was originally non-hereditary:

> *As the son of Shudra can attain the rank of a Brahman, the son of Brahman can attain rank of a Shudra. Even so with him who is born of a Vaishya or a Kshatriya*
> *Manu Smriti X:65*

The various smritis, like the Yagnavalkyasmriti and the Manusmriti strongly disapprove of marrying outside one's caste. The smritis also argue that new, despicable castes are formed out of such cases. According to these smritis, the chamars were born out of the union of a vaideha and a nishada, the chandals were born out of the sexual relations between a Brahmin and a Shudra.

Historical Advantages of the Caste System: Historically, the caste system offered several advantages to the population of the Indian subcontinent:

1. Preservation of order in society through the use of institutional stratification of social groups.
2. Integration of foreigners and invading forces into Indian culture by assigning a caste to them (a process that historian Jawaharlal Nehru referred to as "Indianization"): India has faced repeated invasions from outside the region, dating back to the Macedoniaan invasion by Alexander the Great. Most invaders were swiftly assimilated into ancient Indian society by assigning them specific castes. Examples include the Kambojas, believed to be of Indo-Scythian descent, who were retroactively assigned a social position in the Manusmriti.
3. The Varna system, with its normative interpretation as a division of labour, had and continues to have a heavy bias towards spiritual evolution. The deep religious proclivities and the urge for spiritual uplift had induced the people to search for simpler and effective ways to achieve the spiritual goal which led to innovations like

the Bhakti movement which had a powerful impact on the socio-cultural-spiritual life of the people even at mass level without distinctions of caste or class or other social differences. It is these deeply run cultural roots which caused an abiding following for Hinduism even in the face of unrelenting assaults by other religions and had in fact continued to influence the lives of people even after their conversion to other faiths. Thus, the caste system can be said to have preserved ancient cultural values in Indian society.

4. The caste system played an influential role in shaping economic activities. The caste system functioned much like medieval European guilds, ensuring the division of labour, providing for the training of apprentices and, in some cases, allowing manufacturers to achieve narrow specialisation. For instance, in certain regions, producing each variety of cloth was the speciality of a particular sub-caste.
5. Philosophers argue that the majority of people would be comfortable in stratified endogamous groups and have been in ancient times. Membership in a particular caste, with its associated narrative, history and genealogy would instill in its members a sense of group accomplishment and cultural pride. Such sentiments are routinely expressed by the Marathas, for instance.

Emergence of Rigid Caste Structures: In its later stages, the caste system is said to have become rigid, and caste began to be inherited rather than acquired by merit. In the past, members of different castes would not partake in various activities, such as dining and religious gatherings, together. In addition, the performance of religious rites and rituals were restricted to Brahmins, who were the designated priesthood. In recent years, more egalitarian reforms have enabled lower castes and even outcastes such as the Dalits to become religious clerics.

The "Pandaram" priests are an example of an order of Dalit priests, based in Nepal and South India. The Pandaram maintain the same tradition as the Brahmin priests, including the use of the Sanskrit language (traditionally reserved for the

Brahmins) for the rituals. While they are not generally as well trained as the Brahmin priests, they are highly respected within their community and are addressed with reverence.

According to the Manusmriti, every caste belongs to one of the four varnas (Brahmin, Kshatriya, Vaishya, and Shudra). However, there have been many disputes about the varna of many castes, such as castes being considered Kshatriya by some scholars, while described as Shudra by others.

While texts such as the Manusmriti attempted to rationalize ambiguous castes by placing them in varna-sankaras (i.e. mixed varna), the fact remains that Indian society was, and is, composed of numerous geographically diversified but endogamous groups. With many occupational groups practicing endogamy within a particular region, as well as numerous sub-divisions within the four main castes, a more complex system of sub-castes and jatis is evident. The jatis have broken up into clans like Agarwal, Iyer, etc.

Mobility Across the Castes: The view of the caste system as "static and unchanging" has been disputed by many scholars. For instance, sociolgists such as Bernard Buber and Marriott McKim describe how the perception of the caste system as a static and textual stratification has given way to the perception of the caste system as a more processual, emprical and contextual stratification. Other sociologists such as Y.B Damle have applied theoretical models to explain mobility and flexibility in the caste system in India.. According to these scholars, groups of lower-caste individuals could seek to elevate the status of their caste by attempting to emulate the practices of higher castes.

Flexibility in caste laws permitted very low-caste religious clerics such as Valmiki (of the Naga tribal caste) to compose the Ramayana, which became a central work of Hindu scripture.

According to some economists, mobility across broad caste lines may have been "minimal", though sub-castes (jatis) may change their social status over the generations by fission, re-location, and adoption of new rituals..

Sociologist M. N. Srinivas has also debated the question of rigidity in Caste. In an ethnographic study of the Coorgs of Karnataka, he observed considerable flexibility and mobility in their caste hierarchies. He asserts that the caste system is far from a rigid system in which the position of each component caste is fixed for all time. Movement has always been possible, and especially in the middle regions of the hierarchy.

It was always possible for groups born into a lower caste to "rise to a higher position by adopting vegetarianism and teetotalism" i.e. adopt the customs of the higher castes. While theoretically "forbidden", the process was not uncommon in practice. The concept of sanskritization, or the adoption of upper-caste norms by the lower castes, addressed the actual complexity and fluidity of caste relations.

Historical examples of mobility in the Indian Caste System among Hindus have been researched. The "Noniya" Caste of salt makers have claimed to the higher status of the "Chauhan Rajput". They have risen well above the untouchable line and their leaders have, in the past, mobilized upwards along the caste hierarchy. There is also precedent of certain Shudra families within the temples of the Shrivaishava sect in South India elevating their caste.

British Rule: The caste system was first exposed to the modern Western world during the Portuguese occupation and rule of sections of India. The word 'caste' in this context is derived from the Portuguese, 'casta'. Later, other European empires, including the British, occupied parts of the subcontinent. British anthropologist Herbert Risley's The Tribes and Castes of Bengal, published in 1892, was one of the first works on the caste system in India written by a Western scholar. Some scholars state that the caste system was broken up greatly during British Raj in India. However, some other historians suggest that the impact of British reforms has been greatly exaggerated.

Initially, the British strengthened the caste system. They gave the Brahmins back special privileges the Muslim rulers had taken away. During the initial days of British East India Company's rules, caste privileges and customs were encouraged in the Bengal Army. But, British law courts disagreed with the discrimination against the lower castes. Many believe that the lack of British respect for sepoys' caste traditions was one of the reasons behind the Indian Rebellion of 1857.

During British rule, the reservation of seats for the "Depressed Classes" was incorporated into the Government of India Act 1935, which went into force in 1937. The Act brought the term "Scheduled castes" into use, which was later clarified in The Government of India (Scheduled Castes) Order, 1936 which contained a list of scheduled castes.

British Census Officers determined caste hierarchy based on the principle, e.g. someone who accepts food and water from another person but the other person does not reciprocate the same way, then the other person is superior to the former. It was contested at many places (a notable example is that the Koris of UP who said they won't accept water from Brahmins, and so should be placed higher than them). Because it was met with rampant controversies, arbitration was very common during those days. The most notable arbitration stories are:

1. Caste status of Bhumihar
2. Caste status of Kayastha
3. Caste status of Kurmi
4. Caste status of Yadav

It raised more questions than it answered and subsequent census records varied radically, making it free for all, after some time.

Major Caste Groups: According to the 1891 census data, the major caste groups in India were following (listed in the order of population):

Caste-group	*Example*	*Population %*
Cultivators	Kurmi, Mali, Lodha	20%
Village Menials	Chamar, Dosadh, Dom	13%
Military	Jat, Rajput, Maratha	12%
Artisans	Lohar, Sunar, Julaha	12%
Pastoral	Ahir, Gadaria, Dhangar	7%
Forest tribes	Santhal, Gond, Bhil	7%
Professionals	Nambudri, Bhat, Kayasth	6%
Services	Nai, Dhobi, Kandoi	6%
Traders	Agrawal, Khatri, Balija, Barnwal	5%

Labourers	Musahar, Bagdi, Bawari	3%
Fishers	Kahar, Mallah	3%
Other professionals	Vaidya, Mirasi, Bhand	2%
Vagrants	Waddar, Nat, Beldar	1%

Reform Movements: Traditionally, Dalits (Untouchable Castes) were not allowed to let their shadows fall upon a non-Dalit caste member (particularly a Brahmin, for fear of ritually contaminating them), and they were required to sweep the ground where they walk to remove the 'contamination' of their footfalls. Dalits were forbidden to worship in temples or draw water from the same wells as caste Hindus, and they usually lived in segregated neighbourhoods outside the main village.

However, there have been cases of upper caste Hindus warming to the Dalits and Hindu priests, demoted to outcaste ranks, who continued practising the religion. An example of the latter was Dnyaneshwar, who was excommunicated into Dalit status from society in the 13th century, but continued to compose the Dnyaneshwari, a Dharmic commentary on the Bhagawad Gita. Other excommunicated Brahmins, such as Eknath, fought for the rights of untouchables during the Bhakti period.

Historical examples of Dalit priests include Chokhamela in the 14th Century, who was India's first recorded Dalit poet, Raidas, born into Dalit cobblers, and others. The 15th century saint Ramananda also accepted all castes, including untouchables, into his fold. Most of these saints subscribed to the Bhakti movements in Hinduism during the medieval period that rejected casteism. Nandanar, a low-caste Hindu cleric, also rejected casteism and accepted Dalits.

Many movements in Hinduism have welcomed Dalits into their fold, the earliest being the Bhakti movements of the medieval period. Early Dalit politics involved many Hindu reform movements which arose primarily as a reaction to the advent of Christian Missionaries in India and their attempts to mass-convert Dalits to Christianity under the allure of escaping the caste system (however, the Caste system among Indian Christians remained in full force even after conversions).

In the 19th Century, the Brahmo Samaj under Raja Ram Mohan Roy, actively campaigned against untouchability. The Arya Samaj founded by Swami Dayanand also renounced discrimination against Dalits. Sri Ramakrishna Paramahamsa founded the Ramakrishna Mission that participated in the emancipation of Dalits. Upper caste Hindus, such as Mannathu Padmanabhan also participated in movements to abolish Untouchability against Dalits, opening his family temple for Dalits to worship. While there always have been places for Dalits to worship, the first "upper-caste" temple to openly welcome Dalits into their fold was the Laxminarayan Temple in Wardha in the year 1928 (the move was spearheaded by reformer Jamnalal Bajaj). Also, the Satnami movement was founded by Guru Ghasidas a Dalit himself. Other reformers, such as Mahatma Jyotirao Phule also worked for the emancipation of Dalits. Another example of Dalit emancipation was the Temple Entry Proclamation issued by the last Maharaja of Travancore in the Indian state of Kerala in the year 1936. The Maharaja proclaimed that "outcastes should not be denied the consolations and the solace of the Hindu faith". Even today, the Sri Padmanabhaswamy temple that first welcomed Dalits in the state of Kerala is revered by the Dalit Hindu community.

The 1930s saw key struggles between Mahatma Gandhi and B.R. Ambedkar, most notably over whether Dalits would have separate electorates or joint electorates with reserved seats. The Indian National Congress was the only national organisation with a large Dalit following, but Gandhi failed to gain their commitment. Ambedkar, a Dalit himself, developed a deeper analysis of Untouchability, but lacked a workable political strategy: his conversion to Buddhism in 1956, along with millions of followers, highlighted the failure of his political endeavours. India's first Prime Minister, Jawaharlal Nehru, based on his own relationship with Dalit reformer Ambedkar, also spread information about the dire need to eradicate untouchability for the benefit of the Dalit community.

In more contemporary times, India has had an elected Dalit president, K. R. Narayanan, who has stated that he was well-treated in his community of largely upper-caste Hindus (24 July 2002). Another popular Harijan includes Babaji

Palwankar Baloo, who joined the Hindu Mahasabha and was both a politician and a cricketer. He was an independence fighter. In addition, other Hindu groups have reached out to the Dalit community in an effort to reconcile with them, with productive results. On August 2006, Dalit activist Namdeo Dhasal engaged in dialogue with the Rashtriya Swayamsevak Sangh in an attempt to "bury the hatchet".

Also, the "Pandaram" are an order of Dalit Hindu priests (a task traditionally reserved for the Brahmins) based largely in Nepal and parts of South India. These Pandaram priests maintain the same tradition as the Brahmin priests, including using Sanskrit for the rituals (a language traditionally reserved for the Brahmins). They perform religious ceremonies from weddings to death rituals. They are not generally as well trained as the Brahmin priests, but are highly respected within their community and are addressed reverentially. Also, Hindu temples are increasingly more receptive to Dalit priests, such as Suryavanshi Das, the Dalit priest of a notable temple in Bihar.

Discrimination against Hindu Dalits is on a slow but steady decline. Many Hindu Dalits have achieved affluence in society, although vast millions still remain poor. Recent episodes of Caste-related violence in India have adversely affected the Dalit community. In urban India, discrimination against Dalits in the public sphere is largely disappeared, but rural Dalits are struggling to elevate themselves. Government organizations and NGO's work to emancipate them from discrimination, and many Hindu organizations have spoken in their favour.

Religious form of Caste System

In Hinduism there exists four castes arranged in a hierarchy. Anyone who does not belong to one of these castes is an outcast. The religious word for caste is 'Varna'. Each Varna has certain duties and rights. Each Varna members have to work in certain occupation which only that Varna members are allowed. Each Varna has certain type of diet. The highest Varna is of the Brahman. Members of this class are priests and the educated people of the society. The Varna after them in hierarchy is Kshatriya. The members of this class are the rulers and aristocrats of the society. After them are the

Vaishya. Members of this class are the landlords and businessmen of the society. After them in hierarchy are the Sudra. Members of this class are the peasants and working class of the society who work in non-polluting jobs. The caste hierarchy ends here. Below these castes are the outcasts who are untouchable to the four castes. These Untouchables worked in degrading jobs like cleaning, sewage etc.

The first three castes had social and economical rights which the Sudra and the untouchables did not have. The first three castes are also seen as 'twice born'. The intention in these two births is to the natural birth and to the ceremonial entrance to the society at a much later age. Each Varna and also the untouchables are divided into many communities. These communities are called Jat or Jati (The caste is also used instead of Jat). For example the Brahmans have Jats called Gaur, Kokanastha, Sarasvat, Iyer and others. The outcasts have Jats like Mahar, Dhed, Mala, Madiga and others. The Sudra is the largest Varna and it has the largest number of communities. Each Jat is limited to professions worthy of their Varna. Each Jat is limited to the Varna diet. Each Jat members are allowed to marry only with their Jat members. People are born into their Jat and it cannot be changed.

This is the how the caste system is supposed to be in its religious form. But in reality it is much more complicated and different from its religious form.

Beginning of the Caste System

There are different theories about the establishment of the caste system. There are religious-mystical theories. There are biological theories. And there are socio-historical theories.

The religious theories explain how the four Varnas were founded, but they do not explain how the Jats in each Varna or the untouchables were founded. According the Rig Veda, the ancient Hindu book, the primal man-Purush-destroyed himself to create a human society. The different Varnas were created from different parts of his body. The Brahmans were created from his head; the Kshatriyas from his hands; the Vaishyas from his thighs and the Sudras from his feet. The Varna hierarchy is determined by the descending order of the different organs from which the Varnas were created. Other religious theory claims that the Varnas were created from the body organs of Brahma, who is the creator of the world.

The biological theory claims that all existing things, animated and inanimated, inherent three qualities in different apportionment. Sattva qualities include wisdom, intelligence, honesty, goodness and other positive qualities. Rajas include qualities like passion, pride, valour and other passionate qualities. Tamas qualities include dullness, stupidity, lack of creativity and other negative qualities. People with different doses of these inherent qualities adopted different types of occupation.

According to this theory the Brahmans inherent Sattva qualities. Kshatriyas and Vaishyas inherent Rajas qualities. And the Sudras inherent Tamas qualities.

Like human beings, food also inherents different dosage of these qualities and it affects its eater's intelligence. The Brahmans and the Vaishyas have Sattvic diet which includes fruits, milk, honey, roots and vegetables. Most of the meats are considered to have Tamasic qualities. Many Sudra communities eat different kinds of meat (but not beef) and other Tamasic food. But the Kshatriyas who had Rajasic diet eat some kinds of meat like deer meat which is considered to have Rajasic qualities. Many Marathas who claim to be Kshatriyas eat mutton. The drawback of this theory is that in different parts of India the same food was sometimes qualified to have different dosage of inherent qualities. For example there were Brahmans who eat meat which is considered Tamasic food.

The social historical theory explains the creation of the Varnas, Jats and of the untouchables. According to this theory, the caste system began with the arrival of the Aryans in India. The Aryans arrived in India around 1500 BC. The fair skinned Aryans arrived in India from south Europe and north Asia. Before the Aryans there were other communities in India of other origins. Among them Negrito, Mongoloid, Austroloid and Dravidian. The Negrito have physical features similar to people of Africa. The Mongoloid have Chinese features. The Austroloids have features similar the aboriginals of Australia. The Dravidians originate from the Mediterranean and they were the largest community in India. When the Aryans arrived in India their main contact was with the Dravidians and the Austroloids. The Aryans disregarded the local cultures. They began conquering and taking control over regions in north India and at the same time pushed the local people southwards or towards the jungles and mountains in north India.

The Aryans organized among themselves in three groups. The first group was of the warriors and they were called Rajayana, later they changed their name Rajayana to Kshatriya. The second group was of the priests and they were called Brahmans. These two groups struggled politically for leadership among the Aryans. In this struggle the Brahmans got to be the leaders of the Aryan society. The third group was of the farmers and craftsmen and they were called Vaishya. The Aryans who conquered and took control over parts of north India subdued the locals and made them their servants. In this process the Vaishyas who were the farmers and the craftsmen became the landlords and the businessmen of the society and the locals became the peasants and the craftsmen of the society.

In order to secure their status the Aryans resolved some social and religious rules which, allowed only them to be the priests, warriors and the businessmen of the society. For example take Maharashtra. Maharashtra is in west India. This region is known by this name for hundreds of years. Many think that the meaning of the name Maharashtra is in its name, Great Land. But there are some who claim that the name, Maharashtra, is derived from the Jat called Mahar who are considered to be the original people of this region. In the caste hierarchy the dark skinned Mahars were outcasts. The skin colour was an important factor in the caste system. The meaning of the word "Varna" is not class or status but skin colour.

Between the outcasts and the three Aryan Varnas there is the Sudra Varna who are the simple workers of the society. The Sudras consisted of two communities. One community was of the locals who were subdued by the Aryans and the other were the descendants of Aryans with locals. In Hindu religious stories there are many wars between the good Aryans and the dark skinned demons and devils. The different Gods also have dark skinned slaves. There are stories of demon women trying to seduce good Aryan men in deceptive ways. There were also marriages between Aryan heroes and demon women. Many believe that these incidences really occurred in which, the gods and the positive heroes were people of Aryan origin. And the demons, the devils and the dark skinned slaves were in fact the original residence of India whom the Aryans coined as monsters, devil, demons and slaves.

As in most of the societies of the world, so in India, the son inherited his father's profession. And so in India there developed families, who professed the same family profession for generation in which, the son continued his father's profession. Later on as these families became larger, they were seen as communities or as they are called in Indian languages, Jat. Different families who professed the same profession developed social relations between them and organized as a common community, meaning Jat.

Later on the Aryans who created the caste system, added to their system non-Aryans. Different Jats who professed different professions were integrated in different Varnas according to their profession. Other foreign invaders of ancient India-Greeks, Huns, Scythains and others-who conquered parts of India and created kingdoms were integrated in the Kshatriya Varna (warrior castes). But probably the Aryan policy was not to integrate original Indian communities within them and therefore many aristocratic and warrior communities that were in India before the Aryans did not get the Kshatriya status.

Most of the communities that were in India before the arrival of the Aryans were integrated in the Sudra Varna or were made outcast depending on the professions of these communities. Communities who professed non-polluting jobs were integrated in Sudra Varna. And communities who professed polluting professions were made outcasts. The Brahmans are very strict about cleanliness. In the past people believed that diseases can also spread also through air and not only through physical touch. Perhaps because of this reason the untouchables were not only disallowed to touch the high caste communities but they also had to stand at a certain distance from the high castes.

Caste and Stages of Life in Hinduism

The pattern of social classes in Hinduism is called the "caste system." The chart shows the major divisions and contents of the system. Basic caste is called *varna*, or "colour." Sub-caste, or *jati*, "birth, life, rank," is a traditional subdivision of *varna*.

The *Bhagavad Gita* says this about the varnas:

> *The works of Brahmins, Kshatriyas, Vaishyas, and Shudras are different, in harmony with the three powers of their born nature. The works of a Brahmin are peace; self-harmony, austerity, and purity; loving-forgiveness and righteousness; vision and wisdom and faith.*

These are the works of a Kshatriya: a heroic mind, inner fire, constancy, resourcefulness, courage in battle, generosity and noble leadership. Trade, agriculture and the rearing of cattle is the work of a Vaishya. And the work of the Shudra is service.

There are literally thousands of sub-castes in India, often with particular geographical ranges, occupational specializations, and an administrative or corporate structure. When Mahatma Gandhi wanted to go to England to study law, he had to ask his sub-caste, the Modh Bania, for permission to leave India. ("Bania", means "merchant," and "Gandhi" means "greengrocer"—from *gandha*, "smell, fragrance," in Sanskrit—and that should be enough for a good guess that Gandhi was a Vaishya.) Sometimes it is denied that the varnas are "castes" because, while "true" castes, the jatis, are based on birth, the varnas are based on the theory of the gunas (the "three powers" mentioned in the Gita). This is no more than a rationalization: the varnas came first, and they *are* based on birth. The gunas came later, and provide a poor explanation anyway, since the guna *tamas* is associated with both twice born and once born, caste and outcaste, overlapping the most important religious and social divisions in the system. Nevertheless, the varnas are now divisions at a theoretical level, while the jatis are the way in which caste is embodied for most practical purposes. Jatis themselves can be ranked in relation to each other, and occasionally a question may even be raised about the proper varna to which a particular jati belongs. As jati members change occupations and they rise in prestige, a jati may rarely even be elevated in the varna to which it is regarded as belonging.

Associated with each varna there is a traditional colour. These sound suspiciously like skin colours; and, indeed, there is an expectation in India that higher caste people will have lighter skin—although there are plenty of exceptions (especially in the South of India). This all probably goes back to the original invasion of the Arya, who came from Central Asia and so were undoubtedly light skinned. The people already in India were quite dark, even as today many people in India seem positively black. Apart from skin colour, Indians otherwise have "Caucasian" features—narrow noses, thin lips, etc.—and recent genetic mapping studies seem to show that Indians are more closely related to the people of the Middle East and Europe than to anyone else. Because Untouchables are not a varna, they do not have a traditional colour. I have supplied blue, since this is otherwise not found, and it is traditionally used for the skin colour of Vishnu and his incarnations. Chief among those is *Krishna* whose *name* actually means "black" or "dark," but he is always shown blue rather than with some natural skin colour.

The first three varnas are called the *twice born*. This has *nothing* to do with reincarnation. Being "twice born" means that you *come of age* religiously, making you a member of the Vedic religion, eligible to learn Sanskrit, study the Vedas, and perform Vedic rituals. The "second birth" is thus like Confirmation or a Bar Mitzvah. According to the *Laws of Manu* (whose requirements may not always be observed in modern life), boys are "born again" at specific ages: 8 for Brahmins; 11 for Kshatriyas; and 12 for Vaishyas. A thread is bestowed at the coming of age to be worn around the waist as the symbol of being twice born. The equivalent of coming of age for girls is marriage. The bestowal of the thread is part of the wedding ceremony. That part of the wedding ritual is even preserved in Jainism. Ancient Iran also had a coming of age ceremony that involved a thread. That and other evidence leads to the speculation that the *three* classes of the twice born are from the original Indo-European social system—the theory of George Dumezil. Even the distant Celts believed in three social classes. The three classes of Plato's *Republic* thus may not have been entirely his idea. Although there must have been a great deal of early intermarriage in India, nowhere did such an Indo-European social system become as rigid a system of *birth* as there. The rigidity may well be due to the influence of the idea of *karma*, that poor birth is morally deserved. According to the *Laws of Manu*, when the twice born come of age, they enter into the four *ashramas* or "stages of life."

1. The first is the *brahmacharya*, or the stage of the student (*brahmacharin*). For boys, the student is supposed to go live with a teacher (*guru*), who is a Brahmin, to learn about Sanskrit, the Vedas, rituals, etc. The *dharma* of a student includes being obedient, respectful, celibate, and nonviolent. "The teacher is God." For girls, the stage of studenthood coincides with that of the householder, and the husband stands in the place of the teacher. Since the boys are supposed to be celibate while students, Gandhi used the term *brahmachari* to mean the celibate practitioner that he thought made the best *Satyagrahi*, the best nonviolent activist.
2. The second stage is the *garhastya*, or the stage of the householder, which is taken far more seriously in Hinduism than in Jainism or Buddhism and is usually regarded as mandatory, like studenthood, although debate continued over the centuries whether or not this stage could be skipped in favour of a later one. This is the stage where the principal *dharma* of the person is performed, whether as priest, warrior, etc., or for women mainly as wife and mother. Arjuna's duty to fight the battle in the *Bhagavad Gita* comes from his status as a householder. Besides specific duties, there are general duties that pay off the "three debts": (1) a debt to the ancestors that is discharged by marrying and having children; (2) a debt to the gods that is discharged by the household rituals and sacrifices; and (3) a debt to the teacher that is discharged by appropriately teaching one's wife, children, and, for Brahmins, other students. The three debts are sometimes associated with the three

Gods of the Trimurti—the ancestor debt with Brahma, the gods debt with Vishnu, and the teacher debt with Shiva.

3. The third stage is the *vanaprastya*, or the stage of the forest dweller. This may be entered into optionally if (ideally) one's hair has become gray, one's skin wrinkled, and grandchildren exist to carry on the family. Husbands and wives may leave their affairs and possessions with their children and retire together to the forest as hermits. This does not involve the complete renunciation of the world, for husbands and wives can still have sex (once a month), and a sacred fire still should be kept and minimal rituals performed. This stage is thus not entirely free of *dharma*. The Forest Treatises were supposed to have been written by or for forest dwellers, who have mostly renounced the world and have begun to consider liberation. I am not aware that forest dwelling is still practiced in the traditional way. The modern alternatives seem to consist of the more stark opposition between householding and becoming a wandering ascetic. Nevertheless, forest dwelling is an institution that doesn't really develop as such in Jainism and Buddhism. The idea that husbands and wives would engage in ascetic practices together, without celibacy, would appear extraordinary. In those terms, it is an unfortunate loss if the institution does not continue in modern Hinduism.
4. The fourth stage is the *sannyasa*, or the stage of the wandering ascetic, the *sannyasin* (or *sadhu*). If a man desires, he may continue on to this stage, but his wife will need to return home; traditionally she cannot stay alone as a forest dweller or wander the highways as an ascetic. The *sannyasin* has renounced the world completely, is regarded as dead by his family (the funeral is held), and is finally beyond all *dharma* and caste. When a *sannyasin* enters a Hindu temple, he is not a worshipper but one of the objects of worship. Not even the gods are *sanyasins* (they are householders), and so this is where in Hinduism, as in Jainism and Buddhism, it is possible for human beings to be spiritually superior

to the gods. It has long been a matter of dispute in Hinduism whether one need really fulfil the requirements of the *Laws of Manu* (gray hair, etc.) to renounce the world. The Mahabharata says that Brahmins may go directly to Renunciation, but it also says that the three debts must be paid—and the debt to the ancestors could only be paid with husbands and wives living together either as householders or, if renunciates, as forest dwellers (indeed, the Pandavas are all born in that way). There are definitely no such requirements in Jainism or Buddhism. The Buddha left his family right after his wife had a baby, which would put him in the middle of his *dharma* as a householder. Buddhism and Jainism thus developed *monastic* institutions, with monks and nuns, but these did not really develop as such in Hinduism: While wandering ascetics are rather like mendicant monks, we lack monasteries and nuns, and the ascetics are, traditionally, supposed to have already lived something like a normal, lay life.

The four stages of life may, somewhat improbably, be associated with the four parts of the Vedas: the samhitas with the stage of the student, who is particularly obligated to learn them; the Brahmans with the stage of the householder, who is able to regulate his ritual behaviour according to them; the aranyakas with the stage of the forest dweller, who regulates his ritual behaviour according to them and who begins to contemplate liberation; and finally the upanishads with the stage of the wandering ascetic, who is entirely concerned with meditation on the absolute, *Brahman*.

The twice born may account for as much as 48% of Hindus, though I have now seen the number put at more like 18%—quite a difference but more believable. The Shudras (58% of Hindus) may represent the institutional provision that the Arya made for the people they already found in India. The Shudras thus remain once born, and traditionally were not allowed to learn Sanskrit or study the Vedas—on pain of death. Their *dharma* is to work for the twice born. But even below the Shudras are the Untouchables (24% of Hindus), who are literally "outcastes," without a varna, and were regarded as "untouchable" because they are ritually polluting for caste Hindus. Some Untouchable sub-castes are regarded as so polluted that members are supposed to keep out of sight and do their work at night: They are called "Unseeables."

In India, the term "Untouchable" is now regarded as insulting or politically incorrect (like *Eta* in Japan for the traditional tanners and pariahs). Gandhi's *Harijans* ("children of God") or *Dalits* ("downtrodden") are preferred, though to Americans "Untouchables" would sound more like the gangster-busting federal agent Elliot Ness from the 1920's. Why there are so many Untouchables is unclear, although caste Hindus can be ejected from their jatis and become outcastes and various tribal or formerly tribal people in India may never have been properly integrated into the social system. When Mahatma Gandhi's sub-caste refused him permission to go to England, as noted above, he went anyway and was ejected from the caste. After he returned, his family got him back in, but while in England he was technically an outcaste. Existing tribal people as well as Untouchables are also called the "scheduled castes," since the British drew up a "schedule" listing the castes that they regarded as backwards, underprivileged, or oppressed.

The Untouchables, nevertheless, have their own traditional professions and their own sub-castes. Those professions (unless they can be evaded in the greater social mobility of modern, urban, anonymous life) involve too much pollution to be performed by caste Hindus: (1) dealing with the bodies of dead animals (like the sacred cattle that wander Indian villages) or unclaimed dead humans, (2) tanning leather, from such dead animals, and manufacturing leather goods, and (3) cleaning up the human and animal waste for which in traditional villages there is no sewer system. Mahatma Gandhi referred to the latter euphemistically as "scavenging" but saw in it the most horrible thing imposed on the Untouchables by the caste system. His requirement on his farms in South Africa that everyone share in such tasks comes up in an early scene in the movie *Gandhi*. Since Gandhi equated suffering with holiness, he saw the Untouchables as hallowed by their miserable treatment and so called them "Harijans" (*Hari=Vishnu*). Later Gandhi went on fasts in the hope of improving the condition of the Untouchables, or at least to avoid their being politically classified as non-Hindus.

Today the status of the Shudras, Untouchables, and other "scheduled castes," and the preferential policies that the Indian government has designed for their advancement ever since Independence, are sources of serious conflict, including suicides, murders, and riots, in Indian society. Meanwhile, however, especially since economic liberalization began in 1991, the social mobility of a modern economy and urban life has begun to disrupt traditional professions, and oppressions, even of Untouchables. Village life and economic stasis were the greatest allies of the caste system, but both are slowly retreating before modernity in an India that finally gave up the Soviet paradigm of economic planning.

Varna, Caste, and Other Divisions

Although many other nations are characterized by social inequality, perhaps nowhere else in the world has inequality been so elaborately constructed as in the Indian institution of caste. Caste has long existed in India, but in the modern period it has been severely criticized by both Indian and foreign observers. Although some educated Indians tell non-Indians that caste has been abolished or that "no one pays attention to caste anymore," such statements do not reflect reality.

Caste has undergone significant change since independence, but it still involves hundreds of millions of people. In its preamble, India's constitution forbids negative public discrimination on the basis of caste. However, caste ranking and caste-based interaction have occurred for centuries and will continue to do so well into the foreseeable future, more in the countryside than in urban settings and more in the realms of kinship and marriage than in less personal interactions.

Castes are ranked, named, endogamous (in-marrying) groups, membership in which is achieved by birth. There are thousands of castes and sub-castes in India, and these large kinship-based groups are fundamental to South Asian social structure. Each caste is part of a locally based system of interdependence with other groups, involving occupational specialization, and is linked in complex ways with networks that stretch across regions and throughout the nation.

The word *caste* derives from the Portuguese *casta*, meaning breed, race, or kind. Among the Indian terms that are sometimes translated as caste are *varna*, *jati*, *jat*, *biradri*, and *samaj*. All of these terms refer to ranked groups of various sizes and breadth. *Varna*, or colour, actually refers to large divisions that include various castes; the other terms include castes and subdivisions of castes sometimes called sub-castes.

Many castes are traditionally associated with an occupation, such as high-ranking Brahmans; middle-ranking farmer and artisan groups, such as potters, barbers, and carpenters; and very low-ranking "Untouchable" leatherworkers, butchers, launderers, and latrine cleaners. There is some correlation between ritual rank on the caste hierarchy and economic prosperity. Members of higher-ranking castes tend, on the whole, to be more prosperous than members of lower-ranking castes. Many lower-caste people live in conditions of great poverty and social disadvantage.

According to the Rig Veda, sacred texts that date back to oral traditions of more than 3,000 years ago, progenitors of the four ranked *varna* groups sprang from various parts of the body of the primordial man, which Brahma created from clay. Each group had a function in sustaining the life of society—the social body. Brahmans, or priests, were created from the mouth. They were to provide for the intellectual and spiritual needs of the community. Kshatriyas, warriors and rulers, were derived from the arms. Their role was to rule and to protect others. Vaishyas—landowners and merchants—sprang from the thighs, and were entrusted with the care of commerce and agriculture. Shudras—artisans and servants—came from the feet. Their task was to perform all manual labour.

Later conceptualized was a fifth category, "Untouchable" menials, relegated to carrying out very menial and polluting work related to bodily decay and dirt. Since 1935 "Untouchables" have been known as Scheduled Castes, referring to their listing on government rosters, or schedules. They are also often called by Mohandas Karamchand (Mahatma) Gandhi's term Harijans, or "Children of God." Although the term *Untouchable* appears in literature produced by these low-ranking castes, in the 1990s, many politically conscious members of these groups prefer to refer to themselves as Dalit, a Hindi word meaning oppressed or downtrodden. According to the 1991 census, there were 138 million Scheduled Caste members in India, approximately 16 percent of the total population.

The first four *varnas* apparently existed in the ancient Aryan society of northern India. Some historians say that these categories were originally somewhat fluid functional groups, not castes. A greater degree of fixity gradually developed, resulting in the complex ranking systems of medieval India that essentially continue in the late twentieth century.

Although a *varna* is not a caste, when directly asked for their caste affiliation, particularly when the questioner is a Westerner, many Indians will reply with a *varna* name. Pressed further, they may respond with a much more specific name of a caste, or *jati*, which falls within that *varna*. For example, a Brahman may specify that he is a member of a named caste group, such as a Jijotiya Brahman, or a Smartha Brahman, and so on. Within such castes, people may further belong to smaller sub-caste categories and to specific clans and lineages. These finer designations are particularly relevant when marriages are being arranged and often appear in newspaper matrimonial advertisements.

Members of a caste are typically spread out over a region, with representatives living in hundreds of settlements. In any small village, there may be representatives of a few or even a score or more castes.

Numerous groups usually called tribes (often referred to as Scheduled Tribes) are also integrated into the caste system to varying degrees. Some tribes live separately from others—particularly in the far northeast and in the forested centre of the country, where tribes are more like ethnic groups than castes. Some tribes are themselves divided into groups similar to sub-castes. In regions where members of tribes live in peasant villages with nontribal peoples, they are usually considered members of separate castes ranking low on the hierarchical scale.

Inequalities among castes are considered by the Hindu faithful to be part of the divinely ordained natural order and are expressed in terms of purity and pollution. Within a village, relative rank is most graphically expressed at a wedding or death feast, when all residents of the village are invited. At the home of a high-ranking caste member, food is prepared by a member of a caste from whom all can accept cooked food (usually by a Brahman). Diners are seated in lines; members of a single caste sit next to each other in a row, and members of other castes sit in perpendicular or parallel rows at some distance. Members of Dalit castes, such as Leatherworkers and Sweepers, may be seated far from the other diners—even out in an alley. Farther away, at the edge of the feeding area, a Sweeper may wait with a large basket to receive discarded leavings tossed in by other diners. Eating food contaminated by contact with the saliva of others not of the same family is considered far too polluting to be practiced by members of any other castes. Generally, feasts and ceremonies given by Dalits are not attended by higher-ranking castes.

Among Muslims, although status differences prevail, brotherhood may be stressed. A Muslim feast usually includes a cloth laid either on clean ground or on a table, with all Muslims, rich and poor, dining from plates placed on the same cloth. Muslims who wish to provide hospitality to observant Hindus, however, must make separate arrangements for a high-caste Hindu cook and ritually pure foods and dining area.

Castes that fall within the top four ranked *varnas* are sometimes referred to as the "clean castes," with Dalits considered "unclean." Castes of the top three ranked *varnas* are often designated "twice-born," in reference to the ritual initiation undergone by male members, in which investiture with the Hindu sacred thread constitutes a kind of ritual rebirth. Non-Hindu castelike groups generally fall outside these designations.

Each caste is believed by devout Hindus to have its own dharma, or divinely ordained code of proper conduct. Accordingly, there is often a high degree of tolerance for divergent lifestyles among different castes. Brahmans are usually expected to be nonviolent and spiritual, according with their traditional roles as vegetarian teetotaller priests. Kshatriyas are supposed to be strong, as fighters and rulers should be, with a taste for aggression, eating meat, and drinking alcohol. Vaishyas are stereotyped as adept businessmen, in accord with their traditional activities in commerce. Shudras are often described by others as tolerably pleasant but expectably somewhat base in behaviour, whereas Dalits—especially Sweepers—are often regarded by others as followers of vulgar life-styles. Conversely, lower-caste people often view people of high rank as haughty and unfeeling.

The chastity of women is strongly related to caste status. Generally, the higher ranking the caste, the more sexual control its women are expected to exhibit. Brahman brides should be virginal, faithful to one husband, and celibate in widowhood. By contrast, a Sweeper bride may or may not be a virgin, extramarital affairs may be tolerated, and, if widowed or divorced, the woman is encouraged to remarry. For the higher castes, such control of female sexuality helps ensure purity of lineage—of crucial importance to maintenance of high status. Among Muslims, too, high status is strongly correlated with female chastity.

Within castes explicit standards are maintained. Transgressions may be dealt with by a caste council, meeting periodically to adjudicate issues relevant to the caste. Such councils are usually formed of groups of elders, almost always males. Punishments such as fines and outcasting, either temporary or permanent, can be enforced. In rare cases, a person is excommunicated from the caste for gross infractions of caste rules. An example of such an infraction might be marrying or openly cohabiting with a mate of a caste lower than one's own; such behaviour would usually result in the higher-caste person dropping to the status of the lower-caste person.

Activities such as farming or trading can be carried out by anyone, but usually only members of the appropriate castes act as priests, barbers, potters, weavers, and other skilled artisans, whose occupational skills are handed down in families from one generation to another. As with other key features of Indian social structure, occupational specialization is believed to be in accord with the divinely ordained order of the universe.

The existence of rigid ranking is supernaturally validated through the idea of rebirth according to a person's karma, the sum of an individual's deeds in this life and in past lives. After death, a person's life is judged by divine forces, and rebirth is assigned in a high or a low place, depending upon what is deserved. This supernatural sanction can never be neglected, because it brings a person to his or her position in the caste hierarchy, relevant to every transaction involving food or drink, speaking, or touching.

In past decades, Dalits in certain areas (especially in parts of the south) had to display extreme deference to high-status people, physically keeping their distance—lest their touch or even their shadow pollute others—wearing neither shoes nor any upper body covering (even for women) in the presence of the upper castes. The lowest-ranking had to jingle a little bell in warning of their polluting approach. In much of India, Dalits were prohibited from entering temples, using wells from which the "clean" castes drew their water, or even attending schools. In past centuries, dire punishments were prescribed for Dalits who read or even heard sacred texts.

Such degrading discrimination was made illegal under legislation passed during British rule and was protested against by pre-independence reform movements led by Mahatma Gandhi and Bhimrao Ramji (B.R.) Ambedkar, a Dalit leader. Dalits agitated for the right to enter Hindu temples and to use village wells and effectively pressed for the enactment of stronger laws opposing disabilities imposed on them. After independence, Ambedkar almost single-handedly wrote India's constitution, including key provisions barring caste-based discrimination. Nonetheless, discriminatory treatment of Dalits remains a factor in daily life, especially in villages, as the end of the twentieth century approaches.

In modern times, as in the past, it is virtually impossible for an individual to raise his own status by falsely claiming to be a member of a higher-ranked caste. Such a ruse might work for a time in a place where the person is unknown, but no one would dine with or intermarry with such a person or his offspring until the claim was validated through kinship networks. Rising on the ritual hierarchy can only be achieved by a caste as a group, over a long period of time, principally by adopting behaviour patterns of higher-ranked groups. This process, known as Sanskritization, has been described by M.N. Srinivas and others. An example of such behaviour is that of some Leatherworker castes adopting a policy of not eating beef, in the hope that abstaining from the defiling practice of consuming the flesh of sacred bovines would enhance their castes' status. Increased economic prosperity for much of a caste greatly aids in the process of improving rank

CASTE SYSTEM : EARLY STAGES

One of the most controversial topic regarding the India's society and culture is its stringent caste system. The word "caste" is taken from the Portuguese word casta. It can be defined as a rigid social system in which a social hierarchy is maintained generation after generation and allows little mobility out of the position to which a person is born.

This system dates almost 3000 years back and was formed based on the need to form a social order in ancient India. It is still very prevalent as part of India's society. Today, it occurs more in the rural villages than in big urban cities; and more in the social matters of kinship and marriages than in impersonal day-to-day interaction, such as taking the bus. Having been around for centuries, it is highly doubtful that the caste system will die out completely. Its presence will still be felt in the near future.

History and Description: The original caste system came about when the Aryans migrated from the north to India around 1600BCE. During the Vedic age, Manu, "the founder of this ancient Hindu or Aryan society," and "the great leader who survived the mythical flood and established the new social order, reflecting a return to spiritual values from an earlier and materialistic humanity?" ("The Vedic Social Order", From The River of Heaven, Dr. David Frawley.) founded four social orders based on four main goals of both humans and society. A social classification system of four different classes (varnas) was thus devised so that the human race could have a smooth and ordered life in society.

Difference between Jati and Varna: In each system, each caste (jati)-birth-unit-is an endogamous group into which one is born into and will marry within. There are approximately 3,000 jatis in contemporary society.

By contrast, varna is the typical functional division of an advanced society. It is one of the four large caste groups (Brahman, Kshatriya, Vaishya, and Shudra) from which most jatis are believed to derive.

> *"While the term varna refers to the fours different classes in society, the term jati refers to the different endogamous sections of the Hindu Society which is known as castes." ("An Introduction to Hinduism", Gavin Flood.)*

More about Varna: Varna literally means "colour". It refers to the distinct qualities (guna) that the four functional classes possess in their hearts and minds. There are four different qualities of human beings-white, red, yellow, black.

White (sattva = truthful) represents the quality of purity, love, faith and detachment. Those belonging to this colour seek true knowledge and often exist in ones with spiritual temperament. Those that belong to this colour, belong to the Brahman class.

Red (rajas = energetic) represents the quality of action, will, aggression, and energy. Those belonging to this colour seek honour, power, and status and exist in people with martial and political temperament. Those that belong to this colour belong to the Kshatriya class.

Yellow (rajas) represents the same quality as the red colour but those in this quality seek communication, interchange, trade, and business instead. This colour exists in those of commercial temperament. They make up the Vaishya class.

Black (tamas = inert, solid) represents quality of ignorance, inertia, and dullness. Those belonging to this colour are dependent on the rest of the world for motivation and seek nothing. They exist in those of the servile disposition and make up the Shudra class.

Varna also means "veil". It shows the four different ways in which the Divine Self is hidden in human beings. By this, it refers to the ways in which his four body parts make up the four classes, depending on the nature or values that the human holds. The Brahmans hold spiritual and intellectual values and are in charge of teaching the Vedic Sanskrit, thus are made up of his head. The Kshatriyas are the warriors that protect the countries and thus are made up of his arms. The Vaishyas are the farmers and merchants in the production nature and thus are made up of his belly and the Shudras are the labourers who perform menial chores and thus are made up of his legs.

The 4 Varna Groups: The four ranked varna groups were created from the various parts of the body of the primordial man, which Brahma created from clay. They are described in the earliest part of the Rig-Veda: Brahmans, Kshatriyas, Vaishyas, Shudras. The top four ranked varnas are referred to as "twice-born" (dvijas) in reference to the Hindu sacred thread ritual initiation which is suppose to represent re-birth.

These four groups are considered "clean castes." Typical roles of these four varnas are:

Brahmans-priests, holy men, arbiters

Kshatriyas-kings, warriors, soldiers that protect and guard the country

Vaishyas-businessmen, traders, commercial class

Shudras-farmers, producers, peasants

The Untouchables: Below the four varna castes lays a fifth group-The Untouchables. This group is not mentioned in the Vedas records until the Bhagavad-Gita and is supposed to be considered outside of the human society and of no caste. Unlike the upper four, it is not considered a "twice-born," having not gone through the Hindu sacred thread ritual initiation. The fifth varna is deemed "unclean" and polluting. Their role in life and society is to perform menial, degrading jobs.

The Untouchables are known by a variety of names. They call themselves "Dalits", priding themselves for the struggles they have fought against society. Mahatma Gandhi calls them "Harijans"-Children of God-when he adopted, against the caste rules, an Untouchable child. Finally, the Untouchables are also known as the "Scheduled Castes" after the 1935 constitution was erected to protect them in society both economically and socially.

> *"In India there are approximately 240 million Dalits. This means that nearly 25% of the population is Dalit. It also means that in a country, where everybody is supposed to have equal rights and opportunities, 1 out of 5 persons is condemned to be untouchable."*

Despite the professed equal rights and duties in the Indian society, the Untouchables are still bounded in ways that keeps them in their place. They do not receive any education that can help them climb up in society and they live in poverty with scarce means of amenities, food, health care, and all other key survival needs in life.

Dharma and Reincarnation: Different castes have different designated codes of proper conduct (dharma), according to their ranks on the hierarchy that they are obligated to perform to contribute to their society. For example, Brahman's proper behaviour will be to be nonviolent, religious and have a vegetarian diet; Kshatriyas are expected to be aggressive warriors who fight and defend and consume meat and alcohol.

The original caste system supported the moving of individuals from one caste to another based on one's actions and performances (karma) in society. The mass population believe that the suffering in their present life is a result of the bad deeds they committed in their past life. The karma that they accumulate is the deciding factor as to which position in the caste hierarchy they will belong to in their next lives. They believe that the faithful execution of the duties obligated in their position in life, thus good karma performed, will be a promise to raise them up through the different classes in reincarnation until they reach the top of the ranks and take the next proceeding step to liberation (moksha). The rigid caste system is justified by this belief and it is thus possible to see why the masses stay muted and accept their suffering in life.

Purity vs. Pollution: Other than the roles in life (dharma), what makes the castes different from one another?

Inequalities amongst castes are a part of the ordained natural order and it is explained or justified in terms of purity and pollution. High-caste status is associated with purity and low-castes status, with pollution. Those born into high-ranking class would have inborn purity, like the Brahmans and similarly, the low caste Dalits are born into pollution. The Dalits can easily pollute a Brahman just by physical contact and the latter will have to perform ritual cleanliness like bathing in flowing water and changing clothes. This explains for the distance the upper and lower castes maintain in terms of intercaste relationships. One of the theories of purity is that when a person is alive, both his body and soul are connected spiritually as one. When any part of the body leaves the whole entity, its connection to spirituality is broken and it is considered impure. Polluting. So anything emitted from the body is considered polluting. For example, corpses, manure, dirt, bodily fluids, etc. Similarly, anyone who deals or is in contact with such impure matters is considered tainted and polluting too.

Low-castes that hold perform menial jobs that deal with burying corpses, killing or skinning animals, cleaning toilets and clearing rubbish and body excretion, are considered tainted and polluting. They are kept away from any sacred learning and ritual and away from the mainstream society. The Untouchables have to live outside the villages and have their own wells so as not to pollute the rest of the people.

Since occupational specialization is believed to be in accord with the ordained order of the universe, and since purity or pollution is traditionally hereditary, low castes who hold demeaning jobs have their lives remain polluted forever. For example, a Sweeper will be a Sweeper for his entire life and his children will have to inherit the same job and be polluted as well. Similarly, the upper-class groups like the Brahmins will always retain their inherent purity from their parents, as long as they carry out the daily cleanliness rituals and do not violate any purity codes.

Intercaste Relations

Purity Pollution: Intercaste relations are also affected by the purity and pollution dogma. High-caste groups shun and keep their distance from the lower castes. Dalits are suppose to be so polluting that even the cast of their shadows would stain the higher-castes. In some cases, they even have to wear bells to warn others of their presence.

Distance is maintained in all situations, even in the case of preparation of food. A Brahmin who accepts water or a meal from the hands of a Sweeper or any Dalit will immediately be polluted and could face social rejection from his fellow caste members. Certain exceptions hold. For example, only members of the Waterbearer caste who are employed to supply water from wells to homes can offer water by hand to all castes without polluting them. Only completely raw uncooked food like rice grains, uncooked vegetables, mangoes, or bananas can be accepted by anyone from anybody.

Another instance of inter-caste relation that is forbidden is inter-caste marriage. Given that even the issue of dining has so many regulations, marriage and consummation issues are under even heavier scrutiny. Marriages are traditionally arranged and within one's own caste. The background of each bride and groom are thoroughly studied to make sure they fit. Caste is the key qualification sought, and like how it affects basic socialization of society, is a filter system when seeking potential life partners.

Pollution and Purity have very strict rules and regulations to abide by. Every action in every single day (a drink of water, a meal, talking, touching, bathing) has immediate consequences to it. And one would have to take the necessary purifying rituals to correct the violation. These daily rules and regulations serve as a constant reminder of the multi-ranked caste society and shows how important and essential the hierarchy is to the lives of Indians.

Atrocities: Intercaste Relations can be seen as either economically cooperative or exploitative. In the prior perspective, the lower castes that perform jobs as farmers, carpenters, shoemakers, potters are hired by upper castes who owns lands and business to afford to pay them. In the latter perspective, since the higher-ranking castes are the ones with both social and economic power, they can economically exploit or plainly discriminates the low classes. Such cases range from minor levels of degrade and abuse to shocking states where the low castes are even killed by these high-ranked castes. Evidence of such atrocities appears in several controversial news reports in different parts of India.

> *"In 1990, blatant subjugation of low-caste labourers in the northern state of Bihar and eastern Uttar Pradesh was the subject of many news reports. In this region, scores of Dalits who have attempted to unite to protest low wages have been the victims of some 500 villagers."*

> *"In 1991 the news magazine India Today reported that in an ostensibly prosperous village about 160 kilometres southeast of Delhi, when it became known that a rural Dalit labourer dared to have a love affair with the daughter of a high-caste landlord, the lovers and their Dalit go-between were tortured, publicly hanged and burnt by agents of the girl's family in the presence of some 500 villagers."*

Caste Structure

In Goa, the Bamonn or the Brahmins belonged to the originally priestly class taking upon other occupations like agriculture, trade and commerce (merchants), gold smithy etc. The Chaddho or the Kshatriyas were the noblemen, warriors and related soldiery taking up commercial avocations also. The Vaishya-Vanis were engaged in trade and among them were the 'shetts' or goldsmiths pursuing the craft of gold and gold ornaments. The Sudir or the Sudras were the workers and agricultural labourers engaged in the servicing professions. The Gavddi or Kunnbi were the landless labourers, earlier dislodged by the above high castes and living in their own wards in the village. There were the Gauddo or Gaudde, probably the Vaishya counterparts in Goa of the neighbouring Karnataka's Gowda, as there is 'Gaud' found in the Canacona taluka of Goa on Karnataka's border.

The caste structure in Goa was somewhat like pre-eminence in the social hierarchy based on the nobility of blood, very much resembling the idea of family nobility in the rest of India. All the castes or rather sub-castes or jatis like Saraswats, Karades, Chitpavans, Padhyes etc. among the various segments of the population of Goa, particularly the goldsmiths and some merchants probably, as seen from the surnames of members of communes purportedly all-Brahmin, were lumped into the Christian caste of Bamonn or Brahmin. The various groups among the Kshatriyas or locally known as Chaddho were mainly the noble and warrior class. Some of them engaged in the trading profession, known as Chatim, which was an occupational appellation common to Brahmins also. The caste appellation of Chaddho gradually fell into disuse. Later among the Hindus of this caste in Goa who did not embrace Christianity began preferring the appellation of Maratha. The Marathas and Vanis were incorporated into the Christian caste of Chaddho.

Those of the Vaishya-Vani caste men who could not get themselves merged as Christian Bamonn or Chaddho, appear as Gauddo in place in Bardez Taluka of Goa, among Christians and those among the Hindu remnants of this caste in the present Canacona taluka etc. Gauddo caste among Christians is treated as one of the three high castes. It is believed that large number of Vaishya-Vanis emigrated to the adjoining district of Sindhudurg in Maharashtra. Their descendants trace their origin to Goa and the flight of their ancestors at the time of the conversion fever. The Christian counterpart of the Hindu Vani is the Gauddo Christian caste. The goldsmiths call themselves 'Daivednya Brahmins' and are known in Goa as 'Shetti', they were put into the Christian caste of Sudir or Sudras, which is a lower caste. They did not get into the caste deemed superior because they were known as 'Panchal' or the artisan group of castes.

The aboriginal stock in Goa is known as the 'Gavddi', is a higher caste. The Christian convert of the Gavdi aboriginal was termed as Kunbi. The Kunbis are found in large number in the Salcete taluka than in any other taluka of Goa.

At the time of the conversions carried out by the Portuguese missionaries, there were untouchables like the 'Mahara' and Chambars, who were converted to Christianity. They are found in Chandor village. Chambars have later merged with the Sudras among Christians. Bamonn and Chaddho are the two advanced castes among the Hindus in Goa. They continued to attach their caste to the Christian names and surnames even after conversion. The first mass baptisms or conversions to Christianity were effected in the two prominent villages in the vicinity of the then city of Goa, Divar Island and Carambolim villages, the first of the Bamonn and the second of the Chaddho. The majority of the total number of village communes converted to Christianity belonged to the two high castes. The priests in the Goan community should be recruited from the Bamonn and Chaddho. At some places the Christian name, is mentioned along with the old Hindu name while at others the Christian name is mentioned with the person's father name in the Hindu original or in case of the father being a Hindu. The surnames of Poi, Kamat or Vamotim, Desai Kudav, Naik, Prabhu or Porbu etc. are common to both the high castes of Bamonn and Chaddho. Christian Bahmonns and Chaddhos are the two leading rival classes among the Goan's.

The continued maintenance of the caste system among the Christians in Goa is attributed to the mass conversions of entire villages, as a result of which the religious complexion of the whole village was given a new coat of Christianity without affecting its age-old social structure which was rooted in caste foundations. The old usages and customs and age-old traditions, including superstitions of a varied order, especially the caste-system were transferred. The Portuguese, fearing the relapses of their coverts to Hinduism, destroyed all available material reminiscent of the old religion including literary works which are stated by historians to have been in Konkani, mainly religious or socio-religious in nature.

The Indenture System

In the colonies of the British, French and the Dutch, exploitation in one form or the other stalked the Indian indentured labourers.

The Coolies who arrived to work in the sugar estates in the West Indies were marched to their barracks known as 'Nigger Yard.' It was the same in Mauritius—only the language was different, 'camps des Noirs' or the backbreaking work in the canefields.

In 1843 the first shipload of 217 Indian labourers arrived in Port of Spain in Trinidad in the Caribbean. And in the same decade, others were taken to British Guiana in South America, and Mauritius off the coast of Africa; in the 1860's to the

British colony of Natal in South Africa; in the 1870's to the Dutch colony of Surinam; in the 1880's to Fiji. By 1917-20 the indenture system was abolished but not before 1.5 million Indian bonded labourers had been induced move to remote parts of the globe in the service of British capitalism.

In South Africa they worked from daybreak to nightfall, from four in the morning to seven in the night, and far beyond their capacity. They were strictly confined to the limits of their master's estate. Beating and flogging was part of the regular routine in the plantations. In the West Indies the cattle whip was employed; in Malaya it was the cane, and in South Africa it was the rawhide cattle lash. One callous estate manager reportedly said "As long as the coolie is working for you, you have the right to do what you like with him-that is, short of killing".

Some Caribbean planters solved the problem of the sick by abandoning them to fate. In Grenada the majority of the 2000 Indians were kicked off the estates when they became ill and allowed to die on the road. The editor of a Jamaica newspaper wrote in 1863: 'One must see these wretched hungry, houseless and outcast specters picking up in the streets a chance bone or any putrid offal.... and so crippled, nude, skeletoned before their death, they live on, no parish authority taking them in'.

Unlike the Chinese and the Blacks, the Indians were also wary of the penchant for proselytizing among white missionaries who were on the lookout for 'heathen converts'. Indians were always branded as the dregs of their country, low-born, even criminal. Inspite of this, the Europeans managed to take Indian women for sexual purposes-usually the daughter of a coolie.

Dave Freedholm teaches world religion and philosophy at a nationally recognized independent college preparatory school in the US. and a practitioner of Hindu spirituality for some years, says: 'Caste' was used to justify Christian proselytizing and for continued domination over the Indian population, and this continues to be the case today. Also, the ills of contemporary Indian society (poverty, caste, etc.), which were exacerbated in part due to centuries long foreign occupation, exploitation and domination, are blamed primarily on Hindu thought. Thus, some Western scholars, ignoring the historic subversion of Indian society and Hinduism by the West, align themselves with the 'oppressed' against the 'evils' of Hinduism. The victim is made to feel guilty and hence the 'Hindu shame' I find amongst some Hindus.

Most Christians today (and most scholars of religion) would be scandalized if the feudal system, slavery, capitalist exploitation or anti-Judaism were used to define the essence of Christianity. They would understand these things to be historically and socially bound and not part of Christian universal ideals. In short, descriptions of Christianity in textbooks would distinguish the core or essence of Christian theology from specific social, historical and political contexts. However, Hinduism is not treated in the same way.

It does seem that the caste system, as understood today, was foisted on Indian society by its Western (Christian) oppressors, the British. Efforts within Hindu society to reform itself, and to provide a new vision of Hinduism, are too often ignored or downplayed.

Sociology of Groups in Ancient India

The whole philosophy of Indian social organization may be summarized in one word, varna-ashrama-dharma, which may be appropriately translated as Social Federalism. This principle of social integration or synthesis was understood as early as the times of the Samhitas in the Vedic age. The Vedic seers realized that the best and surest way of saving society from frequent suicidal chaos was to divide its members into specific groups, with well-defined functions and privileges or rewards for each.

The first group was that of the Brahmans, the teachers and the priests. They were the custodians of the social and spiritual heritage of the group and were to pass it on to the succeeding generations. They were to preserve the purity of idealism, point the way to the Eternal discovered by them through study and meditation, while their fellowmen were busy with life's daily tasks which left little leisure. The Brahman was a man of intellect; he came from the mouth of Brahma.

The second group was that of the Kshatriya. They were men of action. They were the guardians of the race. They were soldiers, sailors, civil servants and legislators. They kept the peace and order within the group and protected it from alien aggression. Theirs was a life of service and sacrifice; they came from the arms of Brahma.

The third group was that of the Vaishyas, the merchants. They attended to the distribution of the necessities of life. The vaishya was the merchant who made wealth; he was a man of desire. He was born from the thighs of Brahma.

The fourth and last group was that of the Sudras. The shudra was engaged in producing life's necessities, food, clothing and shelter, so that the physical organism of the group was kept in good health. On this group of working men depended the physical welfare of the whole community, its industries, its prosperity. This working class was psychologically, a group of undefined aptitudes, un-evolved, men of mechanical temperament, the common men. They came from the feet of Brahma. Look where we will, whether it be a primitive community or a modern nation, its population falls easily into these four categories. According to Manu, there are no other groups.

Integration of Various Factors

This division of men into four types, the teacher, the warrior, the merchant and the labourer, is based on sound psychology, ethics, biology and economics. Some men are intellectually by temperament, some are active, some acquisitive and others undefined, none of these. To each are assigned the task true to its type, in conformity with its inherent temperament, svadharma. All together formed an organic whole. Under an arrangement such as this, there is conservation of social energies; there is no necessity of trial and error method. All are not equally endowed with equal physical and mental capacities, but every one should be given an opportunity for putting to use the faculties with which he has been endowed. Man should be treated as man, and not as an economic hand. Danger of exploitation of one group by another can be eliminated. Social harmony and conscious cooperation were made the chief characteristics of human association. The ideal was to evolve a functional and not an acquisitive society. It is this varna dharma that has been the bulwark of Indian civilization and saved it from wreckage of time. Each group had its duties and its own rewards or compensation. The labourer had to work, but he was to be looked after as a younger member of a family. The man of desire, the vaishya, was to acquire wealth; power and authority was vested in the Kshatriya, while all these were to honour the teacher, to obey his religious and spiritual injunctions and accept his guidance. The teacher was to be supported by the gifts of the other three groups.

It was with the aid of this mechanism that India sought to solve her racial problem. The Aryans did not resort to the short cut of annihilating the primitive people with whom they came into contact as the European races have done whenever they have occupied lands in America, Asia, Africa and Australia, but they gave them a place in their body-politic, assigning to them the task befitting their intelligence and subordinate status. Observant scholars of the West have not failed to notice the spiritual significance of the varna-ashrama-dharma and given it its due praise.

Writing of this varna-ashrama-dharma, Auguste Comte (1798-1857) the great French sociologist, wrote in his book Systeme de philosophie positive or Positive Society: "No institution has ever shown itself more adopted to honour, ability to various kinds than this polytheistic organization...In a social view, the virtues of the system are not less conspicuous. Politically, its chief attribute was stability...As to the influence on mortals, this system was favourable to personal morality, and yet more to domestic, for the spirit of caste was a mere extension of the family spirit....As to social morals, the system was evidently favourable to respect for age and homage to ancestors."

These principles formed the background of the Indian social organization; on them was built a superstructure of social institution, such as education, marriage, family and the state.

It was realized by the Indian sociologists that both the individual and the group could find self-expression and fulfilment only in and through a complex of social institutions, based on dharma, cooperation, mutual aid, integration, synthesis, the vision of the whole.

Balance, orderly progress of individual and group, harmonious relationship between both, was the ideal aimed at by the Indian sociologist.

Discrimination in Western Societies

Annie Besant (1847-1933), a prominent leader of India's freedom movement, member of the Indian National Congress, and of the Theosophical Society, delivered lectures in 1895 on Eastern Castes and Western classes and pointed out: "..these distinctions exist and have existed from time immemorial, and are based upon natural divisions. Caste is present in the East and class is present in the West."

> *"Where there is Man, there are social divisions.. That's why you have the Boston Brahmins in the US, the Zaibatsu in Japan, Parisian aristocracy, the Communist Party of China, and what have you."*
>
> *"Christian nations have produced, and indeed in the name of Christianity, things even more hateful than the pariah village of India."-Nicol Macnicol (1870-1952) Professor and author of Is Christianity Unique p. 52.*

Dr. Charles Sabillon author of several books, has observed in his article Christianity and Islam: Which is the Worst?

The origins of both religions are based on the claims of two men, Jesus and Mohammed, and both men proved equally incapable of demonstrating their divine mandate. From that perspective, the two creeds are equally based on false propositions and can be classified as nothing more than lies. Mohammed ordered his followers to do it by the sword, and that is what they did once he died. They launched into one of the most enthusiastic conquering ventures the world has ever seen and forged an empire that extended from Central Asia to the southwest of Europe.

Nations were ruthlessly converted to Christianity by the sword just like Islam converted Arabia, Central Asia, and Africa by the sword. With his armies, Charlemagne preached the Gospel of the cross to the Saxons, the Germans, the Bohemians, and the Hungarians. This was not the only evangelizing military operation. There were also the infamous Crusades from the eleventh to the thirteenth century, the

Inquisition, and the conquest of the American continent from the sixteenth century onwards. Throughout the Middle Ages in Europe, the Christian Church was the most militarily powerful organization in that continent. Being the largest landowner and the biggest tax collector provided the Pope with huge amounts of money, which were used to solidify his power by establishing a potent armed force.

America's Culturally Displaced People? : British bioterrorism in Colonial Era-"Bioterrorism was one of the first things that was imposed against the Native Americans," Oyler said.

We gave them two Blankets and a Handkerchief out of the Small Pox Hospital," trader and land speculator William Trent wrote in a journal. "I hope it will have the desired effect."

Jimmie D. Oyler, chief of the United Tribe of Shawnee Indians, whose territory is based in Kansas, said decedents are aware of their ancestors' struggles. Another common practice among European explorers was to give "smallpox blankets" to the Indians. Since smallpox was unknown on this continent prior to the arrival of the Europeans, Native Americans did not have any natural immunity to the disease so smallpox would effectively wipe out entire villages with very little effort required by the Europeans. William Fenton describes how Europeans decimated Native American villages in his 1957 work "American Indian and White relations to 1830." From 1615 to 1619 smallpox ran rampant among the Wampanoags and their neighbours to the north. The Wampanoag lost 70 percent of their population to the epidemic and the Massachusetts lost 90 percent. Most of the Wampanoag had died from the smallpox epidemic so when the Pilgrims arrived they found well-cleared fields which they claimed for their own.

A Puritan colonist, quoted by Harvard University's Perry Miller, praised the plague that had wiped out the Indians for it was "the wonderful preparation of the Lord Jesus Christ, by his providence for his people's abode in the Western world."

It was not divine intervention that wiped out most of the natives around the village of Patuxet but, most likely, smallpox-embedded blankets planted during an English visit or slave raid.

Indian People Mark 500 Years of Terrorism: The Indian people never knew what act of violence or terror would befall them from the invaders. But death did come. It came in the form of biological warfare when small pox tainted blankets were distributed to the unsuspecting victims. It came to them from the muzzles of guns that did not distinguish between warriors, women, elders or children. It came to them in the ruthless name of Manifest Destiny, the American edict that proclaimed God as the purveyor of expansion Westward.

Christian priests burning the 'heathen' Native Americans.

Countless cultures, rich spiritual traditions and ancient way of life have been destroyed and tramped upon in the name of the "One Jealous God" of Monotheism.

Indian people were often slaughtered like animals and became "inferior" cultures in their own land. The Europeans, through book burning and bayonet, successfully, converted" them, leaving very little trace of their noble civilization.

The (American) Indians of our country have little to be thankful for. They have been decimated and placed on reservations that might as well be concentration camps.

Note: If Columbus had reached India instead of America, it is possible that Indians would today be languishing in reservations!

Indian people were often slaughtered like animals often while waving the American flag in pitiful efforts to convince their killers that they were not bad people.

At Wounded Knee in 1890, a slaughter took place that the white man often called the last great battle between Indians and the United States Army. It was not a battle. It was one the last heinous acts of terror against innocent men, women and children.

Just as the Crusaders believed it was their Christian duty to conquer and kill those Arabs they considered as sub-humans and heathens, so too did America duplicate their misguided logic against the First Americans. The Christians of the Crusade dehumanized the Arabs, the early Americans dehumanized the Indians. A philosopher once said, "Great Nations are judged by how they treat their indigenous people," and I am sad to say that America has failed to pass the test of time.

After 500 years the Indian still lives in fear of the terror that is still lurking just around the corner. The Indian people have lost so much in the past 500 years and they still live in terror of what will come next for them.

Castes and Traditional Economics

The traditional world had three or four castes. In India, they were the brahmana, kstriya, Vaishya, and Shudra. They corresponded, roughly, to the European feudal classes of clergy, nobility, burghers, and servants. More primitively, however, the priestly and warrior functions were united in a single caste. The caste system establishes natural justice; everyone "decides" before birth to incarnate the qualities that make them fit for one caste rather than another. Those in the lower castes were connected to the transcendent by their loyalty to their superiors. Note that this was not personal devotion; traditional loyalty is impersonal, just as the transcendent is nonhuman. The form provided by the caste system is an instance of "creative limitation." The decay of the system is one of the marks of the Kali Yuga.

Work in traditional societies was not work in our sense of the term. All activities, from the sacred sciences to the inferior professions, had their mysteries, anagogic elements that looked upward. The mysteries were preserved by guilds, which eschewed competition and monopoly. The only people who "worked' were slaves, whose activities had no transcendent element. That was what "work" meant. By this definition, the modern West is the civilization of slavery par excellence.

Rigvedic Brahmans and their Social Status

Since the early Rigvedic stage, Brahmans, undoubtedly, had already fixed ritual status: they were the priests, who had a wide circle of duties during soma sacrifices. They were also considered as the assistants of the gods at creation of the world, as the duty of "delivery" of the victim to the gods had been assigned to them.

In time the ritual duties of Brahmans began more and more detail, their universality and the cosmogonic abilities were moved gradually to the second plan in favour of their knowledge of the technical aspects of ritual.

By the end of Rigvedic period this process has resulted in rather precise codification of particular brahmanic qualities and duties, which were based on their personal abilities and skills. Because of that process Brahmans have gradually turned to an independent social class inside the Rigvedic society. Brahmans did not form the triad with Arya-and dAsa-/dasyu-nor regarding the recognizable set of ritual and religious attributes, neither as the opposition of each varna at the Cosmic level. It means that they were not considered as the separate varna. However, already during the Rigvedic period the special social status of Brahmans has been realized de facto. It means, that the Rigvedic society knew some sort of social structure, which had been parallel to the varna one for some time.

It is very well known, that Brahmans were the supreme varna of Ancient Indian society since at least late Rigvedic period. However, most of the modern researchers consider, that Rigvedic Brahmans, like other Rigvedic realities, may not be characterized on the basis of more recent sources, as the former may be of very big time difference from the latter. This is why we consider, that the most productive way of researches of the Brahman subject is to define it with the help of each source as detail as possible and then to compare the results. So, this paper is the Brahman description as they were inside Rigveda.

Of course, this subject has been already searched by scholars and it has brought ahead several points of view.

1. Initially Brahman was one of the four priests (together with hotar, udgatar and adhvaryu), who had supervised over the ceremony with doing nothing else. This position goes from two issues: a) there are many words for priests in Rigveda, b) there are Rigvedic passages, that mention Brahmans as connected to "the way of ration" but not with "the way of speech".
2 Initially Brahman was the priest, who had read hymns to Indra during soma sacrifice, later his functions had been enlarged and he had become the chief of the entire process of sacrifice and also of all the cult procedures. This position is based on some Rigvedic passages which

describes Brahman as a functional priest during soma sacrifice.

3. It has been since Rigvedic time Brahmans formed a separate social group of strata, different from Kshatriya and Vaishya, they were very honoured, read hymns and drank soma. The very word of "Brahman" mivemeant "class of priests-sacrificers". This comes mostly from some passages of non-family Rigvedic hymns (f. e. RV I 108,7).
4. Social meaning of Brahmans passed three stages inside the Rigvedic society. Initially they were poets, who had created hymns, and also wise men, then, it had been any functional priest, and after that Brahmans had formed their own social class. That vision was put ahead by J. Gonda in early 1970s, and was based on detail analysis of considerable number of Rigvedic texts of different mandalas.

Except for historians, "Brahman" subject was researched also by linguists who had created their own theories. We marked only two main ones here.

1. Brahmans formed separate social class since the time of the Indo-European unity, and they preserved their position inside all the historical Indo-European societies, including the Rigvedic one. The theory was based on results of comparative mythology, put ahead in 1950s, and has been under serious critics since that time.
2. Brahmans were those, who provided following of strictly formulated rituals. The concept runs from comparative linguistic studies, mostly of Iranian and Indian languages. It is of the most accepted for now.

So, all those positions we consider as of too fragmented or subjective, as the former come from language data only, and the latter-from few Rigvedic texts without real consideration of the correlation of the mentioned concepts inside Rigveda.

To overcome this situation, we consider to research "Brahman" subject as the Rigvedic one only (i. e. as a sphere of Rigvedic society). Only after this way being covered, one can determine their place and role inside the social structure of Rigvedic society. Here are the results of that vision.

Brahman goes, probably, to verb root barh-/brh-, which forms two semantic fields:

1. barh-/brh-"to grew", "to encrease", "to strengthen". This variant has been put ahead, for instance, by A. Macdonell and M. Mayrhofer.
2. barh-/brh-"to speak". This version of Brahman formation adherents O. Boehtlingk and R. Roth.

We consider, that these both variants form the same semantic field. The reasons for this admittance are: a) goddess vAc possessed cosmological (creative) functions, b) in spite of the recognition of Brahman origin from two semantically different verb roots, both sides give the same semantics for the very Brahman. Let us overlook this more detail.

It is well known, that the word Brahman occurs as of neutral so of masculine gender. It was the stress that had probably made that difference: Brahman (n.) and Brahman (m.). In Vedic language semantically that stress moving meant formation of actor (m.) from action (n.), i. e. action "praying", "life power", "form of religious ceremony" gives actor "poet, singer, form creator", "ritual performer, priest", "the one, who performs the ritual in strictly fixed form".

So, according to the etymology there is no doubt, that Vedic concept of Brahman was the act of verbal putting in order of strengthen; and according to semantics to define the meaning of Brahman as the name of actor one should primarily outcome from Brahman as the name of action.

And one more thing. It is known that there are few words of the same root in Rigveda beside Brahman. Brahman, which one can find in family mandala, is formally the same as Brahman. This paper regards Brahman as the derivatives of Brahman (m.), the Brahman and brahma-as the derivative of Brahman (n.), and the author does not differ those ones from the base form during the analysis.

All the things told above demonstrates very clear, that there was a tendency of transformation of social status of brahmas during the time of Rigveda. Initially they were functional priests, who had wide enough obligations during soma sacrifice.

They also played a role of assistants of gods during creation of the world, the duty of "the delivery" of sacrifice to gods and of dialogue with them was assigned to them. Eventually brahmanic ritual duties began to be specified more and more, their universality was being lost, and their cosmological abilities gradually began to be fixed for "the former" Brahmans. "Present" Brahmans turned more and more to narrow specialized experts-professionals of ritual, which became more and more detailed technically. All that became the basis for brahmanic social allocation from Aryan environment. By the end of Rigvedic times that process has led to rather precise codification of particular brahmanic qualities and duties based on their personal abilities and skills. That was, in our opinion, a doubtless attribute of gradual transformation of Brahmans to an independent social class inside Rigvedic society.

In spite of all the said above, Brahmans did not formed their own varna in Rigvedic society before its very end, because they had not formed any opposition with Arya or dasa/dasyu. However, Brahman had his special social status since very beginning of Rigvedic period, his functions were very important both for that time society and for every Aryan. In time that status was fixed and became formally recognizable by the entire society. By the end of Rigvedic period Aryans had recognized, that they had Brahmans as the special social class de facto. Their next step was to form new social opposition, which had been to become the new basis of cosmological structuring. And it has been done by the time of Purusha sukta. New and the most known varna system has appeared.

Purpose of Varn Vyavastha

Brahman, Kshatriya, Vaishya and Shoodr are 4-Varn that Bhagavan Shri Krishna spoke about. There was a definitive purpose behind 4-Varn System in Hindu society. Necessary occupational training would come from the family itself, and each ancient Hindu village would be self-dependant. There would be No need for migration, like today; self-sufficiency and self-dependence would be the motto of Hindu 4-Varn System.

Brahman parents would provide the child with an environment to grow up as teachers to the society. Kshatriya parents would provide the child with an environment to grow up as protectors of life and land of the society. Vaishya parents would provide the child with an environment to grow up as suppliers of necessities of life to the society. Shoodr parents would provide the child with an environment to grow up as provider of all services to the society.

The necessary training that each would receive would come from the family itself. For instance, son would learn necessary skills from his father. The system would operate in a cyclic pattern from one generation to other. The necessary training would be passed on from one generation to another, by father to the son, and thus ensure continuity of self-sufficiency and self-dependence of each village unit.

The Hindu society would live in small units called villages, and each village would be self-sufficient in respect of its needs with regard to its education, administration, supplies and services. Towns would be few, and the number of those living in towns would be minuscule in comparison to the whole nation.

To ensure that, each village administration would be self-sufficient and self-dependant. It would have Brahman priests and teachers, Kshatriya administrators and defenders, Vaishya producers and agriculturists, and Shoodr service providers with all types of artisans. Here is the documented evidence.

The village communities are composed of those who cultivate the land, the established village-servants, priest, blacksmith, carpenter, accountant, washer-man (whose wife is ex officio midwife of the little village community), potter, watchman, barber, shoemaker, etc. Max Muller, p 255 referring to old Hindu system.

There would be no need for migration of people from one village to another, except by marriages. Thus, women would come from nearby villages, while sons would remain on the soil. For instance, in ancient Hindu society, a child of a barber would learn necessary skills from his father watching his father do the job when the child comes up a certain stage.

Case of India's 'Untouchables'

More than one-sixth of India's population, some 160 million people, live a precarious existence, shunned by much of society because of their rank as "untouchables" or Dalits-literally meaning "broken" people-at the bottom of India's caste system. Dalits are discriminated against, denied access to land, forced to work in degrading conditions, and routinely abused at the hands of the police and of higher-caste groups that enjoy the state's protection. In what has been called India's "hidden apartheid," entire villages in many Indian states remain completely segregated by caste. National legislation and constitutional protections serve only to mask the social realities of discrimination and violence faced by those living below the "pollution line."

For most of the world caste remains an ancient cultural artefact and untouchability a long eradicated practice. This paper attempts to shift the debate on caste and on broader issues pertaining to socially institutionalised discrimination. It begins with a brief description of the characteristics and mechanisms of caste discrimination and a summary overview of the Indian government's response. It then attempts to dismantle those misperceptions that have allowed the system to survive, and comments on the barriers that keep the international community from effectively intervening against a practice that relegates millions of people to a lifetime of segregation, discrimination, and violence.

India's caste system is perhaps the world's longest surviving social hierarchy. A defining feature of Hinduism, caste encompasses a complex ordering of social groups on the basis of ritual purity. A person is considered a member of the caste into which he or she is born and remains within that caste until death, although the particular ranking of that caste may vary among regions and over time. Differences in status are traditionally justified by the religious doctrine of karma, a belief that one's place in life is determined by one's deeds in previous lifetimes. Traditional scholarship has described this more than 2,000-year-old system within the context of the four principal varnas, or large caste categories. In order of precedence these are the Brahmins (priests and teachers), the Ksyatriyas (rulers and soldiers), the Vaishyas (merchants and traders), and the Shudras (labourers and artisans). A fifth category falls outside the varna system and consists of those known as "untouchables" or Dalits; they are often assigned tasks too ritually polluting to merit inclusion within the traditional varna system.

Within the four principal castes, there are thousands of sub-castes, also called jatis; endogamous groups that are further divided along occupational, sectarian, regional, and linguistic lines. Collectively all of these are sometimes referred to as "caste Hindus" or those falling within the caste system. The Dalits are described as varna-sankara: they are "outside the system"-so inferior to other castes that they are deemed polluting and therefore "untouchable." Even as outcasts, they themselves are divided into further sub-castes and practice untouchability against those ranked below; the discrimination is wholly internalised. Although "untouchability" was abolished under Article 17 of the Indian constitution, the practice continues to determine the socioeconomic and religious standing of those at the bottom of the caste hierarchy. Whereas the first four varnas are free to choose and change their occupation, Dalits have generally been confined to the occupational structures into which they are born.

With little land of their own to cultivate, Dalit men, women, and children numbering in the tens of millions work as agricultural labourers for a few kilograms of rice or less than US$1 a day. Most live on the brink of destitution, barely able to feed their families and unable to send their children to school or break away from cycles of debt bondage that are passed on from generation to generation. At the end of day they return to a hut in their Dalit colony with no electricity, kilometres away from the nearest water source, and segregated from all non-Dalits, known as caste Hindus. They are forbidden by caste Hindus to enter places of worship, to draw water from public wells, or to wear shoes in caste Hindu presence. They are made to dig the village graves, dispose of dead animals, clean human waste with their bare hands, and to wash and use separate tea tumblers at neighbourhood tea stalls, all because-due to their caste status-they are deemed polluting and therefore untouchable.

In November 1999, after a cyclone slammed into the eastern state of Orissa, killing thousands and rendering millions homeless, the government brought in 200 Dalit manual scavengers from New Delhi, and planned to bring 500 more from other parts of Orissa, to load animal carcasses onto hand-drawn carts and take them away to be burned. Government officials had offered local upper-caste residents more than the daily minimum wage for each animal burned but they refused citing the decayed conditions of the carcasses and the fact that the task was beneath them: they had "some self-respect left." Even in times of natural disaster, the laws of purity and pollution prevail and the government moves quickly to accommodate the prejudice. At all levels, and under all circumstances, the discrimination is institutionalised.

Dalit women face the triple burden of caste, class, and gender. Dalit girls have been forced to become prostitutes for upper-caste patrons and village priests. Sexual abuse and other forms of violence against women are used by landlords and the police to inflict political "lessons" and crush dissent within the community. According to a Tamil Nadu state government official, the raping of Dalit women exposes the hypocrisy of the caste system as "no one practices untouchability when it comes to sex." Like other Indian women whose relatives are sought by the police, Dalit women have also been arrested and tortured in custody as a means of punishing their male relatives who are hiding from the authorities.

Any attempt to defy the social order is met with physical or economic retaliation. According to the most recent figures available, between 1994 and 1996 a total of 98,349 cases were registered with the police nationwide as crimes and atrocities against Dalits. Given that Dalits are both reluctant and unable (for lack of police cooperation) to report crimes against themselves, the actual number of abuses is presumably much higher. Whether the clashes are social, economic, or political in nature, they are premised on the same basic principle: any attempt to alter village customs or to demand land, increased wages, or political rights sets off a chain of events and leads to social boycotts and acts of retaliatory violence on the part of those most threatened by changes in the status quo. Dalit communities as a whole are summarily punished for individual transgressions; Dalits are cut off from their land and employment, women endure physical attacks, and letter of the law is rarely enforced. Most of the conflicts take place within very narrow segments of the caste hierarchy, between the poor and the not so poor, the landless labourer and the marginal landowner. The differences lie in the considerable amount of leverage that the higher-caste Hindus or non-Dalits are able to wield over local police, district administrations, and even the state government. A theme that is almost universal in its application, it illustrates a crucial aspect of identity politics: one's identity as a person belonging to a certain caste is perceived not only by one's absolute rank but also by the relative treatment meted out to communities that are ranked below.

Building on constitutional provisions, the government of India has pursued a two-pronged approach to narrowing the gap between the socioeconomic status of the Dalit population and the national average. The first approach involves regulatory measures designed to ensure that relevant legal provisions are adequately implemented, enforced, and monitored; the second focuses on increasing the self-sufficiency of the Dalit population through financial assistance for self-employment activities and through development programs to increase education and skills.

The protective component of this two-pronged strategy includes the implementation of legal provisions contained in state and central government legislation, and reservations or quotas in the arenas of government employment and higher education. India's policy of reservations is an attempt by the central government to remedy past injustices related to low-caste status. To allow for proportional representation in certain state and federal institutions, the constitution reserves 22.5 percent of seats in federal government jobs, state legislatures, the Lower House of parliament, and educational institutions for scheduled castes and scheduled tribes. Though some have benefited the reservation policy has not been successfully implemented and has yet to achieve its desired effect. Moreover, most of the landless and illiterate Dalits in the country are not in a position to avail themselves of any of their constitutional privileges. Controversy over the reservations scheme has also allowed the debate to predictably stagnate around the distribution of privilege, taking the focus away from violations of basic rights. India's policy of economic liberalisation is also having an effect on Dalits and their livelihood. As the public sector shrinks due to privatisation, the reservations model is affecting-and able to assist-fewer people, inasmuch as government-related jobs are being drastically reduced. Globalisation has also led to coastal lands increasingly being acquired by multinationals (via the central government) for aquaculture projects. Dalits are the main labourers and tenants of coastal land areas and are increasingly being forced to leave these areas-to live as displaced people, for the most part-as foreign investment rises.

The persistence of caste-based prejudices and the denial of access to land, education, and political power have all contributed to an atmosphere of increasing intolerance. Violence against Dalits, which has steadily climbed since 1994, is only the most extreme form of that intolerance. In 1989 the Scheduled Castes and Scheduled Tribes (Prevention of Atrocities) Act was enacted to prevent and punish caste-based abuses, to establish special courts for the trial of such offences, and to provide for victim relief and rehabilitation. Its enactment represented an acknowledgement on the part of the government that abuses, in their most degrading and violent forms, were still perpetrated against Dalits decades after independence.

A look at the offences made punishable by the act provides a glimpse into the retaliatory or customarily degrading treatment Dalits may receive. They include forcing members of a scheduled caste or scheduled tribe to drink or eat any inedible or obnoxious substance; dumping excreta, waste matter, carcasses or any other obnoxious substance in their premises or neighbourhood; forcibly removing clothes and parading them naked or with painted face or body; interfering with their rights to land; compelling a member of a scheduled caste or scheduled tribe into forms of forced or bonded labour; corrupting or fouling the water of any spring, reservoir or any other source ordinarily used by scheduled castes or scheduled tribes; denying right of passage to a place of public resort; and using a position of dominance to exploit a scheduled caste or scheduled tribe woman sexually.

The potential of the law to bring about social change has been hampered by institutional prejudice and police corruption, with the result that many offences are not registered. Ignorance of procedures or a lack of knowledge of the act itself has also affected implementation. Even when cases are registered, the absence of special courts to try them can delay prosecutions for up to three to four years. Some state governments dominated by higher castes have even attempted to repeal the legislation altogether. Much like other "social welfare" legislation in India, the act remains a paper tiger with little actual effect.

The existence of constitutionally mandated quotas and a large body of legislation and administrative agency mandates assigned exclusively to deal with the plight of Dalits is held up by the government as a panacea to problems of discrimination. These so-called remedies have also shifted attention away from the institutional nature of caste prejudice. It would be difficult to convince the Dalits of Dholapur district, Rajasthan, that after over fifty years of independence, government intervention had made a difference. In April 1998, a Dalit of the area was assaulted by an upper-caste family who forcibly pierced his nostril, drew a string through his nose, paraded him around the village, and tied him to a cattle post-all because he refused to sell bidis (hand-rolled cigarettes) on credit to the nephew of the upper-caste village chief. The message sent from the judiciary on caste discrimination is equally grim: in July 1998 in the state of Uttar Pradesh, an Allahabad High Court judge had his chambers "purified with Ganga jal" (water from the River Ganges), because it had earlier been occupied by a Dalit judge.

India's distinction as the "world's largest democracy" also helps to mask the abuses. For Dalits throughout the country who suffer from de facto disenfranchisement, democracy has not been a self-fulfilling prophecy. During elections, those unpersuaded by typical electioneering are routinely threatened and beaten by political party strongmen in order to compel them to vote for certain candidates. Already under the thumb of local landlords and police officials, Dalit villagers who do not comply have been murdered, beaten, and harassed. Dalits who have contested political office in village councils and municipalities through seats that have been constitutionally "reserved" for them have been threatened with physical abuse and even death in order to get them to withdraw from the campaign. In Tamil Nadu in June 1997, a newly elected Dalit village council president was beheaded by caste Hindus displaced from their once secure elected positions. In 1999, a Dalit woman from Uttar Pradesh considered contesting elections. She was gang-raped and subsequently beaten and murdered as a lesson to other villagers not to disturb the status quo. As with most cases of violence against Dalits, the culprits have yet to be convicted.

Political mobilisation that has resulted in the emergence of powerful interest groups and political parties among middle- and low-caste groups throughout India since the mid-1980s has also largely bypassed Dalits. Dalits are courted by all political parties but generally forgotten once elections are over. The expanding power base of low-caste political parties, the election of low-caste chief ministers to state governments, and even the appointment of a Dalit as president of India in July 1997 all signal the increasing prominence of Dalits in the political landscape but cumulatively have yet to yield any significant benefit for the majority of Dalits. Laws on land reform and protection for Dalits remain unimplemented in most of India's twenty-five states.

Political parties have frequently fashioned their manifestos and campaign slogans around the need for "upliftment" of these marginalised sectors, while political leaders, mostly drawn from higher castes, offer the promise of equal status and equal rights. However, the laws have benefited very few and, due to a lack of political will, development programs and welfare projects designed to improve economic conditions for Dalits have generally had little effect. Dalits rarely break free from bondage or economic exploitation by upper-caste landowners.

Equally insidious, though not as apparent, is the fact that Dalits are denied their place in the public consciousness. The plight of India's "untouchables" elicits only sporadic attention within the country. Public outrage over large-scale incidents of violence or particularly egregious examples of discrimination fades quickly, and the state is under little pressure to undertake more meaningful reforms. Despite ambitious calls for action by central and state governments in the aftermath publicity of massacres and police raids, the Indian authorities have shown little commitment to resolving the root causes of caste conflicts. Society as a whole has turned a blind eye to the institutional character of caste-based abuse and discrimination. Laws are openly flouted, police allegiance is routinely up for sale, and society continues to sanction what the legislature defines as crimes. In the eastern state of Bihar, for example, the first person to be convicted under a decadesold law combating child labour was in 1998.

A loss of faith in the state machinery and increasing intolerance of their abusive treatment has led many Dalit communities into organised movements to claim their rights. In response, state and private actors have engaged in a pattern of repression to preserve the status quo. Unable to find sustainable alliances within, and in an effort to counter their invisibility at home, Dalit movements have from time to time turned outward to look for parallels in struggles abroad. During the 1970s, for example, the Dalit Panthers emerged outside the framework of recognised political parties and aligned themselves ideologically to the Black Panther movement in the United States. During the same period, Dalit literature, painting, and theatre challenged the very premise and nature of established art forms and their depiction of society and religion. Many of these new Dalit artists formed the first generation of the Dalit Panther movement that sought to wage an organised struggle against the varna system. Dalit Panthers visited atrocity sites, organised marches and rallies in villages, and raised slogans of direct militant action against their upper-caste aggressors.

The determined stance of the Dalit Panthers served to arouse and unite many Dalits, particularly Dalit youth and students. The defeat of ruling party candidates and the boycott of elections in some areas forced the government to take notice of the movement: Panther leaders were often harassed and removed from districts for speaking out against the government and Hindu religion. They also became frequent targets of police brutality and arbitrary detentions. Disagreements over the future of the movement and inclusion of other caste groups ultimately led to a dispersal of Dalit Panther leadership. The former aggressiveness and militancy of the Dalit Panthers has for the most part dissipated, though small splinter groups or groups that have adopted the name still survive.

In the 1960s, leftist guerrilla organisations with Marxist, Leninist, and Maoist orientations began advocating the use of violence to achieve land redistribution. By 1970, these so-called Naxalites had initiated a series of peasant uprisings to seize land, burn property records, and assassinate exploitative landlords and others identified as "class enemies" in large areas of the countryside stretching from West Bengal to the southern state of Kerala. Although the Naxalite insurgency was brought to an end in most parts of the country by a brutal police crackdown designed to eliminate the militants and their supporters, the movement continues to survive, albeit with some splits and regroupings, in the rural areas of West Bengal, Orissa, Andhra Pradesh, and Bihar. Higher-caste landlords in Bihar have organised private militias to counter the Naxalite threat. These militias, or senas, also target Dalit villagers believed to be sympathetic to Naxalites. Senas are believed responsible for the murders of many hundreds of Dalits in Bihar since 1987.

Though offshoots of militant movements still thrive in many parts of the country, the strategy for the actualisation of rights has in the past fifteen years undergone a major shift. Beginning in the 1980s, a handful of Dalit organisations began turning to the United Nations as a possible forum for the mobilisation of international support and condemnation of caste-based abuses. However, the difficulty of slotting caste-based abuses into standard categories of human rights violations, and the prevalence of constitutional and legislative protections at the national level, has allowed these abuses to escape international scrutiny. The government of India has consistently asserted that the caste issue does not fall within the mandate of various "race"-based UNHCHR bodies. The government has also refused to allow relevant working groups and special rapporteurs to gain access to the country.

In turn, the response of the international community has been superficial at best. Dalit activists now find themselves struggling to overcome their invisibility abroad. Though caste identity is used as a justification for segregation and exploitation, the discrimination is so entrenched that the victims' shared membership in lower-caste communities is often ignored by upper-caste families and international bodies alike. While the world was united in its condemnation of increasing attacks on India's Christian community this past year, for example, it ignored a significant underlying cause: a majority of Christians in India are Dalits and tribals for whom conversion offers a partial escape from untouchability and exploitation. Conversions are therefore threatening to the social and economic status quo.

Like evaluating the symptoms without diagnosing the disease, most international interventions have also overlooked the fact that Dalits, numbering in the tens of millions, comprise the majority of those driven to bonded labour, manual scavenging, and forced prostitution, under conditions that violate national law and their basic human rights. Despite their mandate of reaching the "poorest of the poor," international development institutions have yet to understand that for those at the bottom of its hierarchy, caste is a determinative factor for the attainment of social, political, civil, and economic rights.

Which strategies then are likely to be effective in reforming socially institutionalised discrimination? Part of the answer lies in supporting the work of grassroots Dalit and human rights activists throughout the country who for many years have assumed many state-like functions and have stepped in where the administration has failed. The second part is to involve the international community in forcing the government to remedy its failures.

In 1998, the National Campaign for Dalit Human Rights was born out of an initiative of grassroots Dalit activists in eight Indian states. Many of these activists were involved in the drafting of over forty recommendations to the government of India and the international community that are contained in a Human Rights Watch report on caste violence released earlier this year. The campaign, which has since expanded to include fourteen states and eleven countries, seeks to mobilise a national coalition that operates at the grassroots level while eliciting the participation of the international community in its struggle. Still, there are other prejudices to be overcome before such participation can be ensured. Internationally, the cyclone in India received little attention in comparison to other recent tragedies of similar or lesser magnitude. Like disparities in responding to crises in Europe and Africa, the "otherness" of those most vividly affected by violence, disaster, or day-to-day deprivation, eases the decision not to respond. When the victims of attacks, even massacres, are non-Christian Dalits, the news barely breaks into international headlines.

Interventions on caste discrimination, if any, have been limited to inquiries regarding the mechanisms of protection offered by the state, without asking for evidence of their effective implementation (which, generally speaking, is a recurring problem in the nature of international intervention on race and ethnicity matters). The Indian government needs to place a priority on strengthening institutional mechanisms aimed at addressing issues of violence and discrimination. But it also needs the active support of-and pressure from-the United Nations, multilateral financial institutions, trading partners, and national and international non-governmental organisations to eradicate the pervasive problem of caste-based abuse. Will the international community respond or even apply the necessary pressure to stimulate domestic political will? Or will it continue to deny Dalits and others their place in the public consciousness? Entrenched forms of discrimination stemming from the world's longest surviving system of social hierarchy may offer some lessons as we prepare for a global forum on modern day "racism." The first and most obvious is to look beyond race as the only arbiter of rights. The second is to look beyond democracy, affirmative action, and the existence of domestic legislation as sufficient guarantors of basic freedoms. The third is to recognise the resilience and adaptability of ancient custom to contemporary global trends. The fourth is to scrutinise the discrimination inherent in the international community's decision to act, and more importantly, in its failure to respond.

Varnasrama Social System

There is a natural system of social organization which can bring about a peaceful society where everyone is happy. This system is described in the timeless Vedic literature of India and it is called Varnasrama dharma.

The purpose of the Varnasrama social system is to provide a structure which allows people to work according to their natural tendencies and to organize society so that everyone, regardless of their position, makes spiritual advancement.

People can only work with a cooperative spirit if there is a central point. Over the years proponents of many different political ideologies have tried to unite society by providing such a central point, however, these attempts have all ultimately failed.

Generally people work for their own pleasure and this is sometimes extended to working for the family, the nation or even the whole world. Because the aims and aspirations of the members of society are so varied it is practically impossible to achieve a peaceful situation as everyone is working to fulfil his own personal goals. The only universal central point around which everyone can work is God. He provides an absolute, eternal centre for all our activities. If we try to make something else the central point the resulting society is doomed to fail.

The Varnasrama system recognizes there are many different types of people who may not be spiritually inclined. The society is organized under the direction of qualified Brahmans and is divided into four occupational and four spiritual divisions in such a way that everyone is serving God simply by performing their occupational duties. As the entire society is arranged to please God, anyone working within the society also pleases God.

The Structure of Varnasrama Society: The practical application of the Varnasrama system is to divide the society according to four occupational and four spiritual orders of life.

The Varnasrama system recognizes the natural talents and abilities of each person and provides work according to a persons qualities. There are four qualities of work, the Brahmans are the intellectual and priestly class, the Kshatriyas are the government, the military and the administrative classes, the Vaishyas are farmers and businessmen, and the sudras are workers.

There are also four spiritual divisions, brahmacary, student life, grhastha, married life, vanaprasta, retired life and sunnyasa, renounced life. If this system is properly implemented under the direction of qualified Brahmans the result will be peace and prosperity throughout the world.

The Corrupt Indian "Caste" System: The Varnasrama social divisions are based on qualities and work. If someone has the qualities of a brahmana and if they work as a brahmana they are accepted as a qualified brahmana. This system should not be confused with the corrupt "caste" system of India.

In India people claim to be Brahmans simply because they are born in a brahmana family even though they do not possess the qualifications or qualities of a brahmana and in most cases they are not working as Brahmans either..

The result of the corruption of the original system has been the destruction of the entire social structure in India and the "caste" system is now being used by the rich to exploit and oppress the poor.

Divisions According to Qualification: In Varnasrama society all members are equally important. An analogy comparing the social body to the human body is given to explain this. The Brahmans are the head of the body as they possess the intelligence and give directions to the other parts of the body. The Kshatriyas are likened to the arms of the body as their business as administrators and the military is to protect the social body from threats from outside (attacks from enemies) and disruption from within. (Thieves and rogues).

The Vaishyas are likened to the stomach. The stomach provides energy to the body. The Vaishyas, as the productive class, are the farmers and businessman who produce and distribute food to the social body. The Vaishyas are also responsible for protecting the cows.

The sudras are likened to the legs as they provide the manual labour required by the social body.

We look after our whole body. It is not that we attend to problems affecting the head and neglect problems in the legs. The body works as a coordinated unit and a problem anywhere in the body causes a disruption to the proper functioning of the whole body and is therefore immediately attended to.

The social body should work as a coordinated unit with different members of the society acting in their respective positions as Brahmans, Kshatriyas, Vaishyas and sudras according to their qualities. The result will be a happy, peaceful and efficient society.

The Brahmans: Although all members of the social body are important, as the Brahmans are the intelligent class directing society by giving guidance and advice to the king or government (Kshatriyas), it is vital that they be properly qualified.

If the head of society is not functioning properly the whole social body is in trouble.

All over the world we are seeing misguided governments make the lives of their citizens hell, simply because they have no qualified Brahmans to give them advice.

The whole planet has become very unfortunate and disturbed due to such unqualified leadership.

The brahmana's position is that of an unpaid adviser to the king or government. The business of the brahmana is to understand the Vedic Scriptures and be expert in applying them in different places and at different times.

The Vedic system doesn't require the creation of any new rules or legislation The perfect laws have been given by Manu, the father of mankind in the Manu Samhita, and the qualified brahmana simply implements these timeless laws. There is no need for imperfect man made laws.

The qualities of a brahmana are given in the Bhagawad Gita as peacefulness, self control, austerity, purity, tolerance, honesty, knowledge, wisdom and religiousness and all of these qualities must be actually manifest before someone can be accepted as a brahmana.

Giving Charity to the Brahmans: On special days such as the birth of a child, marriage and other auspicious occasions it is customary for the Kshatriyas and Vaishyas to give in charity to the Brahmans. The Kshatriya king is wealthy because in return for giving the citizens protection he levies taxes. The Vaishya farmers and businessmen are wealthy because of their farming and trading activity. The brahmana takes whatever small amount is required to maintain himself and his family and he distributes the rest of the charity he receives for the benefit of the people in general.

Because the brahmana is intelligent and an expert in spiritual matters he can understand how best to distribute charity. It is for this reason in Vedic society charity is given to the Brahmans. It is not very intelligent to give charity to unqualified persons, for they will simply squander it. For example if you give a drunkard money, it will be used for purchasing alcohol, not food. Such charity is charity in the mode of ignorance and is not very auspicious.

The Kshatriyas: The Kshatriyas take the positions of king or politicians and the military. They administer society according to the directions and advice of the Brahmans.

Their qualities are given in the Bhagawad Gita as heroism, power, determination, resourcefulness, courage in battle, generosity and leadership.

The Perfect King: A good Kshatriya king is strong and just, he acts according to the advice of the Brahmans, he is loved by the law abiding citizens and feared as death personified by the thieves and rogues.

In a country ruled by a qualified Kshatriya king the citizens are protected and thus they develop good qualities and are peaceful and happy. Because the king is strong and honest the citizens have no fear of being disturbed by thieves and rogues or by attacks from invading armies. They also have no fear of being plundered by unfair or exorbitant taxation or dishonest government officers, as such a strong king will quickly correct any corruption within his own ministry.

The lives of many saintly kings are described in Srimad Bhagavatam and we recommend those interested m hearing more about the qualities and activities of such great souls study the Srimad Bhagavatam..

The Problem With Modern Government: In modern governments we find many politicians and government officers who are simply interested in a good salary and a comfortable life. They achieve this for themselves and their colleagues by levying exorbitant taxes and creating an ineffectual and bureaucratic top heavy government.

The citizens under the rule of such an unqualified government are most unfortunate. They are not protected from thieves and rogues from within the country. Instead they are exploited by the governments taxation system. Excessive taxation is levied to maintain the ineffectual top heavy bureaucratic system. No one can be happy in such a difficult position

Selection of Members of the Government: Unless a person has the qualities of a Kshatriya he should not be given the position of king, president, Prime Minister, minister or a military man.

If the men in these positions do not have the qualities of a Kshatriya (heroism, power, determination, resourcefulness, courage in battle, generosity and leadership) then the government becomes unworkable and the society suffers due to lack of protection.

Currently, all over the world, the people in general are suffering because the governments of the world are full of unqualified persons who have no idea of the process of creating a fair society and maintaining law and order.

The Vaishyas: The Vaishyas are responsible principally for the production food and the protection of the cows. It is the duty of the Brahmans to understand the Vedic Scriptures and give guidance to the Kshatriya government and military who, in turn give directions to the Vaishyas and the sudras.

The qualities of a Vaishya are given in the Bhagawad Gita as farming, cow protection and business and they work to provide the society with the required food, clothing and other goods.

The Sudras: The sudras have little intelligence and must therefore be engaged in the service of one of the other three classes.

Their occupation is to perform manual labour, give service and to engage in arts and craftsmanship.

The sudras are unable to support themselves independently therefore they must take shelter of an employer who can direct and provide for them.

It is described in this age of Kali almost everyone is a Shudra. We can actually see society is now so degraded that practically everyone must work as a Shudra by serving an employer.

Only the sudras take such employment, the Brahmans simply depend on God and this way they get everything required. They receive charity from members of the other divisions of society. The Kshatriya has some land and collects taxes from the citizens and the Vaishya makes some money by trading farm produce and doing business. Only the sudras depend on someone else for their maintenance.

If proper education is provided then the sudras who have the capacity to learn can be elevated to higher positions in the social structure.

A society of sudras means a society of chaos as sudras don't have the intelligence to organize society, therefore, there is great need to train qualified Brahmans to re-establish the "head" of the social body. If this is done there is certainly hope for the future.

Caste is a Variety of Race

Ever Since Dalit groups have started mobilising themselves to fight their centuries old discrimination, the ruling elite have begun to hit back. In recent days, there have been articles in major newspapers on how caste discrimination is very different from race discrimination and that is why it is outside the purview of the U.N. Conference on Racial Discrimination. And all those who have articulated themselves including Andre Beteille, social anthropologist of repute, (in The Hindu of March 10, 2001) have backed the irrational position of the present government and other forces of vested interest.

What is however forgotten in the whole course of the arguments by the ruling elite is their own location in the social hierarchy. Our relationship to other human beings and society depends on our own social location and subjectivity. One can quote from authors and scholars to legitimise one's position and strengthen one's case. Unfortunately, the ground realities are experiential. To be fair to discriminated groups none of the elites who have been part of the oppressive structure should have any business to talk on their behalf since they have not experienced the reality of discrimination. The language and ideas of the ruling elite have been one of subjugation and exploitation since it is purely centred on concepts evolved in ivory towers. The objective of such knowledge is to preserve one's class interests. More than theory, knowledge must be constructed from experience. This position is unlikely to be acceptable to our noble theoreticians, academicians, the politicians and the bureaucrats since this class has benefited through subjugation of certain social groups in the name of caste.

The principle of equality is a fundamental component to the U.N. mechanism of promotion and protection of human rights. Article 1 of the Universal Declaration of Human Rights states that "All human beings are born free and equal in dignity and rights. They are endowed with reason and conscience and should act towards one another in a spirit of brotherhood." As we step into 21st century we need to ask ourselves as a nation whether our social and institutional structures are based on discrimination or not. And if there is discrimination what is it based on?

Endogamy: Whether it is caste or race, the status is entirely ascribed, the status one obtains at birth. Segregation exists in both the systems. Outcasts still remain outcastes. Even in the midst of the recent worst human tragedy that hit the country in the form of an earthquake in Gujarat, the whole institutional mechanism of the state did not move into the Dalit areas and belts while the benefits of relief went to the upper castes as fast as possible. This is no concoction. Papers have reported it. Parliament has discussed it. The Congress party has highlighted it and NGOs have testified to it. In both caste and race those in the lowest rung are not only discriminated against but cursed to do menial jobs. Endogamy is another feature of both. Marriages are rare and few both among different racial and caste groups. Both are stratifications, a hierarchical ordering of social categories, supported by social institutions. Inequality is intergenerationally transmitted in caste and race. Prejudice and discrimination are both a part of race and caste. And what is worse is that such prejudice and discrimination are not merely personal but institutional, a part of the structure and processes of whole society.

In both caste and race theories, there is an attitude of the so-called higher or superior groups that their culture is superior to all other cultures and all the other groups should be judged according to their culture. What is the difference in the claims made by the white race in Europe and the upper castes in India? In any racial or caste society the access to the society's resources including power is proportionately larger to the pure in comparison to the impure or polluted. Take the example of the Dalits in India. The Constitution has made caste illegal and abolished it in 1950. Affirmative action programme was introduced to bring the unequals to the level of equality. Regardless of official policy, the system still permeates Indian life and culture. "When we are working, they ask us not to come near them. At canteens, we have separate tea tumblers and they make us clean them ourselves and make us put the dishes away. We cannot enter temples. We cannot use upper caste water taps. Our children in schools are not treated as children of the others. We live in colonies of our own"-is a testimony of a scavenger in Ahmedabad. Caste has still limited social advancement, job and marriage choices. In spite of 50 years of Independence can one still believe that the SC/ST representation in teaching jobs at the level of higher education is a mere 2 per cent at the all India level, when the affirmative action has provided them with 22 per cent. How do those who oppose the linkage of caste with race explain this? Though skin colour or physical differences may not all the time play a significant part in distinguishing caste as in race, social descent and occupation does. Apartheid exists in both.

On several counts Dalit oppression is worse than racial discrimination. Over 240 million people of this country have been shunned as outcastes. In fact, the Government of India's 1996 state report on the Committee on Elimination of all forms of Racial Discrimination (CERD) clearly notes though caste may not be equivalent to race, it falls within the purview of Article 1 of the Convention due to the clause on descent. Why is the government playing a different tune now? Even the U.N. Committee on Civil and Political Rights has observed "SC/STs continue to endure severe social discrimination and suffer disproportionately from...intercaste violence, bonded labour and discrimination of all kinds." The U.N. bodies have opened up opportunities for Dalit activists, movements and organisations to highlight their oppression in the international forum. When the Indian state has not effectively implemented its constitutional mandate of Dalit Human Rights, what is wrong that the Dalits demand for rights from the World Government, the U.N.? After all, India is a signatory to most of the covenants of the U.N. In the light of India's ratification of CERD in 1969 it is perfectly constitutional, lawful and democratic for the discriminated communities to approach the very body to bring to its notice the discrimination they suffer.

Vested Interests: In spite of ground realities why is our ruling elite thus sound increasingly irrational? The reason is vested interests. It is the same interests that did not permit Ambedkar to raise specific concerns of the Dalits with regard to independence at the Round Table Conference. Once again, it is the very same interests that deny any implementation of affirmative action in the name of efficiency and merit. The caste system has developed a large amount of socioeconomic interests and any change in it affects the existing socioeconomic order. That is why our ruling elite abhor any transformation of the system. What the Dalit cause needs is perception of ground level realities from all concerned and not faithfulness to the position of the state and its academicians. We need to work for the liberation of the marginalisalised based on ground realities as experienced by the discriminated people.

2

CASTE SYSTEM IN MODERN INDIA

The leaders of independent India decided that India will be democratic, socialist and secular country. According to this policy there is a separation between religion and state. Practicing untouchability or discriminating a person based on his caste is legally forbidden. Along with this law the government allows positive discrimination of the depressed classes of India.

The Indians have also become more flexible in their caste system customs. In general the urban people in India are less strict about the caste system than the rural. In cities one can see different caste people mingling with each other, while in some rural areas there is still discrimination based on castes and sometimes also on untouchability. Sometimes in villages or in the cities there are violent clashes which, are connected to caste tensions. Sometimes the high castes strike the lower castes who dare to uplift their status. Sometimes the lower caste get back on the higher castes.

In modern India the term caste is used for Jat and also for Varna. The term, caste was used by the British who ruled India until 1947. The British who wanted to rule India efficiently made lists of Indian communities. They used two terms to describe Indian communities. Castes and Tribes. The term caste was used for Jats and also for Varnas. Tribes were those communities who lived deep in jungles, forests and mountains far away from the main population and also communities who were hard to be defined as castes for example communities who made a living from stealing or robbery. These lists, which the British made, were used later on by the Indian governments to create lists of communities who were entitled for positive discrimination.

The castes, which were the elite of the Indian society, were classified as high castes. The other communities were classified as lower castes or lower classes. The lower classes were listed in three categories. The first category is called Scheduled Castes. This category includes in it communities who were untouchables. In modern India, untouchability exists at a very low extent. The untouchables call themselves Dalit, meaning depressed. Until the late 1980s they were called Harijan, meaning children of God. This title was given to them by Mahatma Gandhi who wanted the society to accept untouchables within them.

The second category is Scheduled Tribes. This category includes in it those communities who did not accept the caste system and preferred to reside deep in the jungles, forests and mountains of India, away from the main population. The Scheduled Tribes are also called Adivasi, meaning aboriginals.

The third category is called sometimes Other Backward Classes or Backward Classes. This category includes in it castes who belong to Sudra Varna and also former untouchables who converted from Hinduism to other religions. This category also includes in it nomads and tribes who made a living from criminal acts.

According to the central government policy these three categories are entitled for positive discrimination. Sometimes these three categories are defined together as Backward Classes. 15% of India's population are Scheduled Castes. According to central government policy 15% of the government jobs and 15% of the students admitted to universities must be from Scheduled Castes. For the Scheduled Tribes about 7.5% places are reserved which is their proportion in Indian population. The Other Backwards Classes are about 50% of India's population, but only 27% of government jobs are reserved for them.

Along with the central government, the state governments of India also follow a positive discrimination policy. Different states have different figures of communities entitled for positive discrimination based on the population of each state. Different state governments have different lists of communities entitled for positive discrimination. Sometimes a specific community is entitled for rights in a particular state but not in another state of India. In modern India new tensions were created because of these positive discrimination policies. The high caste communities feel discriminated by the government policy to reserve positions for the Backward Classes. In many cases a large number of high caste members compete for a few places reserved for them. While the Backward Classes members do not have to compete at all because of the large number of reserved places for them compared to the candidates. Sometimes in order to fill the quota, candidates from the lower classes are accepted even though they are not suitable. Sometimes some reserved positions remain unmanned because there were few candidates from the lower classes causing more tension between the castes. Between the lower castes there are also tensions over reservation.

In the order of priority for a reserved place of the Backward Classes, candidate from the Scheduled castes is preferred over a candidate from the Scheduled Tribes who is preferred over a candidate from the other Backward Classes. As stated earlier Other Backward Classes are about 50% of India's population but only 27% of the Other Backward Classes are entitled for positive discrimination according to central government policy. Some Other Backward Classes communities are organizing politically to be recognized as Backward Classes entitled for positive discrimination.

The Scheduled Tribes who are seen as the aborigins of India got ownership and certain rights over Indian land. Many communities in India claim also to be aborigins of India and they are claiming the same rights as the Scheduled Tribes.

The caste identity has become a subject of political, social and legal interpretation. Communities who get listed as entitled for positive discrimination do not get out of this list even if their social and political conditions get better. In many cases the legal system is involved to decide if a certain person is entitled for positive discrimination. But with all this positive discrimination policy, most of the communities who were low in the caste hierarchy remain low in the social order even today. And communities who were high in the social hierarchy remain even today high in the social hierarchy. Most of the degrading jobs are even today done by the Dalits, while the Brahmans remain at the top of the hierarchy by being the doctors, engineers and lawyers of India.

Changes in Caste System

There have been tremendous changes made to Indians society with regards to providing a more just system for the Dalits. Great leaders have paved the way to help the Untouchables.

In 1967, Dr. Ambedkar, a Dalit, led a mass conversion to Buddhism, partly on the assumption that Buddhism had an anti-cast movement. He also wrote the constitution that outlawed untouchability and sanctioned positive discrimination programs for the Scheduled Castes and Tribes.

Mahatma Gandhi, a Vaishya, broke cast traditions by taking in an untouchable child. He started the name Harijan, meaning "Children of God" for the Untouchable caste. He also "persuaded the Indian National Congress to adopt a resolution in support of Harijan uplift, and published a magazine called Harijan, which was devoted to the welfare of the Untouchables." He helped lead India's independence and in doing so, unified India's social hierachy. Today, more and more Dalits are getting educated and employed. In the academic arena, scholarships have helped increase their literacy rate increase "from 10.3% in 1961 to 21.4% in 1981." This improvement has in turn, led to the emergence of educated Dalits holding higher positioned jobs, even white-collar jobs.

Along with urbanization, caste affiliations are no longer obvious and the observance of purity-pollution regulations is negligible. It is no longer an issue to take the public transport together or to be in the same meeting room. With so many people in such urban public places, it is very easy to forget the rigid, purity-pollution rules.

However, despite the decline in purity-pollution rules, there is still the observance of caste as can be witnessed in caste associations that still organize activities in quest of building numbers and thus influential power in society. Match-made marriages and activities are still present, proving another evidence of caste consciousness in today's time. Still, it would be too general a statement to assume that all purity-pollution consciousness has melted away. In the rural outskirts, it is safe to say that there are still low-caste workers facing discrimination. In the mid-1990s, about 90% of the Dalit population live in rural areas where an increasing proportion-more than 50%-work as landless agricultural labourers. Evasive tactics by high-caste landowners have managed to avoid government regulations that try to secure more even distribution of land. Modernization also posses competition as now, in addition to the minimal pay and benefits, workers have to compete against tractors and other machines for their jobs.

Today's Caste System

According to the Bhagavad-Gita, the Aryan family system has broken down in India over 3000 years ago in Krishna's time. Therefore today, 3000 years later, the social system of natural aptitude has degenerated into the caste system, which only resembles it in form.

So with the modernization and more liberalized and the changes that have been made to fight against caste discrimination, why is there such thing as outcastes still?

One reason might be that the whole ethical code of belief that the Indians uphold is very fatalistic and idealistic. This applies in the dharma and Moksha beliefs where the lower castes have kept quiet and accepted the discriminating treatment as the life God has set for them. Even if the lower castes change their beliefs about being resigned to the fate of their lives and do something about it, it is important to bear in mind that it is almost impossible for one to change their castes. An Untouchable will always be an Untouchable.

There is a backfiring effect to the protected actions administered for the scheduled castes. The affirmative action by the government serves to further perpetuate the discrimination problem because the lower castes are highlighted and made different again compared to the rest of the castes. The special treatments of being on the governments list or schedule, academic entries, voting rights, only make the discrimination glaring, adding onto the existing stigma.

Is Caste System Intrinsic to Hinduism?

This paper, citing evidence from the ancient scriptures, attempts to establish that Hinduism-its vedic and classic variants-did not support the caste system; it rigorously opposed it in practice and principle. Even after the emergence of the caste system, Hindu society still saw considerable occupational and social mobility. Moreover, Hinduism created legends to impress on the popular mind the invalidity of the caste system-a fact further reinforced by the constant efflorescence of reform movements throughout history. The caste system survived in spite of this because of factors that ranged from the socioeconomic to the ecological, which helped sustain and preserve balance among communities in a non-modern world.

> *One need not despair of ever knowing the truth of one's religion, because the fundamentals of Hinduism, as of every great religion, are unchangeable, and easily understood.-MK Gandhi, Young India, October 6, 1921*

It is necessary to demolish the myth that caste system is an intrinsic part of Hinduism. This myth is believed by orthodox elements within Hinduism and also is propagated by elements outside Hinduism with the mischievous intent of proselytising. Ironically both, though opposed to each other, jointly do a lot of damage. Moreover, this myth has harmed relations between the so-called upper castes and lower castes. This paper intends to logically and with documentary proof show that Hinduism-even vedic and classical Hinduism-not only does not support the caste system, but has taken lots of pains to oppose it both in principle and practice, making it obvious that caste system is not an intrinsic part of Hindu canon, philosophy and even practice. It will then show that the caste system emerged and survived due to totally different factors, which had nothing to do with Hindu religion.

What Caste System Means

Caste system as discussed here includes untouchability too, but wherever necessary it will be referred to separately. As we shall note, untouchability came into the caste system much later. The following features are generally taken as essential in characterising caste system.

- It means not simply a division of labour, with each 'varna' associated with a type of occupation, but also a division of labour determined by birth permitting no occupational/ social mobility. This is what distinguishes caste from class. While the former is hereditary, the latter is not-at least in principle.
- It is a rigid system, separating caste from caste, with restrictions on inter-dining and inter-marriage, due to a morbid fear of 'varna-sankara' (mixture of varnas). 'Caste' corresponds to jatis, and each varna is supposed to be a cluster of jatis, though there is sometimes ambiguity about which jati belongs to which varna. It is varnas that are cited in canon, not jatis. Restrictions on inter-dining and inter-marriage pertained not merely to varnas but also to jatis.
- It is a hierarchical system, one below the other in ritual (or purity) status, with several disabilities imposed on the fourth varna of shudras and even more on the untouchables known as 'antyajas'. It was not, however, hierarchical in power and wealth at least as between the upper castes. Dumont thought that the distinction between status and power is basic to understanding caste system [Dumont 1999:65-91].
- The system is associated with a notion of purity vis-a-vis pollution, with utmost purity at the level of Brahmins declining successively with Kshatriyas, vaishyas, and then shudras. At the other end, untouchables are treated as most impure or polluted. A touch of them is supposed to pollute others including shudras. A gradation of hierarchy and pollution was found among untouchables too, for example, bhangis (scavengers) considered as more polluted than say, mahars (agricultural labourers). Initially the notion of purity vs pollution may have been based on the need to maintain cleanliness, but it soon developed into an institutionalised form where pollution was associated with birth. The upper castes when polluted could, however, get rid of their pollution through ritual bath and such other expiatory measures. The notion of purity and pollution developed into a powerful instrument

to discourage and prevent varnasankara.

- The whole system along with its taboos and restrictions is authenticated by religion or canon, giving it a religious sanctity.
- At the foundation of the whole system there is a production system, which is subsistence-oriented and locally based rather than oriented to larger market, and production relations being of patron-client type, based on mutual dependence. Such a system is not necessarily geared for the generation of economic surplus and its appropriation, as it was not oriented to the larger market but to local needs.

Our Approach to the Demolition of the Myth

I reject totally the myth that caste system, as defined by these features either collectively or singly, forms an integral part of Hinduism. Why Hinduism is not varna dharma understood as jati or birth based, will become clear in the course of this paper. Hinduism can be defined, as Gandhiji did, as search for truth, non-violence, compassion for all beings and tolerance. Consistent with its commitment to search for truth, it is also marked by liberalism. Hinduism is a dynamic religion, not fixed or revealed once for all, and hence cannot be identified exclusively with the religion of the Vedas and Upanishads, nor with the religion expounded by 'Dharmashastras', nor with the Hinduism of the three eminent Acharyas-Shankara, Ramanuja and Madhva, nor also exclusively with medieval Hinduism and modern Hinduism. All these phases represent Hinduism, and have contributed to its development. Moreover, there is no disjointedness between different phases of Hinduism, each deriving its inspiration from the previous ones. In that sense, there is both change and continuity in Hinduism. Since however, it is accepted by all as beyond controversy that medieval Bhakti movement was a protest against caste system and since it is equally well known that modern Hinduism as explained by Swami Vivekananda, Aurobindo and others also has rejected caste system, the focus of this paper is on previous or classical phases of Hinduism. It is this earlier Hinduism, which may be termed as classical Hinduism, that is taken as supportive to the caste system, and it is this myth that is being demolished by this paper. Our greater attention to the previous phases of Hinduism is thus not because Hinduism is defined in terms of these phases, but simply because the contention concerns these phases.

The myth is demolished in the following way:

- by showing that there is no strong correlation between Hinduism and caste system, either spatially or temporally;
- by showing that even after the caste system emerged in Hindu society, there was considerable social and occupational mobility, and that none of the defining features of caste system listed above were strictly observed in practice particularly in the classical period;
- by showing that far from supporting the caste system, Hindu canon and philosophy were actually against caste system based on birth;
- by showing that, in addition, Hinduism created legends to impress the popular mind that the caste system is immoral and invalid;
- by showing that within the framework of Hinduism, there took place several movements against caste, starting from Bhakti movements continuing to more modern movements;
- by showing that caste system emerged and survived in spite of Hindu canon and philosophy, because of factors which had nothing to do with Hindu religion.

Reforms in Hindu Caste System

One aspect of Hinduism that is unique, controversial but so intrinsic to the religion is the Caste system. So many saints, reformers and even outsiders have tried to eradicate or avoid it but the system continues to be alive and vitiate the society from attaining the much needed harmony in modern times. The modern education system was expected to produce men and women with no castes and creed. But we have seen that the 'ugly' caste feelings are much more among educated class and more so when it comes to social affairs like marriages and rituals. Instead of wasting time to eliminate an essential feature of our own religion, I feel it is worthwhile exploring mechanisms for effective and quick reforms. Any religion that refuses to reform with the times will be relegated to oblivion and insignificance. We have classic examples of this natural phenomenon in India itself in Buddhism and Jainism. A simple and clear reform, not affecting the basic nature, is the need of the hour if Hinduism is to find its place as one of the best ways of life in twenty first century. A knowledge based liberal democratic religion is indeed the best suited, for the modern age of information, knowledge and freedom.

Mismatch: A clear mismatch exists between the classical four tier Caste system mentioned in the scriptures and the present day Hindu society. We find thousands of castes and sub-castes instead of a clear cut division into four. Across India, we find only the Brahmins having some similarity but other groups are let to choose their Castes according to the political and economic clouts.

For example, in Kerala, no one knows who are the Kshatriyas, Vysyas and Sudras. We have always considered Namboothiris to be the Brahmins in Kerala but there have never been a consensus on the other three castes. Other categories of people like Nairs, Ezhavas, Thiyas, Parayas, Pulayas etc. etc. have been classified under various castes in various times according to different scholars. The situation is very much similar in other states as well.

I strongly feel that we can positively utilize this mismatch between the classical four tier Caste system and the hundreds of castes that exist now. It is possible that we are confused between Gothras and Castes. All these present day categories like Jats, Rajputs, Nairs etc., etc., are essentially Gothras and are akin to the tribes in Africa and Arabia. Even if some scholars feel otherwise, I feel a lot of our problems can be solved if we define it that way. The present day names can continue as such provided they are considered as Gothras (or some other new name) instead of Castes. At one stroke, we can continue with the present naming systems and social groupings but can do away with the Caste problems.

Reform: Since the four tier system is referred in our scriptures at various places and cannot be undone or wished away, all that is required is a different way of looking at the Caste system. I propose a system in which all of us Hindus live through the Sudra, Kshatriya, Vyshya and Brahmin Castes as different stages in our lives.

If one goes back to the origins of Caste system, it is nothing but a scientific and systematic structuring of the then society according to the tastes and talents of the people. The hereditary principle which created bad blood in later years is nothing but a clever move on the part of Brahmins to keep the power within their kith and kin. We find this no longer valid and practical. Most children of Brahmin parents do not study scriptures, do not practice rituals and do not live like Brahmins. So how can they continue to 'enjoy' and monopolize Brahminhood? Similar is the case with all other castes, as they are classified now.

In the classical definition of Caste System, the different qualities attributed are as follows:

Brahmin-Learned & Spiritual

Kshatriya-Strong & Fighting

Vyshya-Intelligent & Creates Wealth

Sudra-Average & Assists all others

Essentially all of us are Sudras at birth and it is evident from the qualities attributed. It is something like starting on a clean slate. The average age of a human being is now 80 years and it is logical to assume that we exhibit Sudra like qualities until one fourth of our lifetime i.e till the age of 20. In the next phase i.e till the age of 40, we are strong, physically active and exhibit qualities of a Kshatriya. This is the period most of us marry and rear children. Strong and fighting qualities are required to protect the family and feed them. In the next phase i.e. 41 to 60, we all become worldly wise and participate in one form or other of wealth creation for the family and society, which makes us good Vaishyas. And finally, in the last phase, we tend to concentrate on spiritual activities and get ready to depart. We all try to become ideal Brahmins in the age group above 60.

Thus all of us Hindus, irrespective of our Gothras, pass through the four tier Caste system as envisaged in our scriptures and live an ideal life fulfilling all the necessary conditions required at various phases. It is this minor reinterpretation of the Caste system that will bring about drastic changes in the way Hindu society would think. All that we need is disassociating the classical Caste system from the present arrangement we have.

Advantages: The distinct advantage of such a reinterpretation of the Caste system is the little or minimum changes that will result in the present social symbols. All the present day laws and rules can continue as such if Caste is replaced by Gothra in the statute. For example, Scheduled Castes and Scheduled Tribes will merge and change to Scheduled Gothras. And they can enjoy the same reservations they are entitled to. The bad name attributed to Hinduism on account of the caste discrimination will vanish in one stroke. All present day names and surnames can continue without any change, but no Gothra will be automatically associated with any one of the four castes. This means nobody is a Brahmin or Kshatriya or Vyshya or Sudra throughout his or her life. It all depends on age and qualities. In the long run, the bad blood generated so far would fade out and Hindu society would be much more harmonious and stronger.

Lack of Access to Agricultural Land and Capital

About three-fourths of the SCs live in rural areas, where the main sources of income are either cultivation of agricultural land, wage labour or some kind of non-farm self-employment. Access to agricultural land for cultivation and capital for undertaking non-farm self-employment is critical. In 1993-94 only one-fifth of all SC households cultivated land as (independent) self-employment workers whereas among the others (i.e. non-SC/ST) the percentage was more than twice this rate. The percentage of those employed in some kind of non-farm self-employment activities, which indicate access to capital, was very low among the Scheduled Castes. Taking both farm and (rural) non-farm self-employment, about one-fourth of SC household seem to be engaged in self-employment activities as compared to more than half for others, in rural area. (Thorat, 2001)

In urban areas the disparity in the access to capital is well reflected in the lower proportion of self-employed workers among the Scheduled Castes. The lower proportion of SC as self-employed in agriculture, in non-farm sector in rural area and in urban area as compared to others, revealed the continuation of lack of access ownership of agricultural land and capital. The limited access is both due to the historical legacy associated with the restrictions of caste system to require means of income by the untouchables and ongoing discrimination in land market and capital market and other related economic spheres. (Thorat, 2001)

Inadequate access to agricultural land and capital (for self-employment activities) leaves no option to SC workers except to resort to manual wage labour, consequently it leads to enormously high level of (manual) wage labour among the SCs, nearly sixty per cent as compared to only one-third for others. In urban areas also disparities in the incidence of wage labour are evident. The proportion of casual labour among the SCs is around one-third as against only 10 per cent among the others. (Thorat, 1999).

Since more than sixty per cent of the SC workers in rural areas and more than one third in urban areas depend on wage employment, their earnings are determined by the level of employment and wage rates. It seems most possible that the SC workers suffer from discrimination in employment. The unemployment rate of SCs is much higher than that of other workers and they suffer from high under-employment as compared to others in Indian society. Higher unemployment rate of SC workers (which is twice that of others) indicates a possible existence of caste-based discrimination against SC workers in hiring. In the earlier section we presented evidence of discrimination against SCs in occupation, employment and wages.

With higher incidence of wage labour associated with high rate of under-employment the SCs would suffer from low income and consumption and a resultant greater level of poverty. This is reflected in the proportion of persons falling below a critical minimum level of consumption expenditure, what is called the poverty line. In 1993-94 about half of SC households were below the poverty line in rural areas as compared to only less than one-third for the general population. The poverty level among the SCs was thus high compared to others. What is striking is the variation in poverty ratio among wage labour across occupation group. The incidence of poverty was about sixty per cent among agricultural labourers, and forty per cent in non-agricultural labour. The level was relatively low for persons engaged in self-employed activities in agriculture (37.71 per cent) and in the non-agricultural sector (38.19 per cent). For each of these occupation groups, however, the proportion of SC household was much higher than their counterparts among the non-SC/ST group.

In urban areas about half of the SCs were below the poverty line in 1993-94, as compared to only one-third among the Others. Further, the incidence was astonishingly high among the casual labour as nearly two third were poor. The disparities in the level of urban poverty between the two social groups were relatively higher in the case of self-employment and regular salaried and wage workers but less in the case of casual labour. This indicates that by the early 1990s still half of the SC population was below the poverty line both in rural and urban areas. The 1993-94 figures revealed that the SCs were at least twenty-five years behind the other group in terms of level of poverty.

This macro-level comparative account of the economic position of the formerly untouchable and upper-caste persons covering relevant economic indicators provides convincing evidence of the continuing economic inequalities associated with caste. It is thus beyond doubt that the historical impact of traditional caste-based restrictions on the ownership of property, employment and occupation are still visible in significant measure, the access of the formerly untouchables to income-earning capital assets and employment is limited, and their segregation into manual labour is overwhelmingly high. The two prime economic attributes of the caste system thus seem to be present in sizeable measure, even today.

Decisive Reasons for Continuity: In the end the question is: why do the higher castes continue to practice untouchability, and discrimination in social, cultural, religious, political and economic spheres. And why do they resort to physical and other violence when the untouchables try to gain lawful access to human rights and equal participation in social, political, cultural, religious and economic sphere of community life? The reasons for widespread practice of untouchability, discrimination and atrocities as well as violent reaction by the higher castes are to be found in their continuing belief and faith in the sanctity of the institution of caste and in untouchability.

The traditional Hindu social order continues to govern the thought process and behaviour of the large majority of Hindus in rural areas. The provisions in the Constitution and law are secular and equal but the customary rules of the caste system and the institution of untouchability are based on the principle of inequality in social, economic, cultural and religious sphere. This obviously brings a conflict between what is contained in the constitution and law, and what is contained in the traditional customary rules, norm, and values of the caste system and untouchability.

People continued to follow the latter because it provides immense privilege and serves their social, political and economic interests. And when the dalits try to get equal access and 'assert' their rights, it often invites the wrath of higher caste persons in the form of atrocities and physical violence. About the reasons for the atrocities on the SC/ST the Report of the Commission of the SC/ST 998 observed, "Some of the major causes of atrocities and other offences against Scheduled Castes and Scheduled Tribes are related to issues of land and property, access to water, wage payments, indebtedness and bonded or forced labour.

Issues of human dignity, including compulsion to perform distasteful tasks traditionally forced on Scheduled Castes, and molestation and exploitation of dalit women are also involved. Caste related tension is exacerbated by economic factors, which contribute to violence. It is the assertion of their rights, be they economic, social or political, by the Scheduled Castes and Scheduled Tribes and their development, which often invite the wrath of the vested interests.

Disputes during elections, animosity due to reservation, jealousy due to increasing economic prosperity, violence related to the process of taking possession and retaining Government allotted land, tension due to refusal of SCs to perform tasks such as disposal of dead cattle or cutting umbilical cord, are manifestations of the resentment of the high caste against increasing awareness among Scheduled Castes, assertion and prosperity among the SCs. Like land, water is another sensitive issue. Accessibility of drinking water and water for irrigation and disposal of water removed from water logged areas become issues that can trigger off atrocities on SCs. Castiest favour during religious and social ceremonies, disputes arising during sowing and harvesting operations, and removal of crops from the granary after harvesting, have also been known to cause tension. Increasing awareness and empowerment of SCs, manifested in resistance to suppression, also result in clashes".

The official evidence and the regional studies based on primary data revealed that in rural India in several spheres, if not in all spheres, the social behaviour of high caste Hindus is still governed by the norms and codes of the traditional caste system, although there are changes in some spheres of social relations. The settlements of the untouchables in rural areas are away from the high-caste locality, endogamy (which is the backbone of the caste system) continues, entries for the untouchables in private houses and temples in rural areas are limited, and common sharing of tea and food is also extremely limited. Pressures and restrictions on voting and political participation also prevail. The restriction on the change of occupation and discrimination in employment, wage rate, share of rent, rate of interest charged and in sale of items from shops owned by the untouchables is still observed in some degree in the rural areas, where three-fourths of the untouchables live.

This goes to shows that the enforcement and practice of universal human rights in society is not conditioned by the formal supportive legal framework (such as the Constitution and other laws) alone. Often, cultural, social, religious and economics notions make the enforcement and practice of human rights difficult. Non-formal institutions; social, religious as well as economic, involve a framework of social behaviour of their own, which may not be in consonance with the principles enunciated by the United Nations, or the Constitution of a nation in which case different sets of values may result in conflicts. It implies that unless inequalities imbedded in the social, economics and cultural structure of the Hindu society are addressed, the legal measures will make little difference in providing access to human rights to the dalits in India.

Table: Untouchability in Practice: Cases Registered, 1955-1997

Year	*Number of cases registered*	*Year*	*Number of cases registered*
1955	180	1956	693
1957	491	1958	559
1959	481	1960	275
1961	489	1962	389
1963	393	1964	371
1965	366	1966	488
1967	353	1968	214
1969	329	1970	364
1971	526	1972	1515
1973	2456	1974	1908
1975	3528	1976	5108
1977	3425	1978	4729
1979	4911	1980	4303
1981	4085	1982	4087
1983	3949	1984	3925
1985	3332	1993	2531
1994	1731	1995	1528
1996	1417	1997	1157

Source: For 1955-1985, Annual Reports of Commissioner for SC/ST; 1993-1997, Commission for Scheduled Caste/ Scheduled Tribe, Delhi.

Table: Crimes and Atrocities Against Scheduled Castes, 1981-1997

Year	*Murder*	*Grievous Hurt*	*Rape*	*Arson*	*Others*	*Crime under POA*	*Total*
1981	493	1492	604	1295	10434	14318	28636
1982	514	1429	635	1035	11441	15054	30108
1983	525	1351	640	993	11440	14949	29898
1984	541	1454	692	973	12327	15987	31974
1985	502	1367	700	980	11824	15373	30746
1986	564	1408	727	1002	11715	15416	30832
1995	571	4544	837	500	11056	13925	31433
1996	543	4585	949	464	13862	9620	30023
1997	504	3462	1002	384	12149	7831	25338

Source: Annual Reports of Commission for the Scheduled Caste and Tribe, Delhi. ***POA:*** Prevention of Atrocities Act.

Table: Occupational Pattern: Scheduled Caste and Other (in percentage)

Occupational Category	1987-88		1993-94	
Rural	SC	OTHER	SC	OTHER
Self-employed in Agriculture	18.90	43.3	19.12	42.42
Self employed in Non-Agriculture	11.0	13.8	10.32	13.89
Self-employed (Total)	29.8	57.1	29.49	56.31
Agricultural Wage Labour	51.7	23.2	50.6	22.37
Non-Agricultural Wage Labour	11.4	09.7	10.22	6.67
Rural Wage Labour Total	63.1	31.1	60.28	29.14
Others	06.9	11.5	9.67	14.62
Urban				
Self-employed	28.0	35.2	24.08	35.05
Regular Wage/Salaries	39.4	45.0	39.27	43.11
Casual Labour	26.0	10.3	26.96	10.57
Others Wage	08.5	09.2	9.67	11.25
All	100	100	100	100

Source: NSS Employment/Unemployment Survey, 1987-88, and 1993-94 CSO, Delhi.

SC = Scheduled Caste; Others = Non SC/ST. (excluding, Scheduled Caste and Scheduled Tribe)

The Indian Caste System as a Means of Contract Enforcement

Estimates put the start of the caste system anywhere between 3000 BC to 1000 BC. Even today it remains an important issue for Indian society with the Indian government's proposals for caste based job quotas in the private sector and increases in caste based reservations at institutes of higher learning. It is still an important determinant of people's economic choices. On the non-academic front, writings on caste tend to be polemic. Rabindranath Tagore called it a "gigantic, cold-blooded repression" and Nehru acknowledged that the caste system was "wholly opposed to modern conditions and the democratic ideal." With the widespread criticism the institution currently faces the persistence of this system of social stratification for 3000 years during periods of changing economic and social environments is puzzling.

Given the long history of this institution and changes in recent decades, covering the whole time period is infeasible. The model of the caste system in the paper is more appropriate to pre-colonial India, or more specifically before the introduction of the British law courts. (Dirks 2001) argues that British policies introduced changes in the caste system. A snapshot of the pre-colonial economy shows a robust thriving economy. Lord Clive in 1757 noted that Murshidabad "is as extensive, populous, and rich as the city of London, with this difference that there were individuals in the first possessing infinitely greater property than in the last city". According to (Maddison 2003), in 1700 India's share of world GDP was 24.4% compared to Western Europe's 21.9%. The economy was largely agricultural but was noted for the high quality its manufactures. Another feature which is often called characteristic of the economy was its ability to sustain a high degree of division of labour. At the same time there is not much evidence of a well developed court system.

This leaves us with two questions. First, can we model the caste system to better understand it and the reasons for its persistence over the years? Second, how was the economy able to sustain a high degree of specialization without a strong enforcement system? In answer to both these questions, I argue that the caste system functioned as a means of contract enforcement, thus providing an economic reason for its persistence over the years. I over a model of how the system provided contract enforcement and check for testable implications. The caste system, like other institutions, shapes an individuals's actions and choices. A model can help us understand the way the system works and by organizing our thinking, help understand its effects on the economy.

The central problem in the economy is sustaining trade in services within a village. Trade is modelled as a one-sided prisoner's dilemma game. The consumer approaches a producer for a service. The producer then provides the service, choosing his effort level. Higher producer effort translates into a better quality service. After the service is rendered, the consumer decides whether he should pay the producer or not, leaving incentives for the consumer to default on payment. For trade to be sustained, there has to be a way of ensuring that default is credibly punished.

The major assumption made about castes is that they serve as a means to share information which can then be used to enforce collective action. Of all the possible equilibria of the game, consider those where punishments are collective and take the form of service denial: If a consumer defaults on payment to a member of caste c, all the members of c refuse to provide the consumer with services in the future. The utility the consumer forgoes by cheating on a member of a caste (the cost of cheating) is what is termed the bargaining power of the caste. It depends on the services which can only be obtained in caste c and nowhere else or if covers a service with higher quality than producers outside the caste. The consumer will not cheat as long as the benefit from cheating is lower than the cost of doing so. This is his incentive compatibility constraint.

The producer has to choose the effort level he will provide. By assumption, the producer always prefers to provide the highest possible effort, since his profits are increasing in effort provision. There is no notion of efficiency wages or of effort unobservability. Both consumers and producers benefit from increasing effort levels. The only thing that restricts the producers effort level is the consumer's incentive to default. Increasing effort levels increases the consumer's benefit from cheating and make him more likely to default. Thus, producer effort is bounded by the bargaining power of his caste through the consumer's incentive compatibility constraint. The higher the punishment for the consumer in default, the higher the effort level the producer can provide. Efficiency of the equilibrium is defined by the effort levels sustainable in equilibrium.

The main part of the paper characterizes equilibria in which trade is sustained with these strategies, showing that the caste system served as a means of contract enforcement. The paper offers three ways to substantiate this claim. The first is anecdotal evidence in support of the assumptions and implications of the model. Section 2 details evidence of collective punishments and the informational capabilities of castes.

The second method of substantiation is by the other implications of the model. Collective punishments are not the best known feature of the caste system. Other features such as occupational specialization by caste, a purity scale and a hierarchy of castes are better known and are used as defining features of the caste system. The second part of the paper shows that these features are implications of the model of contract enforcement. Moreover, these features serve in equilibrium to increase the efficiency of contract enforcement.

Thus the paper integrates the caste system's different aspects and features into one model that is based on a simple economic insight.

The third method of substantiation is empirical. The data used is census data from three different locations and time periods-Cochin (1875), Tirunelveli (1823) and Mysore (1941). Each individual census has limited observations, but together they provide a means to check for patterns in the data and if these patterns are consistent with the implications of the model. The main results will be about two implications-occupational specialization and the relationship between castes and population size.

To return to the features of the caste system briefly: the occupational specialization result argues that increasing the number of occupations that are unique to (monopoly of) some caste increases efficiency. Since punishments take the form of service denial, doing so strengthens the bargaining power of the caste, which then increases effort provision by producers and hence efficiency. The section on purity discusses the role of self production and occupational restrictions by caste.

Self production restrictions allow individuals to commit, ex-ante, to reduce their outside option in the case of default, which strengthens the producer's bargaining power. Occupational restrictions by caste prevents higher caste members from free-riding of the bargaining power of their caste and this allows for unequal bargaining power to be sustained across castes in equilibrium. Both these restrictions could be justified on the basis of purity and it leads naturally into a hierarchy of castes based on purity. In addition, the relationship between the number of castes in a village and population size is also examined. If information collection is costly and increasing in caste size, the prediction is that the number of castes in a village should be increasing in population size. Finally, regarding the ascriptiveness of the system, restricting entry into castes follows naturally from the caste's ability to decide to whom it will extend its punishment power. A person cannot 'belong' to a caste unless the caste is willing to punish consumer's who default on him. If there are rents to be preserved, one could see restricted entry into castes in equilibrium.

Literature Review: One consequence of this institution's persistence and complexity is that it has been a subject of much study not just in economics but in anthropology and sociology as well. On the empirical side, papers such as (Banerjee and Somanathan 2006) and (Anderson 2005) detail the economic effects of caste. The most common explanation given for the persistence of the caste system is religious sanction, based on the ancient texts-the Rig Veda and the Manu Smriti. However, people who converted to other religions like Christianity and Islam, still kept their caste even though their new religion did not have any notion of caste. The racial theory, proposed by (Risley 1892) among others, claims the caste system was a means to prevent racial mixing. But it does not explain the other features of the caste system. (Nesfield 1885) was a main proponent of the 'functional' view of the caste system. He argues that castes were akin to guilds in function. The ranking of castes depending on how 'advanced' in terms of industrial development the occupations they specialized in were. This does not however specify why industrial development would be associated with a purity scale and is inconsistent with evidence showing that castes rise in the rankings with an increase in income without changing their occupation. (Neale 1957) noticed that the caste system governed the exchange of services. Building on this observation, (Klass 1993) proposes that the solution to the division of labour problem that emerged in India was the caste system. The features helped maintain distinct boundaries and thus monopoly power. But he is unable to explain the purity scale. One of the best known papers in economics about the caste system is that of (Akerlof 1976). His model of the caste system depends crucially on people's beliefs and is similar to the literature on discrimination ((Becker 1971)). If beliefs are such that a good will be consumed only if the labour used in its production belongs to a certain group. Then, the caste system can be sustained as an equilibrium as firms hire workers on the basis of which group they belong to. His model has hereditary occupations by group, but he gives no reasons for why such beliefs came about. (Lal 1988) uses the shortage of labour brought about as a result of settled agriculture as a reason for these beliefs. This would require the beliefs only to be about agriculture.

Evidence however suggests that most occupations are monopolies with agriculture being an exception. Most castes are engaged in some type of agricultural activity. Also, blocking coalitions are possible and the caste system will not survive.

The equilibrium analysis of an institution is a separate from the question of institutional origin. This paper focuses on the former and cannot answer the question-what made equilibria with collective punishments a focal point in South Asia over other, possibly be Pareto-dominant equilibria? On this count, the above explanations may be complementary and provide a reason for why this equilibrium was a focal point. What is possible to say, is that given it appeared, it functioned as an effective means of contract enforcement and its various features facilitated this role.

This paper does not argue that the only economic role of the caste system was contract enforcement. It did have other functions, some guild like in nature and others like mutual insurance. However each of these functions alone cannot account for a coherent explanation of all the features of the system. The contract enforcement role of the caste system is crucial to generate the essential features of the caste system. The informational abilities of the caste required to undertake contract enforcement can also assist in a caste's ability to provide other services like insurance. In addition, the paper draws on the literature on collective enforcement. (Greif 1989) and (Greif 1993) use collective punishments to explain the success and failure of the Maghribi traders in the 11th century.

The traders faced a principle-agent problem with their agents overseas which they solved by collectively punishing errant agents. (Greif, Milgrom, and Weingast 1994) consider the role of the merchant guild in the late medieval period. They argue that the guilds served as a means for the rulers to commit to the security of the merchants. In these models the analysis is about one group of people that uses collective punishments against an individual. A model that consider more than one group of people using collective punishments is, for example, (Greif 2002) which models how credit transactions between traders in different localities in medieval Europe were sustained using a collective responsibility system. In a similar vein, (Fearon and Laitin 1996) examine the role of in-group policing to facilitate inter-ethnic cooperation. In both these papers the crucial assumption required is that members of one group cannot individually identify members of another group. This makes collective punishment take the form that members of a defaulter's group are punished at random by the group whose member has been defaulted on. What is new in this paper (as far as I can tell) is looking at a number of groups, each of which uses collective punishments. The groups interact together in a system and individuals are clearly identifiable to all members in the population.

This paper fits into the broader research agenda in Institutional Economics on contract enforcement in societies without an effective legal apparatus. It is also related to the literature that studies the role that information sharing in groups may play in development (for example (Banerjee and Newman 1998), (Cornell and Welch 1996)) and the role social networks can play in situations where enforcement may be limited or lacking. (for example (Besley 1995), (Spagnolo 1999)). On a broader note it is related to the literature that argues that legal and contracting institutions are important influences of long-run economic progress (for example: (North 2002), (Acemoglu, Johnson, and Robinson 2001), (Rodrik, Subramanian, and Trebbi 2004))

Abbé Dubois observes, "In India, where the princes and aristocracy live in extreme indolence, attaching little importance to making their dependents happy and taking small pains to inculcate in them a sense of right and wrong, there are no other means of attaining these desirable ends and preserving good order than by the authoritative rulings of the caste system."

The paper proceeds as follows: section 2 describes the institutional details and the anecdotal evidence in support of the model's assumptions and implications. That is followed by the model and analysis in section 3 and 4. Analysis and anecdotal evidence of the implications of the model with regards to the main features of the caste system are covered in section 5. In section 6 the model's implications are tested using census data. Section 7 concludes.

Implications of the Model: other Features of the Caste System

Features of the caste system, namely occupational specialization, purity scale, hierarchy and commensality are used in the definition of the caste system in section 2, but have not been addressed in the model yet. In this section I show that they can be obtained as implications of the model of the contract enforcement.

Anecdotal Evidence

Occupation Choice: At the start of the Manu Smriti, the occupations assigned to each caste are set out: " But in order to protect this universe He, the most resplendent one, assigned separate (duties and) occupations to those who sprang from his mouth, arms, thighs, and feet. To Brahmans he assigned teaching and studying (the Veda), sacrificing for their own benefit and for others, giving and accepting (of alms). The Kshatriya he commanded to protect the people, to bestow gifts, to offer sacrifices, to study (the Veda), and to abstain from attaching himself to sensual pleasures; The Vaishya to tend cattle, to bestow gifts, to offer sacrifices, to study (the Veda), to trade, to lend money, and to cultivate land. One occupation only the lord prescribed to the Sudra, to serve meekly even these (other) three castes.

What is important to interpret the results later on is what Manu has to say about castes following occupations that are the domain of other castes. He does make the broad statement that "It is better (to discharge) one's own (appointed) duty incompletely than to perform completely that of another; for he who lives according to the law of another (caste) is instantly excluded from his own." However, he qualifies that with exceptions in the case whereby individuals are not able to subsist by following their caste occupations. He allows castes to follow occupations of castes lower than them but very categorically prohibits them from following the occupations of castes above them. "A man of low caste who through covetousness lives by the occupations of a higher one, the king shall deprive of his property and banish." Even though a higher caste member may be allowed to perform the occupations of a lower caste restrictions are placed on him to ensure that the occupations are not entirely profitable. If those restrictions are ignored then the upper caste individual is reduced to a lower caste. " But a Brahmana, unable to subsist by his peculiar occupations just mentioned, may live according to the law applicable to Kshatriyas; for the latter is next to him in rank. If it be asked, 'How shall it be, if he cannot maintain himself by either (of these occupations?' the answer is), he may adopt a Vaishya's mode of life, employing himself in agriculture and rearing cattle. But a Brahmana, or a Kshatriya, living by a Vaishya's mode of subsistence, shall carefully avoid (the pursuit of) agriculture, (which causes) injury to many beings and depends on others. By (selling) flesh, salt, and lac a Brahmana at once becomes an outcast; by selling milk he becomes (equal to) a Sudra in three days. But by willingly selling in this world other (forbidden) commodities, a Brahmana assumes after seven nights the character of a Vaishya. A Kshatriya who has fallen into distress, may subsist by all these (means); but he must never arrogantly adopt the mode of life (prescribed for his) betters. A Vaishya who is unable to subsist by his own duties, may even maintain himself by a Sudra's mode of life, avoiding (however) acts forbidden (to him), and he should give it up, when he is able (to do so). But a Sudra, being unable to find service with the twice-born and threatened with the loss of his sons and wife (through hunger), may maintain himself by handicrafts".

Purity, Hierarchy and Commensality: The purity scale was a central feature of the caste system. A leading anthropologist on the caste system, Louis Dumont, conceived of Indian hierarchy as "a purely relative non-competitive ranking oriented to a single idea of higher and lower". Louis Dumont considered the relative opposition of pure and impure to be the defining characteristic that kept the caste system together. In his book (Dumont 1970) he says " [caste] rest on one fundamental conception and are reducible to a single true principle, namely the opposition of the pure and the impure. This opposition underlies hierarchy, which is the superiority of the pure to the impure, underlies separation because the pure and the impure must be kept separate, and underlies the division of labour because the pure and impure occupations must likewise be kept separate". (Miller 1975) argues that "some occupations are attributed certain polluting qualities and are identified with the pollutability of certain castes associated with them." Occupations are ranked on the basis of purity. The key word being 'relative'-the pure occupations are only so relative to the occupations at the lower end of the ranking. In addition to occupations being ranked, castes were ranked too. The rank of a caste had two sources. The first was the number of services they could get someone else to provide for them. The more 'impure' services a caste would get someone else to perform for them rather then having to do it themselves, the higher the ranking of the caste. (Kolenda 1978) notes "In Khalapur, the servants saved their high caste jajmans from work deemed to be dirty (the Barber, Laundryman, Sweeper), or manual (Potter and Carpenter), or menial (Watercarrier)". This can be seen clearly in cases when castes rose and fell in the hierarchy. (Srinivas 1960) defines 'Sanskritization' as a means by which a low caste tries to raise its ranking by emulating the "customs, rituals, beliefs, ideology and style of life" of the castes higher in the ranking. He notes that an attempt to move up in the hierarchy is usually preceded by an improvement in the economic or political fortunes of the caste. (Rowe 1968) undertakes a case study of the Noniya caste, a Shudra caste trying to raise their status to that of the Cauhan Rajputs, over North India. He finds that the claim made gains " whenever a group of Noniyas existed whose wealth enabled them to attempt social emulation of the Rajput style of life". (Gupta 1991) discusses Rowe's study of the Noniya caste trying to raise their ranking to that of Cauhans. " The importance of the economic factor cannot be overemphasized for very often the claims of the well-to-do sections of a depressed jati are accepted by the powerful and dominant castes, while the identical claims of their indigent jati brethren do not win such acceptance. The prosperous Noniyas, for instance were accepted by the privileged castes as Chauhans but the poorer Noniyas were not accorded similar status". (Srinivas 1996), based on his study on Rampura, finds that "a caste which is numerically strong and wealthy will be able to move up in the ritual hierarchy if it Sankritizes its ritual and way of life, and also loudly and persistently proclaims itself to be what it wants to be ". (Marriott 1950) discusses how the carpenter caste tries to raise their rank by emulating the ceremonies and lifestyles of the Brahmins.

The second source of purity that affected the rank of the caste was the occupation of its members (O'Malley 1932) says that "One section of a caste having taken up an occupation which is considered more respectable than those followed by other members of the caste, claims superiority on that account, refuses to let its women marry men belonging to other sections, and becomes a separate sub-caste.". (Desai 1911) says "A section of Kohlis left off their traditional occupation of menial labour and took to the making of bricks. They came to be known as Dalwadi or Talvar, that is cutter, because they dug up ponds and made bricks. This new and honourable profession gave them a higher social status and in the course of time, they came to be know as a new caste of Kohlis. Kalal (liquor sellers) were originally Kanbis or Rajputs. Owing to the degrading nature of their profession, they had to separate themselves from the parent castes and formed a new caste of their own".

Commensality was usually a means for people to keep track of the ranking of the castes. (Marriott 1965) finds that "residents of both Kishan Garhi and Ram Nagla villages say that they are able to form exact opinions about the relative ranks of castes according to certain ritual interactions-i.e., formalized symbolic gestures between persons of different castes resembling the gestures used in religious worship. The ritual interactions which are said to be most significant for precise ranking are those which concern the giving and receiving of food, and the giving and receiving of a variety of honorific gestures and service". (Miller 1975) gives evidence of the case when a change in hierarchy is accompanied by a change in commensal relationships. More importantly he stresses that the commensal relations are based on a perceived 'purity/ pollution' basis. Castes that are deemed to be more 'pure' find that their food is more readily acceptable and social interactions become easier.

Castes and Population Sizes: The relation between the size of a village and the number of castes has not been explored in detail in the literature with the exception of (Marriott 1965). In his data description he notices that the number of castes in a village seem to be increasing with population size. Most of the current literature treats the number of castes as fixed. This is not entirely true as growth of local caste groups due to migration, fission and fusion was a common occurrence.

One reason for the fission of castes was changes in occupation. (Nesfield 1885) examines the fission and fusion of castes on the basis of occupation changes in detail. He gives the example of the "Peshiraj or stone-quarrier, on the sides of the Mirzapur hills, who seems inclined to separate himself from the parent stem of Ahir or cattle-grazer; for it is in the neighbourhood of these stone quarries that the Ahir finds woods and pasture for his herds...at Saharanpur, some fruit sellers, whose trade, it may be presumed, has been encouraged by the large public gardens at that station, have separated themselves from the common herd of Kunjras and decorated their small community with the Persian title of Mewafarosh". The best sources for evidence of formation of new castes locally are (Gait 1913), (Blunt 1912), (Desai 1911), (Martens 1912) and (Nesfield 1885). (Gait 1913) best summarizes this when he says "When one section of a caste develops peculiarities of any kind-a different occupation, habitat or social practice, more rarely a different religious cult-the tendency is for it to regard itself and be regarded by the rest of the caste, as something different. This feeling grows with time, until at last it, or the main body of the caste, withdraws from the marriage league. The result is a new sub-caste, and often, in the end, a new caste. On the other hand, when a section of one caste adopts the occupations characteristic of another, the tendency is for it to be absorbed into the latter.

Occupational Specialization: This section examines the role that monopolies play in this economy. Taking occupation choice as given, examine the game in the service trade subperiods (t > 0). The punishment power of the caste depends on how large the set of occupations unique to a caste is. The larger it is, the easier it is to provide incentives for consumer j to pay for services as the bargaining power of the caste is higher. This in turn raises the effort level that producers are willing to supply thus improving efficiency. Define the set of occupations unique for some caste as Kunique = Sc

Empirical Evidence

This section tests the predictions of the model on the relationship between castes and population size. It also considers the relationship between occupation diversity and the bargaining power of the caste. The predictions tested are:

1. Castes and population size: Keeping the number of occupations fixed, an increase in population size will be accompanied by a rise in the number of castes.
2. Occupational diversity:

o If castes have unequal bargaining power, castes with higher bargaining power have more occupation choices open to them.

o larger castes should have occupations with a higher bargaining power or they should have a monopoly over a larger number of occupations.

The model is more appropriate to pre-colonial India, but data from this period that is amenable to testing the predictions are difficult to find. The censuses used are from Tirunelveli (1823), Cochin (1875) and Mysore (1941). These particular censuses are used because they are the earliest available census that have the approprate data. The Tirunelveli data is before India was under direct control of the British Crown.

Also, both Cochin and Mysore at the time of the census were native states and not under direct control of the British. The model focuses on intra-village trade and the narrowest definition of what constitutes a caste. Testing requires detailed village level caste data that is difficult to obtain. Individual level data was collected, however, due to resource constraints, all census data were presented in reports that tabulated this information. Individual level information has long since been lost.

The Tirunelveli and Mysore censuses are used to test the castes and population size implications. The caste data available are the number of castes and the number of people in the largest castes and detailed economic data for the villages are also available. The 1941 census, though not pre-colonial, it is useful as it 86 I'm very grateful to David Ludden for sharing his Tirunelveli data is one of the few censuses with village level data, narrow caste definitions and it also provides some measure of geographic variation.

The occupational predictions are tested using data taken from a report on the census of the native state of Cochin in 1875. It has a breakdown of occupations by caste. Other census undertakings also collected this data but usually prioritized economic information about the region over a detailed breakdown of occupation by caste. In the case of this census, no detailed economic information was available as a revenue survey of the region was yet to be undertaken so the census focuses on caste information. However, a lack of economic data restricts our testing. This data is at the district level. Castes are grouped into 23 categories and the data is for each caste category. This information is also available in the later British Censuses but they are by definition colonial censuses. In addition, the British census information is worse as it is for broader categories of castes, occupations as well it aggregates information over much larger areas.

As the observations in each census are limited, the results should be interpreted with caution. These empirical results should be treated as suggestive evidence only. It is extremely difficult to establish causality in this context due to the paucity of data and instruments. It should be seen more as checking for patterns in the data-Are the implications of the model consistent with the patterns in the data? One general caveat about data on caste in general is that the data are noisy because of people's confusion regarding the degree of specificity required when answering the caste question, confusion by the census enumerators and other problems (see (Barrier 1981)).

Occupational Specialization

Data Description: This part uses data from the 1875 census of Cochin. The purpose of the Cochin census was to update information on the condition of the people. In particular it focused on age, occupation, education, infirmities, caste and religion. The state had attempted to ascertain the numbers of people on five earlier occasions, the last being 17 years before this census. This though, was the first attempt at a systematic enumeration. Data was reported at the district level. The state had 7 districts. If a person had two or more occupations the one he considered most important by him was returned as his occupation. There are 18 occupation categories which together with the occupations included in each category. Castes were categorized into 23 broad categories. The population of these castes is broken down into 18 occupation categories. In addition for each caste the population, number of houses and number of women is available.

Implications from the Theory: In the model, a caste is able to sustain trade in the services it supplied if it had some bargaining power. Its bargaining power depends on the services unique to the caste and/or the services which the caste provides at a better quality than other castes. A caste can increase in bargaining power by increasing the number of services it has a monopoly over or by specializing in services that have a high bargaining power. If castes have unequal bargaining power, castes with higher bargaining power have more occupation choices open to them.

The section on castes and population sizes (section 5.3) also provides some implications on occupational choice by caste. If the optimal caste size is determined by the trade-off between information costs and the benefits due to increased monopoly power, then larger castes should also have occupations with a higher bargaining power or they should have a monopoly of a larger number of occupations.

To test these implications there needs to a measure of what practically constitutes bargaining power. Three measures are used: economic bargaining power, social bargaining power and occupational bargaining power. One of the occupation categories is property ownership. The first measure of bargaining power is a measure of how a caste is able to monopolize control over land resources. This is a proxy for economic bargaining power. The second is the social rank of the caste. Caste categories in the native state are ranked into

5 categories according to the perception of the census enumerators. This roughly corresponds to the average social rank of the caste across districts, as the census report does not give this ranking by district.

For the third measure of occupational bargaining power, occupation categories are further categorized into high or low bargaining power. A caste's bargaining power is that of the occupation that the caste has either the highest fraction of people following or the occupation they have the largest monopoly in. The relative measure of caste size used in the regressions is the fraction of district population in the caste. Other caste characteristics considered are the fraction of the caste engaged in cultivation and interactions of the various measures of bargaining power with the relative size of the caste. The main district characteristic considered to affect occupational specialization is the population of the district. Economic measures of the district such as the fraction of the population literate, a weak measure of poverty of the district (the fraction of houses classified as class 3 or the lowest category), a measure of agricultural surplus (the fraction of population engaged in cultivation) and the fraction of the caste engaged in cultivation are also controlled for. In addition, papers like (Banerjee and Somanathan 2006), (Anderson 2005) and (Chaudhary 2005) highlight the role of social diversity, economic inequality and the fraction of upper castes in determining economic outcomes. These measures are also controlled for in the regression to check if they are correlated with caste occupational diversity.

There are insufficient data to include occupation fixed effects, however summarizes how specialized occupations are across the various districts. The labour category appears to be the most diversified across castes with almost all castes in the district having at least one person following an occupation classified as labour. The book binding occupation on the other hand is the most specialized by caste.

As the data is categorized both by caste and occupation this introduces certain biases into the results. Since occupations are classified into categories, two castes may be in reality specialized in different occupations but if these occupations fall in the same category, then the castes will appear as if they are both following the same occupation and hence do not have a monopoly over those services. This makes castes appear less specializaed than they actually are. Lumping various occupations also biases the bargaining power of occupation measure. Occupations in the same category need not have the same bargaining power.

For example the category religious service includes servants attached to religious buildings of all ranks. It is likely that people attached to religious buildings as priests have a different bargaining power than those attached as servants. To counteract this other measures of bargaining power namely economic and social are used in the analysis.

Empirical Specification: Occupational specialization has two aspects in this paper. The first is determining how many occupations are unique to a caste (i.e. those that the caste has a monopoly over). The second is capturing the diversity of occupations caste members may follow that are not unique to the caste. The measure of occupational specialization used would need to capture both these dimensions.

One standard way of capturing diversity is a Herfindhal like measure of occupational specialization for each caste c:

diversityc = Xk, Kc µnc,k

nc 2

nc,k: number of people in caste c following occupation k

nc,k: number of people in caste c

An decreasing index value implies a higher diversity of occupations in a caste. This index works well in most cases, but in this context there is a problem. Suppose a caste has a monopoly over two occupations and its members only follow those two occupations, say half in each occupation. This would show up as a measure of diversity of 0.5. Another caste whose members are also equally divided between two occupations but which has a monopoly over one of those occupations will also have the same measure of 0.5. However, according to our definition of occupational specialization, the first caste is more specialized than the second because it has a monopoly over more occupations.

Consider a measure that just considers the degree of monopoly each caste has over the occupations of its members:

monopolyc = Xk,Kc μnc,k

nk 2

nc,k: number of people in caste c following occupation k

nc,k: number of people in occupation k in the district

This measure has the following problem: two castes may be in reality specialized in different occupations but if these occupations fall in the same category, then they will appear as if they are following non-unique occupations. This is due to data limitations, but the problem is confounded as the relative population sizes of castes will matter. Castes that have a larger fraction of the population will show up as having more monopolies over occupations than they actually have. For example consider a caste that has a small population relative to the other castes. Just considering the monopoly index above, even if all the members of the caste followed one occupation, if the occupation was a small fraction of service providers in its occupation category, it will show up as a small index value when in reality since all the members follow the same occupation the index value should be high.

It uses the maximum of the degree of monopoly the caste has in an occupation and the fraction of the caste engaged in that occupation. It should counteract the effect discussed above. It is not the only possible index but it is a simple way of capturing the intuition. The monopoly and diversity indices are also used as robustness checks and to check for additional insights. The relationship between the indices in graphical form is given in figure 3 The index excluded the occupation categories property and cultivation. There is evidence that agriculture/cultivation was an occupation undertaken by most castes. Property will be used as a measure of economic bargaining power (discussed later) and so will be excluded from the index.

The specification is as follows:

indexc,i = a + ß1Di + ß2Ci + ß2Ei,c + eic

where:

Di: District i characteristics

Cc: Caste c characteristics

Ei,c: District-caste interactions

Results: The dataset contains 7 districts. This makes isolating district factors that affect occupational choice difficult.

Putting district factors alone into a regression gives a maximum R2 of 0.02 and none of the variables are significant. In the interests of space district level results are not reported. They are however controlled for in the caste regressions by adding district dummies.

The results with caste factors. In support of the second implication, the larger the caste relative to the population in the district the higher the degree of specialization. To check if this is purely coming from the size effect discussed earlier, I run the same regressions on the diversity index that just measures the degree of occupational diversity in a caste. From those regressions larger castes are on average following more occupations, lending further credence to the implication.

All the bargaining power indices when considered separately are negatively correlated with specialization, indicating that castes with higher bargaining power on any dimension on average follow more occupations.

This supports the implication that castes with higher bargaining power have a larger choice of occupations they can follow. When the three indices are considered together, the occupation rank measure and the social rank measure still retain their negative signs, but lose their significance. However, the economic bargaining power is the only significant coefficient, but with the sign switched. This indicates that wealthier (more propertied) castes on average follow a fewer number of occupations. The correlation between economic bargaining power and occupational diversity seems to be the least robust finding. The sign is positive when factors like other measures of bargaining power and caste interactions are introduced. This suggests a potential channel that economic factors of a caste may play on occupation choice.

The fraction of the caste engaged in cultivation is negatively correlated with occupational diversity indicating that castes that take up agriculture tend to be more diversified on average. Interacting the relative size of the caste with the measures of bargaining power gives a negative coefficient. This indicates that as the bargaining power of larger castes rises, they tend to be more diversified using the combined index. To check if this is coming due to monopoly or occupational diversity, the coefficients are compared to those using the diversity index. For the diversity index, the social and occupational bargaining power interactions seem to be positively correlated indicating that as the bargaining power of larger castes rises, they tend to be less diversified using the diversity index. Bargaining power comes from two sources-the number of unique occupations and the bargaining power of those occupations. This supports the implication that if larger castes follow occupations that have higher bargaining power, then they do not need to have a monopoly over many occupations. The monopoly index regression are not reported as the only significant variable there is the relative size of the caste.

Castes and Population Size: Belonging to a caste is costly because of informational considerations and this cost is rising in caste size (see section 5.3). The benefit from belonging to a caste is increasing in the number of occupations unique to a caste. If all occupations are unique to some caste, the trade-off between costs and benefits determines the optimal number of castes in a village. Increasing the population for the same number of castes will raise the size of each caste, increasing the cost of belonging. For the same number of occupations, this changes the balance between costs and benefits and the number of castes in the village rises. This gives rise to the following testable prediction: Keeping the number of occupations fixed, an increase in population size will be accompanied by a rise in the number of castes.

Data Description

1823 Data: The data is from the Dehazada and Census of the Province of Tirunelveli (Tinnevelly), 182390. Tirunelveli is situated in the present day state of Tamil Nadu. The dataset consists of 152 census villages in four contiguous taluks. This enables us to control for a variety of village characteristics. The census was collected by offers of the Survey of India department and was commissioned by the Collector of Tirunelveli.

1941 Data: These data are from the British India Census. Most of the data on caste collected by the British Census are reported at the District level. These districts are extremely large and the caste categories are reported only if the caste was considered 'large' enough. The exception to this is the Mysore Census of 1941, which is (are far as I know) the only village level data reported by the Census that has data on castes. For each of the 235 villages in the survey, there is detailed economic information. On castes they report the name of all the castes present in the village (no exclusions) and for the biggest castes, some caste level information. I conduct the same investigations as with the 1823 data. The variables do not correspond exactly to the ones in the 1823 dataset but I keep them as close as possible.

The variable of interest is population. The theory holds the number of occupations in a village constant, so factors in the village that may be correlated with the number of occupations are controlled for. Irrigated land may be more productive than dry cultivation. Having more productive agriculture would allow for the village population to specialize in other services, which may affect the number of occupations in the village. The faction of land under irrigation is a control for this. Population pressures may also affect the agricultural surplus available and is controlled for by adding population density as a control. The results of this basic specification for both 1823 and 1941 are given in tables 2b and 3b. In the 1823 census villages may have sub-villages under them and this is controlled for by adding the number of sub-villages as an additional control.

Results: The total population of the village is strongly positively correlated with the number of castes in a village in both datasets. Looking at the 1823 data, an increase in village population by 1% is associated with a 0.54% increase in the number of castes in the village. Similarly for the 1941 data, a 1% increase in population size is associated with a 0.57% increase in the number of castes in the village. The coefficient is similar to the one in the 1823 data, however the R2 is much lower. In both datasets, factors that increase agricultural surplus in the village, namely the fraction of cultivated land under irrigation and lower population density are associated with a higher number of castes in the village. This is consistent with the view that a higher agricultural surplus allows for a larger non-agricultural economy, which would be associated with a larger number of castes. Apart from these factors other factors that may influence agricultural productivity like the number of plows per acre, bullocks per acre and waterworks per acre are also controlled for. None of these controls significantly affect the coefficient on population.

In the 1823 data, the occupational structure of the village is also directly controlled for by adding variables like the number of looms per capita and artisan shops per capita among others. They are on average significant and positively correlated with the number of castes in the village. However, the significance of the population coefficient remains unchanged. It does however drop to a 0.48% increase in the number of castes in the village for a 1% change in population. In the 1941 data, I am unable to control for the various service/occupations available in the villages. However an attempt is made by including controls for whether the village is interior or not, the fraction of income sent as remittances and spent on travel. The coefficient on population does drop to 0.55% but again the significance is unaffected.

Another way of controlling for the strength of the local economy is to control for market activity. In the 1823 data this is done by using factors such as bazaars per capita. These are also associated with a larger number of castes without taking away from the population coefficient. To check if wealth of the village on average makes a difference, factors such as the fraction of houses that are tiled, animals per capita, and taxable tree per capita are controlled for. In the 1823 data these are all associated with a higher number of castes in the village leaving the population coefficient unchanged. In 1941 an increase in the fraction of houses tiles is associated with a lower number of castes. Whether this is due to the fact that the data is from a different part of the country or due to the colonial policies one cannot distinguish. However, it is related to (Banerjee and Somanathan 2006)'s findings where social heterogeneity is not a positive for the economic conditions of a village. Literacy is another source of difference in the datasets. Unlike 1823 where villages with a larger number of schools per capita are associated with a larger number of castes, in 1941 literacy is not strongly correlated with the number of castes.

Robustness Checks: Various interaction terms are also considered to check for other possible patterns. However, none of them are statistically significant. The results are not included in the interests of space. The same regressions are repeated for average caste size and the results are shown in tables 2c and 3c. In the 1823 data a rise in village population is associated with a rise in the average caste size. An increase of a 100 people in the village is associated with 1.6 extra people per caste. The corresponding number is 3.3 for 1941. In 1823 population density seems to have the biggest effect and is positively correlated with the number of people per caste. All the measures that are correlated with agricultural surplus, wealth or market activity are associated with a lower caste size. In 1941 all these factors seem unimportant and only population seems to matter for the average caste size.

Instrumental Variables: Reverse causality is a problem here. For example, economic factors that cause castes to migrate to an area, would increase the population size purely because the number of castes increased. An appropriate instrument would be one that is correlated with population size but not with the number of castes. Appropriate instruments would be fertility rates and death rates. Unfortunately, these are not available for the 1823 Census. Deaths from small-pox, cholera and plague in each village in the 1941 census are available. This is not the best instrument for total population due to the presence of a large number of zeros.

Summary: The empirical evidence presented serves to substantiate the implications of the theory model. The bargaining power of the caste seems to be an important factor in determining the occupational decisions of the caste. The higher the bargaining power of the caste, the more occupational diversified the caste. Secondly, there seems to be a trade-off between the number of occupations and the bargaining power of the occupations the caste specializes in. If the caste specializes in occupations with high bargaining power, it does not need to specialize in as many occupations.

The castes and population size implication is empirically verifiable. An increase in the population of the village is correlated with a larger number of castes. The results holds even after factors that may affect the number of castes in the village such as agricultural productivity, population density, wealth and occupational distribution are controlled for.

Conclusions: The caste system is difficult to define, complex and it changes over time and place. Because of this, it has often proved difficult to analyse and conceptualize. However, we know that it has real effects on the economy. To sufficiently understand the effects, the reasons for the effect and the mechanism of transmission a model is invaluable. This paper provides a model of the caste system with its features as an equilibrium of a game where the central problem is contract enforcement. The implications of the model provide a coherent explanation for why we see features like the purity scale and occupational specialization in equilibrium. This should not be interpreted as saying that the caste system was free of inefficiencies. In fact features like restricting occupations by caste may cause inefficiencies in the economy on other dimensions which are not considered in this paper. The focus is on the role the features of the system play in increasing the efficiency with which the system can undertake contract enforcement.

The first part of the analysis shows that trade is sustainable with collective punishments. The various features of the system are shown to be implications of the model that increase efficiency. The bargaining power of a caste is a key concept in the analysis. Factors that increase the bargaining power of the caste increase effort provision by the producer and hence efficiency. Increasing the number of occupations unique to some caste in the economy increases efficiency, providing a reason for occupational specialization by caste. Self-production restrictions increase bargaining power as by giving up the option of producing the service for himself a consumer lowers his outside option. Each individual also has an incentive to free-ride off the bargaining power of his caste. To prevent this, the paper discusses the role of occupational restrictions by caste. Since bargaining power is so important to the analysis, data from Cochin (1875) is used to check how occupational patterns are correlated with bargaining power of the caste. The last part of the analysis examines the ascriptive nature of castes. Reasons for why this is observed may be tied to a caste's attempts to preserve rents. Restricting entry into castes in equilibrium is tantamount to choosing whom to extend the caste's punishment power.

The determinants of the number of castes in a village are also examined. The central assumption about castes is that they serve as information sharing devices. Coordinating and enforcing collective punishments is assumed to be costly and increasing in the size of the caste (see (Olson 1971)). This introduces a trade-off that determines the size of the caste and the optimal number of castes in a village. The prediction being that the optimal number of castes in the village is increasing in the population of the village. This implication is tested using data from Tirunelveli (1823) and Mysore (1941) and found to be consistent with patterns in the data.

Institutions are a key determinant of economic outcomes because they affect individual's incentives. In the developing world setting up an environment in which countries can achieve their growth potential has become the current push for policy makers. In order to do that effectively current institutions must be better understood. The caste system is a persistent institution that governs a large fraction of people in the developing world. Nehru, writing on the eve on Indian independence summed it up well when he said about the caste system "we have to pay attention to the human material we have to deal with, to the background of its thoughts and urges, and to the environment in which we have to function.

To ignore all this and to fashion some idealistic scheme in the air, or merely to think in terms of imitating what others have done elsewhere, would be folly. It becomes desirable therefore to examine and understand the old Indian social structure which has so powerfully influenced our people." This paper models the caste system in a tractable way. Future work will involve delving into the role of the caste system in post-colonial India.

Changes in Caste Equations

Historians who have attempted to draw a straight line between the Manusmriti and post-independence India are clearly unfamiliar with those patterns of Indian history that contradict such a linear view. While some of the social evils of modern India may have ancient roots, many others have a fairly recent history. And even those that may have ancient precedence were modulated and modified as a result of numerous struggles for social equality that have taken place throughout Indian history.

For example, after independence one could find temples built in the late 18th or 19th century that restricted entry to dalits and menstruating women. But it is not at all clear if such strictures were widespread prior to colonization. Research indicates that during the Pratihara period, caste categories were relatively flexible and popular temples were constructed by those considered low-caste. Temple construction was often a way of gaining social respect and upward mobility.

Restrictions on temple entry most likely reached a peak during the British period partly because only the upper castes had the means to build temples, and also because the control of existing temples passed into the hands of trusts who were hand-picked by the British, and were given free license (possibly even encouraged) to promote discriminatory practices. The iron hand of the colonial state made it much more difficult to challenge such reactionary tendencies

Economic factors were also crucial in determining caste rank and caste relationships. In periods of intense economic exploitation, caste discrimination intensified, and the reverse took place in periods of economic expansion. For instance, most historians are in agreement that the Gupta period was a period of rising prosperity and also a period of increasing social mobility. Improvements in agricultural productivity led to concomitant improvements in the social rank of the cultivators.

Similiarly, (though much later) there is evidence for the rise in status of the telis-cooking oil manufacturers and traders whose earlier low caste status did not fit with their growing economic importance, and were thus granted a higher caste rank. Besides, all through Indian history, phony lineages for non-Kshatriya rulers were constructed to create the aura of continuity and legitimacy. Hence, the mere existence of a document like the Manusmriti should not cause serious social scientists to jump to broad conclusions without greater scrutiny and dispassionate analysis of the Indian historical record.

It is also important not to judge an older society by modern standards. Social relations cannot be entirely separated from how productive activities are carried out and what the level of available technology makes socially possible. In today's world, the widespread availability of printed matter, of computers and other means to store and develop knowledge systems makes the older systems of learning and skill-preservation largely redundant. But in older times, the artisans guild system helped in the development and preservation of specialized knowledge and perfection of important manufacturing skills. In India, artisans guilds were closely correlated to jati or caste. It was not only the Brahmins and upper castes who favoured hereditary continuity, but skilled carpenters, weavers, metalworkers, painters and numerous categories of other artisans also saw certain benefits in maintaining their jati identities. While the artisan castes often fought for greater social equality-the complete breakdown of caste identities was never a serious option except for those at the very bottom of the caste totem pole.

The caste system survived not just because it was enforced by the legal writ of an elite class, but as much because it served a social purpose in an era in which it was difficult if not impossible to organize the educational and productive activities of society in a more flexible and democratic way.

Caste System in Bengal

Even though formally there are four castes in Hinduism: Brahmins, Kshatriyas, vaishyas and shudras, the social reality is very different in different parts of India. The social rules enjoined by the religions also differ in different regions. In Bengal, much of the development of the first distinct Bengali Hinduism took place during the rule of the sena and barman kings: and is described in the writings of bhavadeva, aniruddhabhatta, vallalasena, laksmanasena, gunavisnu, halayudha etc., as well as in the brhaddharma and brahmavaivarta puranas. To a large extent, they codified, formalized and made immutable some of the existing social structure, as well as making it very much more rigid. In fact according to traditional stories, which however are not history, Brahmins originated in bengal during this time.

The society described therein does not contain (though they still appear in origin myths) any Kshatriyas or vaishyas except when some of the rulers are referred to as Kshatriyas and today most of the people who call themselves Kshatriyas have variations of varman or malla as their surname. The Brahmins were divided geographically into radhi and barendri with a variety of village associations, but according to aniruddha had forgotten their vedic tradition. In addition, there were vaidika Brahmins who came (according to tradition, during shyAmalavarmA's rule) from the north (including sarasvati region) and south (including utkala) India, who according to halayudha were the only Brahmins who knew the vedic tradition. Mention is also found of Brahmins from shakadvipa (who, according to tradition, came during shashagka's rule and were called grahavipra; the latter, according to brahmavaivarta purana, however, are children of devalas, who are true shakadvipi Brahmins, and vaishya women) who were not respected in society. A sub-caste of them called agradani used to perform shraddha ceremony for the shudras. Also found is another group of Brahmins not respected in society: the bhatta Brahmins.

According to the rules developed in this period, the respected or shrotriya Brahmins could not perform priestly duties for anyone other than the 20 high shudra sub-castes. (According to vrhaddharma purana, these shudra sub-castes arose from mixture of castes forced by king vena; the upper sub-castes had parents belonging to unmixed caste, the middle ones had fathers of unmixed caste, and the lowest had both parents of mixed caste.) Those that violate the rule get the sub-caste of that person and thus we find, in addition, varna Brahmins who could not even serve water to the true Brahmins. In additions, certain occupations like teaching shudras, doing priestly duties for them, practicing medicine or astrology, or performing painting or other artistic activities, were forbidden; though certain others like farming and fighting, or working as a minister, go-between, religious leader or general were all allowed.

The non-Brahmins in Bengal were almost all classified as formally 36, but actually 41, sub-castes of shudras and came in three categories. The exact enumeration varies somewhat, but the list in vrhaddharma purana is presented here as an example. The top sub-caste (from whom the Brahmins can drink water, and for whom they can be priests) consist of record keepers (karana or kayastha; karana seems to become less prevalent with time, kayastha more, though there are exceptions), doctors and medicine makers (ambastha or vaidya; doctors in the early part are being described as karana; in south India some doctors were also Brahmins; in bihara, one can also find the ambastha kayastha caste, said to be descendants of citragupta and zobhavati; in bengal, ambasthas seem to merge into vaidyas), fighters (ugra), envoys and messengers (magadha), weavers (tantuvaya), scent traders (gandhikavanika), barbers (napita), writers (gopa), ironsmiths (karmakara), betelnut traders (taulika), potters (kumbhakara), brass smiths (kamsakara), conch smiths (shagkhika), farmers (dasa), betelleaf farmers (varujivi), sweetmeat makers (modaka), florists (maiakara), praise singers (suta), rajaputra, and betelleaf traders (tambull). Some of these people, the kayastha/vaidyas (these terms have taken much broader meanings) often call themselves (in accord with their origin myths as found in, for example, brahmavaivarta purana) Kshatriyas or vaishyas, and some of their origin myths are closely tied to those of the Brahmins.

Manu also provides origin myths for many of these as arising out of violation of caste rules: thus ambasthas of Brahman father and vaishya mother (two degrees apart is not considered proper), karanas of some Kshatriyas who had given up his duties. As a result, some of them consider themselves vaidya-Brahmins (and use both the vaishya indicator Gupta and Brahman indicator Sharma), and like the non-shudra castes in ancient texts have limited rights to the veda and sacred thread ceremony. The middle sub-caste consisted of engravers (taksana), washermen (rajaka), goldsmiths (svarnakara), gold traders (svarnavanika), milkmen and cowherds (Abhira), oil traders (tailakaraka), fish traders (dhivara), alcohol traders (shaundika), actors and magicians (nata), descendants of Buddhist leaders, fishermen (jalika; possibly, buffalo keepers arose from these later) and another unidentifiable category (shabaka).

The lowest sub-caste (who are untouchables) consist of cleaners (malegrahi), those that cremate the dead (candala), carpenters (taksa), leatherworker (carmakara), boatmen (ghattajlvi), chairbearers (dolavahi), wrestlers (malla) and two unidentified groups (varuda and kudava). In addition are described the Mlechchh or foreign groups like pukkasha, pulinda, khasa, thara, kamboja, yavana, sumha, shavara etc., who were left outside the entire classification.

In contrast, brahmavaivarta purana mentions the top sub-caste exemplified by gopa, napita, bhilla, modaka, kuvara, tambull, svarnakara (later demoted), and vanika; followed by karana and ambastha. Then of the nine sons of vishvakarma by a shudra: maiakara, karmahara, shagkhakara, kuvindaka, kumbhakara, and kamsakara are explained as being high, and sutradhara and citrakara are also demoted, suvarnavanika is also demoted because of association with svarnakara. After this there is a long list of fallen sub-castes including attalikakara, kotaka, tivara, tailakara, leta, malla, carmakara, shundi, paundraka, mamsaccheda, rajaputra, kaivarta, rajaka, kauyail, gaggaputra, and yuggi.

The really low sub-castes included vyadha, bhada, kola, kojca, haddi, Doma, jola, vagatata, vyalagrahi, and candala. Traditional stories try to explain the bizarre patterns with mythological stories: thus the goldsmiths claimed they were vaishyas who were insulted by vallalasena who invited and placed them with the satshudras at dinner, and who, furthermore borrowed a lot of money by force. When they tried to revolt against him, he lowered their status; and he further disallowed wearing of the sacred thread by traders.

The rules developed in this period prescribe strict limits on Brahmins intermixing with the rest of the society. Some examples can be provided. They were not allowed to eat food cooked by shudras, except for fried items, rice cooked in milk and in time of distress. However they could not drink even water touched by the untouchables, neither could they be touched by untouchables.

Elaborate rituals were needed to clean oneself of violations of these rules. Similarly, even though intermarriage between upper caste men and lower caste women was allowed, the normal rule was marriage within ones own caste. Rules made it clear that a wife of a lower caste had less rights than one of the same caste. Marriage rules for Brahmins, and possibly upper category of shudras, had to follow the endogamy/exogamy rules of sapinda (exogamy for parts of an extended family), sagotra (exogamy for a group of paternally inherited markers called gotra) and samanapravara (exogamy outside related gotras).

Marriage was also forbidden if it took place according to high ceremony and any of the seven male ancestors along the father's line and five along the mother's line coincided. Low marriage ceremony only required exclusion for five and three generations, but pushed one to the shudra caste. Note that this does not imply that the society, either before or during the sena period, was very spartan or puritanical in the modern sense of the word, vatsayana's kamasutra (3rd/4th cent AD), as well as kalhana's rajataraggini (describing 8th cent AD pundra), describes the dancers who attracted the young men, bhatta bhavadeva's writings, sandhyakara nandi's ramacarita and poet dhoyi's pavanaduta sings praises of the beauty of the city and temple prostitutes, thus providing supporting contemporary and internal evidence.

Though Brahmins marrying shudra women was looked down upon, extramarital relationship between them was overlooked. During the 10th day of Durga puja, during the sharadotsava festival, men and women with mud and leaves only on their body used to sing and dance to primal images; as described in the contemporary kalviveka and slightly later kalikapurana, brhaddharmapurana seems to speak against it, unless the participants were followers of shakti. Similar festivals during holaka=holi and kama-mahotsava are also known. Poetry (e.g. govardhana's Arya satashati, jayadeva etc.) also describe physical love. Descriptions of fine clothes, gold, silver and pearl ornaments, palatial houses and temples also abound. The village society, however, often shunned many of these behaviour and considered them shameful as is clear from descriptions in saduktikarnamrta.

Up to the Ancient Period in the History of Bengal

The Aryans were an invading people, and their first arrival

into the subcontinent was probably to be dated about 1500 BC Perhaps some 200 years after this, there began to come into being the collection of the hymns of the Rigveda.

The Aryans were a series of related tribes, settled mainly in the Punjab and the adjacent regions, speaking a common language, sharing a common religion and designating themselves by the name Arya, and they were represented as being in a state of permanent conflict with a hostile group of native peoples called by the Aryans variously as "Dasu" or "Dasyu."

During the period of the Samhitas and the Bramanas the Aryans were seen to have extended their habitation towards the east, down the Gangetic plains; and the third stage of their expansion was made towards the Bengal region, approximately by the 8th century BC. During this stage "other terms e.g. Mleccha and Nishada-are used as designations of the non-Aryan tribes, while the word 'dasa' becomes the usual word for 'slave'."

> *"On the other hand, the term 'Arya' is opposed not only to the external barbarian, but also to the lowest of the four varnas, the 'Sudra'."*
>
> *"In the latter context the word Arya naturally acquires the meaning 'noble, honourable,' and the word continues in use in both the senses down to the classical period."*

Hence North India referred to as Arya Varta. By the end of 6th century BC the Aryan India was vastly increased in area and would probably correspond with "the boundaries of the Indo-Aryan" in a modern linguistic map.

But, "the Aryan influence in the south, i.e., in the Dravidian India, was a matter of cultural penetration, and not, as previously, of conquest and settlement."

In this historical setting of ancient India, it was generally stated by many of the historians and ambiguously understood by the average Indians that when the means of subsistence had been provided, the people were simultaneously divided into four varnas, on the basis of their occupations:

The Brahmins for praying;

The Kshatriyas for fighting;

The Vaishyas for producing goods;

The Sudras for manual tasks, i.e. to assist the other three upper varna-people in their respective professions.

This favoured those varnas who prayed and fought and was resented by the classes producing goods.

Castes and the Caste System

The Caste System: Caste is the fundamental institution of traditional Indian society. The caste system divides the whole society into a large number of hereditary groups, which are distinguished from one another and connected by separation in matters of marriage and contact, division of labour and hierarchy, which ranks the groups as relatively superior or inferior to one another.

The boundaries between castes are maintained by exquisitely detailed rules of ritual purity: contact with, in some instances even sight of, lower castes is viewed as polluting; intimate contact, especially in marriage or at meals, is especially defiling. Despite the fact that untouchability was abolished under India's constitution in 1950, the practice of untouchability-the imposition of social disabilities on persons by reason of their birth in certain castes-remains very much a part of rural India. More than one-sixth of India's population lives a precarious existence, shunned by much of society because of their rank as lower castes.

These people are discriminated against, denied access to land, forced to work in degrading conditions, and routinely abused at the hands of the police and of higher-caste groups that enjoy the state's protection. In what has been called India's "hidden apartheid," entire villages in many Indian states remain completely segregated by caste.

As a defining feature of Hinduism, caste encompasses a complex ordering of social groups on the basis of purity. A person is considered a member of the caste into which he or she is born and remains within that caste until death, although the particular ranking of that caste may vary among regions and over time. Differences in status are traditionally justified by the religious doctrine of karma, a belief that one's place in life is determined by one's deeds in previous lifetimes.

Traditional scholarship has described this more than 2,000-year-old system within the context of the four principal varnas, or large categories.

In order of precedence these are the Brahmins (priests and teachers), the Ksyatriyas (rulers and soldiers), the Vaishyas (merchants, and traders), and the Shudras (labourers and artisans). A fifth category falls outside the varna system and consists of those known as 'untouchables'. They are often assigned tasks too ritually polluting to merit inclusion within the traditional varna system. In Sanskrit, the classical language of northern India and of Hinduism, this ideology is called varna dharma. Its essential claim to acceptance among Hindu believers is that it is ordained by God.

It is sacred. Its historicity is uncertain, but scholars think that varna dharma originated in the conquest and subjugation more than a millennium before Christ of the darker completed people of northern India by fairer completed Aryan invaders from central Asia. There are mythological descriptions of this in the earliest Sanskrit hymnals, and one of the meanings of varna is colour. However, Hinduism is disinclined to search the historical past for validation, and the validity of varna dharma is not as a memory of the past but as a living ideology.

Dumont argues that, in contrast to the competitive Western system, which emphasizes individual ambition, the caste system involves a 'holism', an orientation toward the welfare of all. Certainly, not all castes receive equal rewards; but this, he explains, is because all do not contribute equally, as judged by the underlying values of the caste system.

Thus, Dumont argues that although all castes are not equally rewarded, all are integrated into the system. By Hindu ideals, all are cared for; the system exists for the benefit of all (Dumont 1970: 107).11 In the traditional Indian society a person's status vis-a-vis his caste rank was determined by his birth in the caste and by its place in the ritual hierarchy, though other factors also, like economic and political power, added substantially to his esteem. But, according to Dumont (1970: 24), both status and power were separate in their functions in the caste system even in the early periods, and power was subordinate to status. Thus, a person having more power had inferior ritual and social status in the caste hierarchy if he belonged to a lower caste.

Nevertheless, even in this system which seems very rigid mobility is possible. In Indian sociological literature, the various mobility courses that the castes lower in the hierarchy have adopted for improving their status are characterized as Sanskritisation. But according to Pradip Kumar Bose there seems to be at least two distinct courses, which need to be differentiated. In the one, caste mobility depended upon gaining access to some source of wealth, substantiated by a plausible genealogy and also by mobilizing the caste group by forming caste associations and by petitioning and appealing to the colonial administrators to change the status of the caste in the decennial census. The attitude of these caste groups was totally loyalist to colonial rulers because their primary intention was to consolidate their social status after improving their economic position. As a result, these caste groups maintained their separation from equivalent castes whose economic status was lower; they were for continuing the relationship which made it possible for them to acquire wealth and hence they were for alliance with the colonial rulers. (In Bihar, examples of such castes are the Kayasthas and the Bhumihars.)

The other mobility course has its roots in the exploitation suffered by the castes. These caste mobility movements were the social representation of their economic grievances and deprivations. Here the caste groups favoured association with the equivalent caste groups; they were antagonistic to colonial rulers and wanted change in existing economic relations. In contrast to the emphasis on 'consolidation' of the first group, this mobility movement can be called a movement of assertion. (In Bihar, the movement by the Yadavs, Kurmis and Koeris are examples of such a mobility course.)

But although mobility of castes within the system is possible, this mobility is not large-scale and even though some castes achieved a higher ranking this did not change the system. Today, however, caste still has great social, economic, and political relevance, especially for the rural lower castes, but the traditional coincidence of caste, class, and power is increasingly under attack, both indirectly through the processes of economic modernization and political democracy, and directly through political action by and on behalf of the 'backward' or 'depressed' communities.

Type 1	Type 2
Due to improved economic status	Due to deteriorated economic status
Loyalty to the ruling class	Antagonistic towards the ruling class
Perpetuation of existing economic relations	Removal of existing economic relations
Separation from other castes	Association with other castes
Consolidation of social status	Assertion of social status

Several legislative measures, taken by the government of post-independence India, have shaken the very foundation of the traditional pattern of social interaction. The most important of these measures were the legal reforms to recognise the panchayats (village councils), the abolishment of zamindari (absentee landlords) and the outlaw of untouchability. The conflict-regulating mechanisms like the practice of keeping social distance between different castes and the hereditary allocation of occupational roles which controlled drastic structural changes are being abolished. In the Hindu community, the different castes have now begun to view each other with suspicion, hate and fear.

SOME THOUGHTS ON CASTE SYSTEM

All developed social systems are stratified. No society is a mass of individuals. European society was organized along class, guilds, and religion (Jews and gentiles, Protestants and Catholics, etc.) India had castes, or more properly, jatis.

As a political category, caste is a British invention. The British introduced the category of caste for purposes of counting population in the census that began in 1871. The British began to rank order castes by status and economics. Many petitions were filed by new resurgent groups to seek higher ranking. Caste began to be organized as political movement. In a similar fashion, the counting of people by tribal identity in Africa led to tribalism. Sikhism was defined as a separate religion by the British, and it became so. These points are elaborated in an excellent book by Nicholas Dirks, Castes of Mind: Colonialism and the Making of Modern India, 2001.

Castes in India are different than classes in the West. Castes are not economically structured. Each caste has its own rich and its own poor. There are rich Brahmins and poor Brahmins. As a general rule, Brahmins were among the poorest section of society. This observation runs counter to the prevalent view that Indian society is Brahmin dominated and Brahmin exploited. Different castes in India are like different ethnic groups within the United States. There are rich Italians and poor Italians, rich Irish and poor Irish. Also like caste groups in India, till recently the ethnic groups in America married in their own community, i.e. Jews would marry other Jews, the Polish would marry other Polish, and so on.

The caste system in ancient times was not static. Castes rose and fell. Castes became static and rigid during extended foreign rule. Under Muslim rule, some caste groups that fought against domination were pushed to the outer edges of the social system. I have been told that among the sweeper castes in India, one finds many Rajput gotras.

Why is caste denied in the West and replaced by 'class'? Why are dowry murders denied when husbands in the West shoot their wives more frequently than dowry murders in India? Why is idolatry denied when Westerners worship celebrities and money and brand names as their idols? Is the American flag not an idol that is worshipped by the Pledge of Allegiance? The third world non Christian phenomenon is always given a separate term so as to be able to demonize it whereas the western equivalent is spared by saying the term does not apply.

This is linguistic sleigh of hand.

"The European colonizers wanted to impose their ideal of equality so profoundly contrary to that of liberty, that the Western peoples sought to impose their ideas,

culture, religion, language, and ways of living and thinking on the people of their empires who preferred to live and think differently. Whole races and civilizations have been destroyed by the European conqueror so that he can preserve the illusion of living in a world of justice, equality, and democracy."

"The moneyed elite in the United States have long coveted their neighbours' land, resources, and cheap labour forces. Eager to invade, annex, and exploit, the plutocracy began to disseminate the warped notion of Manifest Destiny in the Nineteenth Century. Purporting to have the unwavering support of the Almighty, the "superior" Anglo-Saxons rationalized slavery, the Native American Genocide, the conquest of half of Mexico, the annexation of Hawaii, and their eradication of over 300,000 "savages" in conquering the Philippines."

Racial and Social inequities continue to plague modern Western industrial societies who claim to be the beacon of Human Rights. Historically, nations in Europe and America have had a similar structure: the class system. A Westerner who has had occasion to witness the rise of the new castes in industrial societies, or status-oriented thinking and bureaucratic hierarchies would not praise the modern or industrial culture. Exploitation exists in all societies-in India, it is caste, while in the West, it is based on class. Casteism in India is a terrible injustice. No thoughtful person will deny that. So is crime, homelessness, social inequality and racism in Western nations. Ancient Hindus have never discriminated against people based on their colour or race. Hindus worship God Krishna and Goddess Kali. Both, Krishna and Kali, means black and are depicted as such as well.

"In Europe and America, which are said to be the most democratic and highly individualistic, individual life is least regarded. In the land of liberty, fundamentalism, Ku Klax Klan, and Nordic assaults on all other races and cultures prevail."

Degeneration of the Varna System

The Varna system was started as analogous to professional guilds, but as a result of exploitation by some priests, and socioeconomic elements of society, this system became hereditary and degenerated over the centuries. The ancient culture of India was based upon a system of social diversification according to spiritual development.

Four orders of society were recognized based upon the four main goals of human beings and established society accordingly. These four groups were the Brahmins, the priests or spiritual class; the Kshatriya, the nobility or ruling class; the Vaishya, the merchants and farmers; and the Shudras or servants. These four orders of society were called "varna", which has two meanings; first it means "colour" and second it means a "veil". As colour it does not refer to the colour of the skin of people, but to the qualities or energies of human nature. As a veil it shows the four different ways in which the Divine Self is hidden in human beings.

In ancient India, these divisions were not based on birth but based on qualifications. According to the Bhagavad Gita this Aryan family system broke down in India over three thousand years ago at the time of Krishna. Hence after three thousand years this system of determining natural aptitude has degenerated into the caste system which resembles it now only in form.

As the Varna system became increasingly rigid and based on inheritance, it was enveloped by another system known as the caste system. Thus, this varna system determined the social structure of ancient Hindu society. The caste system could not have been part of Hindu religious philosophy, since it violates fundamental Hindu doctrine, according to which there is no absolute distinction between individuals, since the atman dwells in the hearts of all beings. There is no religious sanction whatsoever to the concept of the caste system in Hinduism.

Swami Sivananda (The Divine Life Society, Rishikesh), in his commentary on Gita, Ch.18, verses 41, and 45 says: "Mankind is organized into the four castes and each man's life is divided into four stages, according to the nature of the Gunas (traits) and the degree of growth or evolution. This is the division of labour for which each caste is fitted according to its own nature. The duty prescribed is your sole support, each devoted to his own duty in accordance with his own nature or caste, and the highest service you can render to the Supreme is to carry it out wholeheartedly, without expectation of fruits, with the attitude of dedication to the Lord. The caste system is, indeed, a splendid thing. It is quite flawless. But the defect came in from somewhere else. The classes gradually neglected their duties. The test of ability and character slowly vanished. Birth became the chief consideration in determining castes. All castes fell from their ideals and forgot all about their duties."

Varna-Not Racial Colour

Varna was conferred on the basis of the intrinsic nature of an individual, which is a combination of the three gunas. The term, 'Varna', has nothing to do with racial colour. It is related to the three 'gunas' or traits-white (sattva or sagacity), red (rajas or aggressiveness), and dark (tamas or ignorance) which all men and also all living beings possess, albeit in different proportions-varying from species to species, from man to man and even from sibling to sibling.

Alain Danielou has said: "That abusive caste practices were introduced when the administrative power ceased to be in Hindu hands, thus making the repression of abuses legally impossible. Such abuses as there are have been greatly exaggerated in order to justify Western domination and are normally quite local. In most of India, the caste system functions today as it always has; as a harmonious whole in which each is satisfied with his social lot, in which the freedom of each tribe, and religious group to live according to its customs, traditions, and convictions is respected as it is in no other country and no other form of society.

Manu Smrti: Not a Religious Book:

"The Seniority of Brahmans is from Sacred Knowledge, that of Kshatriyas from valour, that of Vaishyas from wealth in grain, but that of Sudras is from age alone." (Manu Smriti II, 155)

"Manu has declared that those Brahmans who are thieves, outcasts, eunuchs, or atheists are unworthy to partake of oblations offered to gods and ancestors." (Manu Smriti III, 150)

" A Brahmin who departs from the Rule of Noble Conduct, does not gain the fruit described in the Veda, but he who duly follows the Rule of Noble Conduct, will obtain the full reward." (Manu Smriti I,109)

" He who possesses faith may receive pure learning even from a man of lower caste, the highest law even from the lowest, and an excellent wife even from a base family." (Manu Smriti II, 238)

Manu Smriti which outlines the scheme of the four varnas (socioeconomic classes) and four ashramas (stages of life of the individual) refuses a provide for the fifth varna. The four classes are adequate to cover all the sections of the society. Manu Smriti is a sociological treatise and not a religious or theological work. It has never been held on par with the Vedas and has never been claimed to be a Holy Book whose authority is unquestionable. Manu Smriti does not deal with the Absolute, a field specialized in by the Upanishads. Manu Smriti is as this-worldly as the Arthashastra is. Manu was also only a Codifier (Documenter of the then-existing codes) of the Caste System and was not to be interpreted as the creator of the Caste System.

"Only the British administrators and jurists who dominated the scene since 1757 found it expedient for their purposes to present it as a religious code binding all the Hindus. The original text of Manu Smriti has been tampered with is acknowledged by Sir William Jones who introduced it as the law book of the Hindus, as he agrees that ' it is accommodated to the improvements of a commercial age'. The extant text of Manu Smriti is a doctored version, doctored to benefit the commercial class of Britain which had sponsored the East India Company, the company for which he was serving as a judge at Calcutta."

Varnashrama Dharma, said to be the mainstay of the Hindu Social Order has no sanction in the Vedas.

In ancient India, these divisions were not based on birth but based on qualifications. According to the Bhagavad Gita this Aryan family system broke down in India over three thousand years ago at the time of Krishna. Hence after three thousand years this system of determining natural aptitude has degenerated into the caste system which resembles it now only in form.

Manu made it clear that superiority is not by birth but by Conduct. This Principle was further emphasized later by Maharishi Veda Vyasa in Mahabharata. Manu himself says that if there is anything in his Smriti which is not acceptable to the conscience of any person, that person should reject it and act according to his/her own conscience.

> *"For choosing your course of conduct at any time and place, keep in view the instructions given first in Sruti (Vedas), then in Smritis, Itihaas (History of grèat personalities) and finally you act according to your conscience." (Manu Smriti, 11, 6).*

> *"Just as a wooden toy elephant cannot be real elephant, and a stuffed deer cannot be a real deer, so, without studying scriptures and the Vedas and the development of intellect, a Brahmin by birth cannot be considered a Brahmin. " (Manu Smriti 11-157).*

Louis Francois Jacolliot (1837-1890), who worked in French India as a government official and was at one time President of the Court in Chandranagar, translated numerous Vedic hymns, the Manusmriti, and the Tamil work, Kural. His masterpiece, La Bible dans l'Inde, stirred a storm of controversy.

Manu-Hindu Law: The Hindu law were codified by Manu more than 3,000 years before the Christian era, copied by entire antiquity and notably by Rome, which alone has left us a written law-the code of Justanian, which has been adopted as the base of all modern legislations.

Jurisprudence: "Observe, enpassant, this striking coincidence with French law, that the Hindu wife, in default of her husband's authority may release from her incapacity, by authority of justice. " "The contract made by a man who is drunk, foolish, imbecile or grievously disordered in his mental condition...." Manu further adds, "What is held under comprehension-held by force is declared null."

Would not this be thought a mere commentary on the Code of Napoleon? Of 4-5,000 years after "How far is all this from those barbarous customs of first ages, when every question was solved by violence and force, and what admiration should we feel for a people who, at the epoch at which Biblical fall would date the world's creation, had already reached the extraordinary degree of civilization indicated by laws so simple and so practical."

Caste System and Code of Manu

The Hindus have been an intensely practical people. The magnificence of daring glimpses into the cosmos as their meditations or scientific investigations revealed to them, convinced them beyond doubt that the complexity of earthly existence could be reduced to some order and the march of human progress subjected to some form of control. They embraced in their researches such subjects as astronomy, physics, chemistry, biology, medicine, ethics, logic, psychology, aesthetics, politics, economics, sociology, and metaphysics. Indeed, in sociology alone, they have left us over twenty treatises; and the Code of Manu, the subject of the present study, is only one of them.

Manu, Manas, manava, all have the same philological root, man, to think. Manu's Code, therefore, is a treatise of social relations for human beings. It lays emphasis on reason, the thinking faculty (manas), in the ordering of man's social relations. It stands for a planned society. Manu's social theory is an art of life; it is a technique, not mere congeries of consistent concepts.

An individual's life is divided into four parts-1. studentship, 2 householding 3. partial retirement or hermitage, 4. and complete retirement. Correspondingly, there are four groups: 1. the manual worker, 2. the merchant, 3. the warrior, and 4. the teacher. A unity of function ties each stage of individual life to the corresponding group. This unity, which lays emphasis on harmonious relations, is the dharma, or the ethics of Manu. There are thus presented four social institutions: 1. the educational, 2. the family-economic, 3. the political, 4. and the religious.

Stable Human Societies

Alain Danielou says: "The Hindus assert that their social formula meets the requirements of man's individual and collective nature. The fact that the Hindu civilization has been able to survive over thousand of years, despite disorders caused by invasions, schisms, and internal wars, and has been capable of constant renewal, as demonstrated by one brilliant period after another, merits all our attention in the study of a social system whose longevity is unique in history."

Aryan Invasion Theory and Caste System

Guy Sorman visiting scholar at Hoover Institution at Stanford and the leader of new liberalism in France, writes: "The Invasion theory has today become the standard explanation for the caste system, though it came up only in the 19th century. Besides, all we have to attest the Aryan invasion is a specious interpretation of the Mahabharata, which is like searching the origins of European aristocracy in the works of Homer! In any case, it is doubtful whether a single invasion, which was more likely a slow infiltration of the North, could have succeeded in structuring so perfectly Indian society along ethnic lines for over three thousand years. Finally, in South India the caste system among the dark, skinned Dravidians is as rigid as it is in the North, though the Aryans in all probability never reached there.

The racial origin of caste hypothesis tells us little about India but it does tell us a great deal about the 19th century Westerners who invented the Aryan invasion theory. It was at the same time that Sieyes and Augustin Thierry claimed that the French nobility was of Germanic stock, whereas the lower classes were of Gallic origin; so the 1789 Revolution was a race war rather than a class war! It was also in the 19th century that appeared the myth of the Indo-Europeans being at the source of all Western civilization and for this we have to thank British authors who were taken up with evolutionist theory. Indian historians trained in Europe have fallen victim to this myth but that does not make it any more authentic. Later on, at the beginning of the 20th century, it became fashionable to support the Marxist theory which replaced race with class, though its premises were just as shaky."

3

GENETIC EVIDENCE OF INDIAN CASTE

INTRODUCTION

The origins and affinities of the 1 billion people living on the subcontinent of India have long been contested.

This is owing, in part, to the many different waves of immigrants that have influenced the genetic structure of India. In the most recent of these waves, Indo-European-speaking people from West Eurasia entered India from the Northwest and diffused throughout the subcontinent. They purportedly admixed with or displaced indigenous Dravidic-speaking populations. Subsequently they may have established the Hindu caste system and placed themselves primarily in castes of higher rank. To explore the impact of West Eurasians on contemporary Indian caste populations, we compared mtDNA (400 bp of hypervariable region 1 and 14 restriction site polymorphisms) and Y-chromosome (20 biallelic polymorphisms and 5 short tandem repeats) variation in 265 males from eight castes of different rank to 750 Africans, Asians, Europeans, and other Indians. For maternally inherited mtDNA, each caste is most similar to Asians. However, 20%-30% of Indian mtDNA haplotypes belong to West Eurasian haplogroups, and the frequency of these haplotypes is proportional to caste rank, the highest frequency of West Eurasian haplotypes being found in the upper castes. In contrast, for paternally inherited Y-chromosome variation each caste is more similar to Europeans than to Asians. Moreover, the affinity to Europeans is proportionate to caste rank, the upper castes being most similar to Europeans, particularly East Europeans. These findings are consistent with greater West Eurasian male admixture with castes of higher rank. Nevertheless, the mitochondrial genome and the Y-chromosome each represents only a single haploid locus and is more susceptible to large stochastic variation, bottlenecks, and selective sweeps. Thus, to increase the power of our analysis, we assayed 40 independent, biparentally inherited autosomal loci (1 LINE-1 and 39 Alu elements) in all of the caste and continental populations (600 individuals). Analysis of these data demonstrated that the upper castes have a higher affinity to Europeans than to Asians, and the upper castes are significantly more similar to Europeans than are the lower castes. Collectively, all five datasets show a trend toward upper castes being more similar to Europeans, whereas lower castes are more similar to Asians. We conclude that Indian castes are most likely to be of proto-Asian origin with West Eurasian admixture resulting in rank-related and sex-specific differences in the genetic affinities of castes to Asians and Europeans.

Shared Indo-European languages (i.e., Hindi and most European languages) suggested to linguists of the nineteenth and twentieth centuries that contemporary Hindu Indians are descendants of primarily West Eurasians who migrated from Europe, the Near East, Anatolia, and the Caucasus 3000–8000 years ago (Poliakov 1974; Renfrew 1989a,b). These nomadic migrants may have consolidated their power by admixing with native Dravidic-speaking (e.g., Telugu) proto-Asian populations who controlled regional access to land, labour, and resources (Cavalli-Sforza et al. 1994), and subsequently established the Hindu caste hierarchy to legitimize and maintain this power (Poliakov 1974; Cavalli-Sforza et al. 1994). It is plausible that these West Eurasian immigrants also appointed themselves to predominantly castes of higher rank. However, archaeological evidence of the diffusion of material culture from Western Eurasia into India has been limited (Shaffer 1982). Therefore, information on the genetic relationships of Indians to Europeans and Asians could contribute substantially to understanding the origins of Indian populations.

Previous genetic studies of Indian castes have failed to achieve a consensus on Indian origins and affinities. Various results have supported closer affinity of Indian castes either with Europeans or with Asians, and several factors underlie this inconsistency. First, erratic or limited sampling of populations has limited inferences about the relationships between caste and continental populations (i.e., Africans, Asians, Europeans).

These relationships are further confounded by the wide geographic dispersal of caste populations. Genetic affinities among caste populations are, in part, inversely correlated with the geographic distance between them (Malhotra and Vasulu 1993), and it is likely that affinities between caste and continental populations are also geographically dependent (e.g., different between North and South Indian caste populations).

Second, it has been suggested that castes of different rank may have originated from or admixed with different continental groups (Majumder and Mukherjee 1993). Third, the size of caste populations varies widely, and the effects of genetic drift on some small, geographically isolated castes may have been substantial. Fourth, most of the polymorphisms assayed over the last 30 years are indirect measurements of genetic variation (e.g., ABO typing), have been sampled from only a few loci, and may not be selectively neutral. Finally, only rarely have systematic comparisons been made with continental populations using a large, uniform set of DNA polymorphisms (Majumder 1999).

To investigate the origin of contemporary castes, we compared the genetic affinities of caste populations of differing rank (i.e., upper, middle, and lower) to worldwide populations. We analysed mtDNA (hypervariable region 1 [HVR1] sequence and 14 restrictionsite polymorphisms [RSPs]), Y-chromosome (5 shorttandem repeats [STRs] and 20 biallelic polymorphisms), and autosomal (1 LINE-1 and 39 Alu inserts) variation in 265 males from eight different Teluguspeaking caste populations from the state of Andhra Pradesh in South India (Bamshad et al. 1998). Comparisons were made to 400 individuals from tribal and Hindi-speaking caste and populations distributed across the Indian subcontinent (Mountain et al. 1995; Kivisild et al. 1999) and to 350 Africans, Asians, and Europeans (Jorde et al. 1995, 2000; Seielstad et al. 1999).

Results: Analysis of mtDNA Suggests a Proto-Asian Origin of Indians MtDNA HVR1 genetic distances between caste populations and Africans, Asians, and Europeans are significantly different from zero ($p < 0.001$) and reveal that, regardless of rank, each caste group is most closely related to Asians and is most dissimilar from Africans. The genetic distances from major continental populations (e.g., Europeans) differ among the three caste groups, and the comparison reveals an intriguing pattern. As one moves from lower to upper castes, the distance from Asians becomes progressively larger. The distance between Europeans and lower castes is larger than the distance between Europeans and upper castes, but the distance between Europeans and middle castes is smaller than the upper caste-European distance. These trends are the same whether the Kshatriya and Vysya are included in the upper castes, the middle castes, or excluded from the analysis. This may be owing, in part, to the small sample size ($n = 10$) of each of these castes. Among the upper castes the genetic distance between Brahmins and Europeans (0.10) is smaller than that between either the Kshatriya and Europeans (0.12) or the Vysya and Europeans (0.16). Assuming that contemporary Europeans reflect West Eurasian affinities, these data indicate that the amount of West Eurasian admixture with Indian populations may have been proportionate to caste rank.

Conventional estimates of the standard errors of genetic distances assume that polymorphic sites are independent of each other, that is, unlinked. Because mtDNA polymorphisms are in complete linkage disequilibrium (as are polymorphisms on the nonrecom-bining portions of the Y-chromosome), this assumption is violated. Alternatively, the mtDNA genome can be treated as a single locus with multiple haplotypes.

However, even if this assumption is made, mtDNA distances do not differ significantly from one another even at the level of the three major continental populations (Nei and Livshits 1989), the standard errors being greater than the genetic distances. Considering that the distances between castes and continental populations are less than those between different continental populations, the estimated mtDNA genetic distances between upper castes and Europeans versus lower castes and Europeans would not be significantly different from each other. Therefore, to resolve further the relationships of Europeans and Asians to contemporary Indian populations, we defined the identities of specific mtDNA restriction-site haplotypes. The presence of the mtDNA restriction sites

Ddei 10,394 and Alui 10,397 defines a haplogroup (a group of haplotypes that share some sequence variants), M, that was originally identified in populations that migrated from mainland Asia to Southeast Asia and Australia (Ballinger et al. 1992; Chen et al. 1995; Passarino et al. 1996) and is found at much lower frequency in European and African populations. Most of the common haplotypes found in Telugu-and Hindi-speaking caste populations belong to haplogroup M and do not differentiate into language-specific clusters in a phylogenetic reconstruction. Furthermore, these Indian haplogroup-M-haplotypes are distinct from those found in other Asian populations and indicate the existence of Indian-specific subsets of haplogroup M (e.g., M3). As expected if the lower castes are more similar to Asians than to Europeans, and the upper castes are more similar to Europeans than to Asians, the frequencies of M and M3 haplotypes are inversely proportional to caste rank.

Of the non-Asian mtDNA haplotypes found in Indian populations, most are of West Eurasian origin. However, most of these Indian West-Eurasian haplotypes belong to an Indian-specific subset of haplogroup U, that is, U2i (Kivisild et al. 1999), the oldest and second most common mtDNA haplogroup found in Europe (Torroni et al. 1994). In agreement with the HVR1 results, the frequency of West Eurasian mtDNA haplotypes is significantly higher in upper castes than in lower castes ($p < 0.05$), the frequency of U2i haplotypes increasing as one moves from lower to higher castes. In addition, the frequency of mtDNA haplogroups with a more recent coalescence estimate (i.e., H, I, J, K, T) was fivefold higher in upper castes (6.8%) than in lower castes (1.4%). These haplotypes are derivatives of haplogroups found throughout Europe (Richards et al. 1998), the Middle East (Di Rienzo and

Wilson 1991), and to a lesser extent Central Asia (Comas et al. 1998). Collectively, the mtDNA haplotype evidence indicate that contemporary Indian mtDNA evolved largely from proto-Asian ancestors with Western Eurasian admixture accounting for 20%-30% of mtDNA haplotypes.

Y-Chromosome Variation

Confirms: Indo-European Admixture Genetic distances estimated from Y-chromosome STR polymorphisms differ significantly from zero ($p < 0.001$) and reveal a distinctly different pattern of population relationships. In contrast to the mtDNA distances, the Y-chromosome STR data do not demonstrate a closer affinity to Asians for each caste group. Upper castes are more similar to Europeans than to Asians, middle castes are equidistant from the two groups, and lower castes are most similar to Asians. The genetic distance between caste populations and Africans is progressively larger moving from lower to middle to upper caste groups.

Genetic distances estimated from Y-chromosome biallelic polymorphisms differ significantly from zero ($p < 0.05$), and the patterns differ from the mtDNA results even more strikingly than the Y-chromosome STRs. For Y-chromosome biallelic polymorphism data, each caste group is more similar to Europeans, and as one moves from lower to middle to higher castes the genetic distance to Europeans diminishes progressively. This pattern is further accentuated by separating the European population into Northern, Southern, and Eastern Europeans; each caste group is most closely related to Eastern Europeans. Moreover, the genetic distance between upper castes and Eastern Europeans is approximately half the distance between Eastern Europeans and middle or lower castes. These results suggest that Indian Y-chromosomes, particularly upper caste Y-chromosomes, are more similar to European than to Asian Y-chromosomes. This underscores the close affinities between Hindu Indian and Indo-European Y-chromosomes based on a previously reported analysis of three Y-chromosome polymorphisms (Quintana-Murci et al. 1999b).

Overall, these results indicate that the affinities of Indians to continental populations varies according to caste rank and depends on whether mtDNA or Ychromosome data are analysed. However, conclusions drawn from these data are limited because mtDNA and the Y-chromosome is each effectively a single haploid locus and is more sensitive to genetic drift, bottlenecks, and selective sweeps compared to autosomal loci.

These limitations of our analysis can be overcome, in part, by analyzing a larger set of independent autosomal loci. Consequently, we assayed 1 LINE-1 and 39 unlinked Alu polymorphisms.

Affinities to Europeans and Asians Stratified

Genetic distances estimated from autosomal Alu elements correspond to caste rank, the genetic distance between the upper and lower castes being more than 2.5 times larger than the distance between upper and middle or middle and lower castes (upper to middle, 0.0069; upper to lower, 0.018; middle to lower, 0.0071). These trends are the same whether the Kshatriya and Vysya are included in the upper castes, the middle castes, or excluded from the analysis (data not shown). Furthermore, a neighbour-joining network of genetic distances between separate castes (Fig. 3) clearly differentiates castes of different rank into separate clusters. This is similar to the relationship between genetic distances and caste rank estimated from mtDNA (Bamshad et al. 1998). It is important to note, however, that the autosomal genetic distances are estimated from 40 independent loci. This afforded us the opportunity to test the statistical significance of the correspondence between genetic distance and caste status. The Mantel correlation between interindividual genetic distances and distances based on social rank was low but highly significant for individuals ranked into upper, middle, and lower groups ($r = 0.08$; $p < 0.001$) and into eight separate castes ($r = 0.07$; $p < 0.001$). Given the resolving power of this autosomal dataset, we next tested whether we could reconcile the results of the analysis of mtDNA and Ychromosome markers in castes and continental populations.

Genotypic differentiation was significantly different from zero ($p < 0.0001$) between each pair of caste populations and between each caste and continental population. Similar to the results of both the mtDNA and Y-chromosome analyses, the distance between upper castes and European populations is smaller than the distance between lower castes and Europeans. However, in contrast to the mtDNA results but similar to the Ychromosome results, the affinity between upper castes and Europeans is higher than that of upper castes and Asians. If the Kshatriya and Vysya are excluded from the analysis or included in the middle castes, the genetic distance between the upper caste (Brahmins) and Europeans remains smaller than the distance between the lower castes and Europeans and the distance between upper castes and Asians. Analysis of each caste separately reveals that the genetic distance between the Brahmins and Europeans (0.013) is less than the distance between Europeans and Kshatriya (0.030) or Vysya (0.020). Nevertheless, each separate upper caste is more similar to Europeans than to Asians.

Because historical evidence suggests greater affinity between upper castes and Europeans than between lower castes and Europeans (Balakrishnan 1978, 1982; Cavalli-Sforza et al. 1994), it is appropriate to use a one-tailed test of the difference between the corresponding genetic distances. The 90% confidence limits of Nei's standard distances estimated between upper castes and Europeans (0.006-0.016) versus lower castes and Europeans (0.017-0.037) do not overlap, indicating statistical significance at the 0.05 level. Significance at 0.05 is not achieved if the Kshatriya and Vysya are excluded. These results offer statistical support for differences in the genetic affinity of Europeans to caste populations of differing rank, with greater European affinity to upper castes than to lower castes.

Discussion: Previous genetic studies have found evidence to support either a European or an Asian origin of Indian caste populations, with occasional indications of admixture with African or proto-Australoid populations (Chen et al. 1995; Mountain et al. 1995; Bamshad et al. 1996, 1997; Majumder et al. 1999; Quintana-Murci et al. 1999a).

Our results demonstrate that for biparentally inherited autosomal markers, genetic distances between upper, middle, and lower castes are significantly correlated with rank; upper castes are more similar to Europeans than to Asians; and upper castes are significantly more similar to Europeans than are lower castes. This result appears to be owing to the amalgamation of two different patterns of sex-specific genetic variation.

The majority of Indian mtDNA restriction-site haplotypes belong to Indian-specific subsets (e.g., M3) of a predominantly Asian haplogroup M, although a substantial minority of mtDNA restriction site haplotypes belong to West Eurasian haplogroups. A higher proportion of proto-Asian mtDNA restriction-site haplotypes is found in lower castes compared to middle or upper castes, whereas the frequency of West Eurasian haplotypes is positively correlated with caste rank, that is, is highest in the upper castes.

For Y-chromosome STR variation the upper castes exhibit greatest similarity with Europeans, whereas the lower caste groups are most similar to Asians. For Y-biallelic polymorphism variation, each caste group is more similar to Europeans than to Asians, and the affinity to Europeans is proportional to caste rank, that is, is highest in the upper castes.

Importantly, five different types of data (mtDNA HVR1 sequence, mtDNA RSPs, Y-chromosome STRs, Ychromosome biallelic polymorphisms, and autosomal Alu polymorphisms) support the same general pattern: relatively smaller genetic distances from European populations as one moves from lower to middle to upper caste populations. Genetic distances from Asian populations become larger as one moves from lower to middle to upper caste populations. It is especially noteworthy that the analysis of Y biallelic polymorphisms, which involved an independent set of comparative Asian, European, and African populations, again indicated the same pattern. Additional support is offered by the fact that the autosomal polymorphisms yielded a statistically significant difference between the uppercaste-European and lower-caste-European genetic distances.

With additional loci, other differences (e.g., the distances between different caste groups and Asians) may also reach statistical significance. The most likely explanation for these findings, and the one most consistent with archaeological data, is that contemporary Hindu Indians are of proto-Asian origin with West Eurasian admixture. However, admixture with West Eurasian males was greater than admixture with West Eurasian females, resulting in a higher affinity to European Y-chromosomes. This supports an earlier suggestion of Passarino et al. (1996), which was based on a comparison of mtDNA and blood group results. Furthermore, the degree of West Eurasian admixture was proportional to caste rank. This explanation is consistent with either the hypothesis that proportionately more West Eurasians became members of the upper castes at the inception of the caste hierarchy or that social stratification preceded the West Eurasian incursion and that West Eurasians tended to insert themselves into higher-ranking positions. One consequence is that shared Indo-European languages may not reflect a common origin of Europeans and most Indians, but rather underscores the transfer of language mediated by contact between West Eurasians and native proto-Indians.

West Eurasian admixture in Indian populations may have been the result of more than one wave of immigration into India. Kivisild et al. (1999) determined the coalescence (50,000 years before present) of the Indian-specific subset of the West Eurasian haplotypes (i.e., U2i) and suggested that West Eurasian admixture may have been much older than the purported Dravidian and Indo-European incursions. Our analysis of Indian mtDNA restriction-site haplotypes that do not belong to the U2i subset of West Eurasian haplotypes (i.e., H, I, J, K, T) is consistent with more recent West Eurasian admixture. It is also possible that haplotypes with an older coalescence were introduced by Dravidians, whereas haplotypes with a more recent coalescence belonged to Indo-Europeans. This hypothesis can be tested by a more detailed comparison to West Eurasian mtDNA haplotypes from Iran, Anatolia, and the Caucasus. Alternatively, the coalescence dates of these haplotypes may predate the entry of West Eurasians populations into India. Regardless of their origin, West Eurasian admixture resulted in rank-related differences in the genetic affinities of castes to Europeans and Asians. Furthermore, the frequency of West Eurasian haplotypes in the founding middle and upper castes may be underestimated because of the upward social mobility of women from lower castes (Bamshad et al.

1998). These women were presumably more likely to introduce proto-Asian mtDNA haplotypes into the middle and upper castes.

Our analysis of 40 autosomal markers indicates clearly that the upper castes have a higher affinity to Europeans than to Asians. The high affinity of caste Y-chromosomes with those of Europeans suggests that the majority of immigrating West Eurasians may have been males. As might be expected if West Eurasian males appropriated the highest positions in the caste system, the upper caste group exhibits a lower genetic distance to Europeans than the middle or lower castes. This is underscored by the observation that the Kshatriya (an upper caste), whose members served as warriors, are closer to Europeans than any other caste (data not shown). Furthermore, the 32-bp deletion polymorphism in CC chemokine receptor 5, whose frequency peaks in populations of Eastern Europe, is found only in two Brahmin males (M. Bamshad and S.K. Ahuja, unpubl.). The stratification of Y-chromosome distances with Europeans could also be caused by malespecific gene flow among caste populations of different rank. However, we and others have demonstrated that there is little sharing of Y-chromosome haplotypes among castes of different rank (Bamshad et al. 1998; Bhattacharyya et al. 1999).

The affinity of caste populations to Europeans is more apparent for Y-chromosome biallelic polymorphisms than Y-chromosome STRs. This could be attributed to the use of different European populations in comparisons using STRs and biallelic polymorphisms.

Alternatively, it may reflect, in part, the effects of high mutation rates for the Y-chromosome STRs, which would tend to obscure relationships between caste and continental populations. A lack of consistent clustering at the continental level has been observed in several studies of Y-chromosome STRs (Deka et al. 1996; Torroni et al. 1996; de Knijff et al. 1997). The autosomal Alu and biallelic Y-chromosome polymorphisms, in contrast, have a slower rate of drift than Ychromosome STRs because of a higher effective population size, and their mutation rate is very low. Thus, the Y-chromosome biallelic polymorphisms and autosomal Alu markers may serve as more stable markers of worldwide population affinities. Our analysis may help to explain why estimates of the affinities of caste groups to worldwide populations have varied so widely among different studies. Analyses of recent caste history based on only mtDNA or Y-chromosome polymorphisms clearly would suggest that castes are more closely related to Asians or to Europeans, respectively. Furthermore, we attempted to minimize the confounding effect of geographic differences between populations by sampling from a highly restricted region of South India. Because of the ubiquity of the caste system in India's history, it is reasonable to predict similar patterns in caste populations living in other areas. Indeed, any genetic result becomes more compelling when it is replicated in other populations. Therefore, comparable studies in caste populations from other regions of India must be completed to test the generality of these results.

The dispersal and subsequent growth of Indian populations since the Neolithic Age is one of the most important events to shape the history of South Asia.

However, the origin and dispersal route of the aboriginal inhabitants of the Indian subcontinent is unclear.

Our findings suggest a proto-Asian origin of the Indian-specific haplogroup-M-haplotypes. Haplogroup-M-haplotypes are also found at appreciable frequencies in some East African populations-18% of Ethiopians (Quintana-Murci et al. 1999a) and 16% of Kenyans (M. Bamshad and L.B. Jonde, unpubl.). A comparison of haplogroup-M-haplotypes from East Africa and India has suggested that this southern route may have been one of the original dispersal pathways of anatomically modern humans out of Africa (Quintana-Murci et al. 1999a). Together, these data support our previous suggestion (Kivisild et al. 1999) that India may have been inhabited by at least two successive late Pleistocene migrations, consistent with the hypothesis of Lahr and Foley (1994). It also adds to the growing evidence that the subcontinent of India has been a major corridor for the migration of people between Africa, Western Asia, and Southeast Asia (Cavalli-Sforza et al. 1994).

It should be emphasized that the DNA variation studied here is thought to be selectively neutral and thus represents only the effects of population history.

These results permit no inferences about phenotypic differences between populations. In addition, alleles and haplotypes are shared by different caste populations, reflecting a shared history. Indeed, these findings underscore the longstanding appreciation that the distribution of genetic polymorphisms in India is highly complex. Further investigation of the spread of anatomically modern humans throughout South Asia will need to consider that such complex patterns may be the norm rather than the exception.

Methods

Sample Collection: All studies of South Indian populations were performed with the approval of the Institutional Review Board of the University of Utah, Andhra University, and the government of India. Adult males living in the district of Visakhapatnam, Andhra Pradesh, were questioned about their caste affiliations and surnames and the birthplaces of their parents. Those who were unrelated to any other subject by at least three generations were considered eligible to participate.

We classified caste populations based upon the traditional ranking of these castes by varna, occupation, and socioeconomic status. According to various Sanskrit texts, Hindu populations were partitioned originally into four categories or varna: Brahmin, Kshatriya, Vysya, and Sudra (Tambia 1973; Elder 1996). Those in each varna performed occupations assigned to their category. Brahmins were priests; Kshatriya were warriors; Vysya were traders; and Sudra were to serve the three other varna (Tambia 1973; Elder 1996). Each varna was assigned a status; Brahmin, Kshatriya, and Vysya were considered of higher status than the Sudra because the Brahmin, Kshatriya, and Vaishya are considered the twice-born Bamshad et al. castes and are differentiated from all other castes in the caste hierarchy. This is the rationale behind classifying them as the upper group of castes (Tambia 1973).

The Kapu and the Yadava are called once-born castes that have traditionally been classified in the Sudra, the lowest of the original four varna. However, the status of the Sudra was actually higher than that of a fifth varna, the Panchama. This fifth varna was added at a later date to include the so-called untouchables, who were excluded from the other four varna

(Elder 1996). The untouchable varna includes the Mala and Madiga. The position of the Relli in the caste hierarchy is somewhat ambiguous, but they have usually been classified in the lower caste group. Therefore, prior to the collection of any data, males from eight different Telugu-speaking castes

(n = 265) were ranked into upper (Niyogi and Vydiki Brahmin, Kshatriya, Vyshya [n = 80]), middle (Telega and Turpu Kapu, Yadava [n = 111]), and lower (Relli, Madiga, Mala [n = 74]) groups (Bamshad et al. 1998). This ranking has been used by previous investigators (Krishnan and Reddy 1994).

After obtaining informed consent, 8 mL of whole blood or 5 plucked scalp hairs were collected from each participant. Extractions were performed at Andhra University using established methods (Bell et al. 1981).

DNA Polymorphisms

The mtDNA data consisted of 68, 116, and 73 HVR1 sequences and 79, 159, and 72 restriction-site haplotypes from largely the same individuals in upper, middle, and lower castes, respectively. These data were compared to data from 143 Africans (15 Sotho-Tswana, 7 Tsonga, 14 Nguni, 24 San, 5 Biaka Pygmies, 33 Mbuti Pygmies, 9 Alur, 18 Hema, and 18 Nande), 78 Asians (12 Cambodians, 17 Chinese, 19 Japanese, 6 Malay, 9 Vietnamese, 2 Koreans, and 13 Asians of mixed ancestry), and 99 Europeans (20 unrelated males of the French CEPH kindreds, 69 unrelated Utah males of Northern European descent, and 10 Poles) (Jorde et al. 1995, 1997).

In addition to our samples, the phylogenetic analyses also included data from 98 published HVR1 sequences from two castes (48 Havlik and 43 Mukri), and a tribal population

(7 Kadar) living in south-western India (Mountain et al. 1995) and restriction-site haplotypes from one caste (62 Lobana) from Northern India, three tribal populations from Northern

(12 Tharu and 18 Bhoksa) and Southern (86 Lambadi) India, and 122 individuals from various caste populations in Uttar Pradesh (Kivisild et al. 1999). Phylogenetic relationships of HVR1 sequences assigned to haplogroupMwere estimated for Indians (this study), Turks (this study), Central Asian

populations (Comas et al. 1998), Mongolians (Kolman et al. 1996), Chinese (Horai et al. 1996), and Japanese (Horai et al. 1996; Seo et al. 1998).

The mtDNA HVR1 Sequence was Determined by Fluorescent: Sanger sequencing using a Dye terminator cycle sequencing kit (Applied Biosystems) according to the manufacturer's specifications (Bamshad et al. 1998). Sequencing reactions were resolved on an ABI 377 automated DNA sequencer, and sequence data were analysed using ABI DNA analysis software and SEQUENCHER software (Genecodes). To identify mtDNA haplotypes and haplogroups (a group of haplotypes that share some sequence variants), major continent-specific genotypes (Torroni et al. 1994, 1996; Wallace 1995) for the following polymorphic mtDNA restriction sites were determined: Hpai 3592, Ddei 10394, Alui 10397, Alui 13262, Bamhi 13366, Alui 5176, Haeiii 4830, Alui 7025, Hinfi 12308, Acci 14465, Avaii 8249, Alui 10032, Bstoi 13704, and Haeii 9052.

Y-Chromosome and Autosomal Polymorphisms

Y-chromosome-specific STRs (DYS 19, DYS 288, DYS 388, DYS 389A, DYS 390) were amplified using published conditions (Hammer et al. 1998). PCR products were separated on an ABI 377 automated sequencer and scored using ABI Genotyper software. Y-chromosome STR data were collected from 622 males including 280 South Indians, 200 Africans (Seielstad et al. 1999; this study), 40 Asians, and 102 Europeans. Autosomal data were collected from 608 individuals including 265 South Indians, 155 Africans, 70 Asians, and 118 Europeans.

The Y-chromosome-specific biallelic polymorphisms tested included: DYS188792, DYS194469, DYS 211105. DYS 221136, DYS 257108, DYS 87, M3, M4, M9, M12, M15, SRY 4064, SRY 10831.1, SRY 10831.2, p12f2, PN1, PN2, PN3, RPS 4Y711, and Tat (Hammer and Horai 1995; Hammer et al. 1997, 1998, 2000; Underhill et al. 1997; Zerjal et al. 1997; Karafet et al. 1999). All individuals tested negative for the Y Alu insert (DYS287). A complete description of the Ychromosome STR loci can be found in Kayser et al. (1997).

For the Y-chromosome biallelic dataset, comparisons were made to a different set of worldwide populations including:

East Asians from Japan, Korea, China, and Vietnam (n = 460); Western Europeans from Britain and Germany (n = 77); Southern Europeans from Italy and Greece (n = 148); and Eastern Europeans from Russia and Romania (n = 102) (M.F. Hammer, unpubl.). The complete dataset of Indians consisted of 55 Brahmin, 111 Yadava and Kapu, and 74 Relli, Mala, and Madiga.

Statistical Analysis

Genetic distances for Y-chromosome STRs were estimated using the method of Shriver et al. (1995), which assumes a stepwise mutation model. Genetic distances for mitochondrial and autosomal markers were calculated as pairwise FST distances, using the ARLEQUIN package (Schneider et al. 1997).

For autosomal polymorphisms, Nei's standard distances and their standard errors were estimated using DISPAN; and 90% confidence intervals were estimated by multiplying the standard error by 1.65. The significance of the FST distances between populations was estimated by generating a null distribution of pairwise FST distances by permuting haplotypes between populations. The p-value of the test is the proportion of permutations leading to an FST value larger than or equal to the observed one. Genotypic differentiation was estimated using GENEPOP (Raymond and Rousset 1995) vers. 3.2. The null hypothesis tested is that there is a random distribution of K different haplotypes among r populations.

Estimates of significance for the correlation between interindividual caste rank differences and interindividual autosomal genetic distances were made by forming two n - n matrices, where n is the number of individuals. For the first matrix, interindividual genetic distances were based on the proportion of Alu insertions/deletions shared by each pair of individuals. To form the second matrix, each individual was assigned a score according to his rank in the caste hierarchy for caste groups (i.e., upper caste = 1, middle caste = 2, lower caste = 3) and also for separate castes (i.e., Brahmin = 1, Kshatriya = 2, Vyshya = 3, Kapu = 4, Yadava = 5, Relli = 6, Mala = 7, and Madiga = 8). An interindividual matrix of score distances was formed by comparing the absolute value of the difference between the scores of each pair of individuals. The matrix of genetic distances was compared to 10,000 permuted matrices of score distances using a Mantel matrix comparison test (Mantel 1967).

To illustrate phylogenetic relationships we constructed reduced median (Bandelt et al. 1995) and neighbour-joining networks (Felsenstein 1989). Coalescence times were calculated as in Forster et al. (1996), using the estimator, which is the average transitional distance from the founder haplotype.

Acknowledgments: We thank all participants, the faculty and staff of Andhra University for their discussion and technical assistance, as well as Henry Harpending for comments and criticisms. We acknowledge the contributions of an anonymous reviewer who suggested that the Kshatriya and Vyshya be analysed separately from the other upper castes. Genetic distances between STRs were estimated by the program DISTNEW, kindly provided by L. Jin. This work was supported by NSF SBR-9514733, SBR-9700729, SBR-9818215, NIH grants GM-59290 and PHS MO1-00064, the Estonian Science Fund (1669 and 2887), and the Newcastle University small grants committee. The publication costs of this article were defrayed in part by payment of page charges. This article must therefore be hereby marked "advertisement" in accordance with 18 USC section 1734 solely to indicate this fact.

REVOLT AGAINST CASTE SYSTEM

Hence, the State power was largely influenced by varna on the one hand, and law and politics on the other. The Puranic texts establish a casual connection between the rise of the varnas and the origin of the State. The importance of the social order and the king as the promulgator of dharma, jatidharmia and varna dharma were stressed since the Brahmans, the Artha Sastra and the Dharma Shastras. According to Manu, "people of the med caste sully the purity of caste, and the State will perish." Narada says that "if the king does not punish the breakers of the Varnashrama Dharma the world would perish."

However, the story that the Varnashrama is based on occupation is not wholly correct. In fact the Varnashrama Dharma as a social classification emerged after two stages, of which, while "race distinction" alone was the basis for the first classification, the profession became the basis in the second classification.

The terms such as Brahmana, Kshatriya, Vaishya and Sudra were in use even when the Aryans were still in the Punjab region. The Rigveda says that since these terms were used as professional nomenclatures, one could find a Brahmana, Kshatriya, Vaishya and Sudra among members of the same family. Therefore, during the Rigvedic period the argument of Manu that people of mixed caste sullied the purity of caste and the State would perish did not arise and seemed meaningless! There was no caste system existing in the Rigvedic society, and therefore, it is historically ascertained that the terms Brahmana, Kshatriya, Vaishya and Sudra of the Rigvedic society meant differently at different times. At the end of the Rigvedic period, the Aryans were divided into a larger number of independent tribes, normally ruled by kings who, when not fighting the Dasas or Dasyus, were frequently engaged in fighting each other. Nevertheless, the Aryans were highly conscious of their ethnic unity, based on a common language, a common religion and a common way of life, and also conscious of the contrast between themselves and earlier inhabitants. The latter were partly absorbed into the Aryan community in the capacity of the Sudras and partly withdrew to such regions temporarily that were out of the reach of the Aryans.

Therefore, the Aryans in the Gangetic plains introduced and executed this system of Varnashrama Dharma in two stages. The highly self-conscious Aryans first divided this mixed society into Brahmins and "others" or non-Brahmins. Accordingly the Brahmins were supposed to be the custodians of the dharma (the law) of the society, i.e. "the Brahmana Dharma" or "Brahminical Dharma." The second classification was made only among the "others," i.e. the non-Brahmins, the Kshatriyas, Vaishyas and Sudras.

This category of "others" or non-Brahmins did not include all the non-Aryans of India, rather this threefold division was made only among those who were subjugated by or surrendered to the Aryans. They might be the Dasus or Dasyu, or the Yakshas, for Dasa or Dasyu means "slave" and Yaksha means "docile and meek" to the Aryans.

The remaining non-Aryan Indians were known by the Aryans as the Asuras who lived scattered in the Aryavartha and concentrated in the South. It took many centuries after the establishment of the dharma for the Aryans to achieve the surrender or subjugation of the Ashuras. And since they were not to be identified with any of the existing varna, or its division of dharma, they were considered as the most backward in relation to the Brahminical culture, and hence though exploited, were condemned as "untouchables."

Ever since its introduction, the Varnashrama Dharma system was resented by the people of the three varnas after the Brahmins.

It is evident through the ages that the Brahmins as a varna never resented or opposed the existence of the Varnashrama system in their society.

That sense of protest and the incidents of revolt against the Varnashrama system could be seen throughout history. But this fact was not focused upon propey. Instead it was comfortably neglected and misinterpreted by Brahmin-oriented historians.

Let me cite a few examples from the legends, the Puranas or the epics of these people called the Aryans.

The Vayu Purana exposes the resentment of the producing classes against the Varnashrama division in the following lines:

> *"The duties of the castes were settled long ago but they did not fulfil their respective duties and came into 'mutual conflict.' Having become aware of this fact the Lord Brahma prescribed criminal justice (danda) and war as the profession of the Kshatriyas."*

Viswamithra wanted to be recognised as Brahma Rishi. Being classified as Kshatriya, Vishvamitra posed a great challenge to the monopoly of the Brahmins over knowledge or the Shastras.

In Mahabharatha the "Sudra" Ekalavia learned the martial arts of the Kshatriya. Though ultimately he lost his thumb, this he did not at the request or demand of Dhronacharya, his Guru.

Sambuga of Ramayana became learned and well versed in dharma, etc. Though he was also killed for breaking the Varnashrama restrictions by Rama of Ayodhya-the so-called compassionate, humane, avatar or Vishnu, the fact still remains clear that the non-observance, protesting and revolt against Varnashrama system was accepted and cannot be hidden by the Aryan writers of the epics and the Puranas.

Since the Varnashrama Dharma itself is the creation of the Brahmins, by the Brahmins and for the Brahmins, they have no reason to resent it. Hence they do not only maintain the system but are determined to see it observed at any cost. This system of caste is not challenged or shattered by any force, internal or external. And this they said and did as the custodians of the so-called "Indian traditions and Indian culture."

Whenever they claim "Indian tradition or Indian culture," the Brahmins never mean any non-Aryan traditions or culture. They systematically and collectively manipulate to make us believe that it is nothing but the Brahmin tradition and Brahmin culture. So, in this divided Indian society, the revolts against the Varnashrama Dharma can be classified, qualitatively and quantitatively, into three kinds. They were (1) individual protests, (2) individual varna protests and (3) the Asura protests.

Almost all the legends, Puranas and Ithihasas of the Aryans provide us a number of stories about the suppression, humiliation and taming of the Ashuras. Particularly the Rama-'avatar' was meant specifically for the purpose of destroying Ravana, the chief of all the Ashura kings.

The protest against the Brahmin supremacy in the Varnashrama society was not successful for many centuries for the simple reason that by enjoying social and cultural supremacy in the society, the Brahmins allowed the Kshatriyas to have a full sway over political authority and exploit society.

So far as there existed a good understanding between the Brahmins and the Kshatriyas, no rebellion against the Varnashrama Dharma, either by the Vaishyas, Sudras or Ashuras, could succeed.

The Sixth-Century Revolt

In the Sixth Century BC there was a tidal wave of revolt against the priestcraft of the ancient world. This wave shattered the power of the old religions, though their cults continued to exist as backwaters for centuries. Seven world religions appeared within fifty years of each other and all continue to this day.

The wave seems to have had its origin in Persia. Zoroaster's actual teaching is still obscure. Scholars are still discussing whether he was a Dualist or a Monotheist. Some have given him a very early date, but the most likely seems to be some time in the first half of the sixth century. He must certainly have influenced Cyrus, who overthrew the Babylonian Empire in 539 BC, and sent the first group of Jews back to Palestine to rebuild their temple. By the time the temple was completed in 516 BC four religious giants in India and China had dared to question the authority of the Brahmin and Chinese priests. Socrates (470-399 BC) came at least a hundred years after Zoroaster, but he was preceded by the Sophists, who probably indicate the first arrival of the tidal wave of religious revolt in Greece.

The first causes of this great movement are probably as complex as the Renaissance and Reformation in Europe 2,000 years later. One obvious possible source is the preaching of Isaiah (c. 740 BC onwards) and the other eighth-century prophets of Israel, with the refrain from Jeremiah and Ezekiel a century or so later. Certainly we can find most of the ethical emphases of Zoroaster, Buddha (c. 563-483 BC), Mahavir (599-527 BC) and Confucius (551-479 BC) in the great prophets.

It is hard to believe that the prophets were heard by no-one else but Israel and Judah. Isaiah's language was intelligible without translation in cities all over the Fertile Crescent. The transmission of religious ideas, especially when they were so revolutionary, would be exceedingly rapid. By the time it takes us to write and publish a book, the ancient world would have gossiped the ideas far more extensively. The number of major cities from Athens to China were comparatively few, and all were cosmopolitan with several languages spoken by the various national groups who lived there. Religious teachers and their disciples travelled constantly and, most important of all, people had the time and interest to listen to them.

Whatever the cause of the tidal wave, the actual force of its impact can be seen most clearly in India. The sequence of the Vedas, and Brahmans, the Upanishads, and the writings of the early Buddhists and Jains give us a picture of what happened with a clarity which is unequalled except in the Bible. From a study of the sixth-century revolt in India we can postulate with some degree of certainty what must have happened in other parts of the ancient world.

Indian life was dominated by the Brahmin priests. From the primitive simplicity of animal sacrifice a thousand years before, they had developed an elaborate system of ritual. Specialization into various schools with their own literature, the leisure to study, and access to weighty books, all enabled them to increase their hold on the common people. They, and they only, could offer sacrifice, and their sacrifices and magical prayers were so powerful that men and even gods had to submit to them. Economically their rapacious demands had become intolerable. For every occasion of birth, puberty, marriage, war, death, or transgression of the ritual laws, the Brahmins demanded dakshina (money gifts). All these might have been tolerated, but when they insisted on interfering in politics the pressure of discontent among the second caste of warriors, nobles and kings increased till a revolt was inevitable. The actual spark may or may not have come from Israel via Persia, but it is significant that the revolt was simultaneous in both India and China. It took several different forms.

Atheism

Some of the warrior caste became Atheists (Charvakas). They said that since God did not exist the whole system of priests, sacrifices and the mumbo-jumbo Vedic prayers was all nonsense. The first recorded example of true Atheism is in Jerusalem, 'The fool says in his heart, "There is no God" ' (Psalm 14:1). It is interesting that the second should be a vigorous group of Atheists in India five centuries before Christ. Of course in the ancient world it was impossible just to declare Atheism. The Atheist had to state his way to salvation. Since there is no God, what must man do? The answer that the

Charvakas gave was that the only good that man knows is happiness, so the highest good was to do what made one truly happy. In this modern opinion they preceded the Epicureans of Greece by two centuries and our Atheists by twenty-four. We shall study their philosophy with other kinds of religious Atheism in the second part of this book.

Buddhism

Buddha, who lived c. 563-483 BC, was a prince of this second or warrior caste. The first written accounts of his life are at least two hundred years after his death, and scholars agree that the two main forms of Buddhism existing today have moved far from their founder's teachings. Certain facts, however, do seem established. The tradition is that he was shocked into seeking the meaning of life by the sight of a leper, an old man and a corpse. He practised austerities for many years till he attained the illumination he was seeking. He certainly knew about the religion offered by the Brahmin priests, and rejected this decisively. He seems to have been an Atheist, or at least to have abandoned the usual worship of the gods. He had no time for animal sacrifice, Brahmin priests, or even the caste system.

Buddha's doctrine was simple and down to earth. The cause of all unhappiness is desire. The lust for power, success, money, sex, comfort and other bodily pleasures causes all the ills of life. Salvation (Nirvana) is therefore the losing of all desire. It is not necessary to become a hermit or stop doing the necessities of life, but it is essential to have no passion in doing them. The practising Buddhist tends as a result to develop a quiet, serene type of personality, but the desire for the good of others and the passion for social justice is eradicated along with the desires for self. Jesus expected us to love our neighbours as ourselves. Buddha denied love for self so that practical love for others was also lost. The main sects of Buddhism vary enormously in their basic practices and philosophy, so they will be looked at under their own religious species. Here we have only noted that Buddha fits exactly into his time and the movement of revolt against priestcraft that swept the ancient world.

Ethicism

A contemporary of Buddha, also a prince of the warrior caste, was Vardhamana Mahavir (599-527 BC). His reaction against the amorality of priestcraft was to stress the need for good deeds. Priests and sacrifices and even God were unnecessary, since this world had an inbuilt, ruthless moral order which automatically rewarded goodness and punished evil. Salvation was therefore attained by destroying the evil of one's heart through doing good. The details of his philosophical system, called Jainism, need not concern us since they were recorded nearly a thousand years later, and in any case are held by only a small fraction of the people of India. An interesting fact is that Mahavir's ethical system for the first time required vegetarianism to the extent that no animal life was to be harmed. Jainism gave to India the word Ahimsa (no-harming), which was taken up and used with a very different meaning by Gandhi. Originally it was connected with the sacredness of all animal and insect life, which is very hard to practise in the modern world, though it was professed by the late Albert Schweitzer in Africa.

If we omit the inclusion of respect for animal life as part of his system of ethics, it is obvious that Mahavir's 'way' was similar to that of his predecessor Zoroaster in Persia, and his contemporary Confucius (551-479 BC) in China. All three of them were first and foremost preachers of ethics. The desire to do what is right and good, quite apart from any doctrines about God, is a recurring theme in the history of philosophy. Aristotle (384-322 BC) and the Stoics of Greece, the high-principled Chinese, Roman, and English 'gentleman', the modern Humanist, and many Liberal Jews, adhere to this religious genus. I have called Ethicism a type of religion because it has a 'way' enforced by a real conscience, and an experience of feeling right or righteous. Whether or not God exists, the devotee has an assurance that all is and will be well. There are many examples of this kind of thinking in nineteenth-and twentieth-century Modernism in the West.

In this introduction to religions I am embarrassed to dismiss Chinese Confucianism with so few words in this section on Ethicism. Since millions in China and elsewhere have been influenced by his teaching, Confucius deserves more extensive treatment. My purpose is, however, to indicate the origin of Ethicism as one of the reactions against priestcraft, and to show that this type of religious life has been common in many well-ordered civilizations. More information about Confucius and the other ethical teachers is readily available in any encyclopedia. Having recognized the genus, there is no point in labouring the details.

We have looked briefly at three types of revolt against an intolerable priestcraft. They all agreed in their rejection of animal sacrifice, the priests who controlled it and even the God to whom the sacrifices were directed. Because of this direct attack on Brahminism and the caste system, the three forms of revolt were excommunicated from Hinduism for over 2,000 years. Now that the Brahmins have found other ways of establishing their position through education and the key positions in India, Buddhism, Jainism and even Atheism have been readmitted as accepted paths within Hinduism. Protestantism has also come perilously close to including Ethicism and even Atheism as acceptable 'ways' within the Christian fold.

Monism

We must now look at a fourth kind of revolt, which is philosophically far more important, and may in this century become the main threat to Christian Theism. Monism is a type of thinking which first appeared in the Hindu Upanishads (teachings for a disciple). Over 200 of these writings exist. The main group belongs to our period in the sixth century BC, although some are much later additions. The writers of the Upanishads did not seek to banish the gods and priests and sacrifices, but offered a parallel and deeper way of union with the Absolute. The sacrifices are spiritualized, and God is given a new meaning. He is no longer a Theistic Creator, but the Absolute, the Deepest Self, Ultimate Reality, or what modern writers call 'the ground of all being'. Priests and sacrifices were suitable for the uninitiated, but the true Monist had a direct access to the Absolute which bypassed the need for ritual. The discipline developed to attain this union with the absolute was called Yoga. It is still widely practised in India, and is now being vigorously propagated in the West.

The extensive literature of Hinduism describes the various types of Monism in the greatest detail, and we must devote a whole chapter to contrasting its philosophy at every point with Christian Theism. Our task here is to note that this type of religion has appeared again and again in the history of the world. The Chinese teacher Lao-Tse (born c. 550 or 600 BC) was a contemporary of Confucius, and obviously belongs to the same wave of revolt against priestcraft. He insisted on freedom from elaborate ritual and regulations. He rejected the man-made restraints typical of Ethicism, so that Confucius found him incomprehensible. Positively he recommended conformity to the Way (Tao) of the Universe. As we shall see in chapter 9, there are four kinds of Monism. Of these Taoism would appear to have been closer to Pantheism or Modified Pantheism than to the typical Vedanta type of Hindu Monism. Instead of a stress on meditation, it was more a seeking to be natural, or at one with the course of nature. But in any case Taoism was certainly monistic as opposed to the ancient Theism and Polytheism of China.

Monism has since had a long history, not least in Christianity. After the powerful attack from the direction of Gnosticism in the second century, the Christian church had to face a monistic counter-attack from the Neo-Platonists in the third century. Plotinus (c. 205-270) made a journey to the East and returned with an arsenal of monistic ideas against the rapidly growing Christian church in the Roman Empire. To claim the Greek philosophical heritage he included some ideas from Plato, but his system of contemplation was identical with the Yoga of Hindu Monism.

Plotinus failed to rally the Roman Empire against Jesus Christ, but he was rediscovered and introduced through the back door many centuries later. An Italian philosopher, Giordano Bruno (1548-1600), represented the first Western monistic reaction to medieval priestcraft, and his Pantheism influenced the Jew Spinoza (1632-77). Meanwhile many of the mystics had been influenced by Neo-Platonism through a forgery attributed to Dionysius the Areopagite. Most of the readers of Pseudo-Dionysius thought that they were still Christians, but their piety had become strangely Hindu, and one of them, Eckhart (c. 1260-c. 1327), was nearly condemned for heresy.

Philosophical Monism entered the German church through Johann Fichte (1762-1814), who is described as an ethical Monist. He was dismissed from the University of Jena for Atheism in 1799, but was later appointed to the University of Berlin. Through G. W. F. Hegel (1770-1831) one wing of the Idealists became the true materialists like Feuerbach (1804-72) and Karl Marx. Friedrich Schelling (1775-1854) led a group who had a less materialistic view of reality which was closer to the Hindu Vedanta type of Monism. Another wing was championed by the mighty Schleiermacher (1768-1834), who tried to show that true Christianity is in fact a kind of Monism. The newest exposition of this view is Bishop Robinson's Honest to God, which claims to be Christian but follows exactly the philosophical position called Modified Monism, which has been known in India since the Upanishads.

We can now conclude this chapter with a chart showing the main religious systems preached in the sixth century BC and the later developments classified under them. Priestcraft was a degeneration from the original religion of man. Atheism, Buddhism, Ethicism and Monism are the four possible reactions of a thinking man against it, and all are at least twenty-five centuries old.

This chart could be developed under each category from standard works such as: M. Hiriyanna, Outlines of Indian Philosophy, Frederick Coplestone, A History of Philosophy, and many modern treatments such as Theodore Roszak's The Making of a Counter Culture. It is striking that the typical forms of revolt against priestcraft and polytheism appear suddenly in Greece at the same time as they erupted in India. Whether the relationship is one of borrowing, or merely due to similar minds facing similar problems, is an interesting question, but it does not affect the thesis that the sixth-century revolt against ritualism did sweep across the known world from the Middle East to China and to Greece.

A similar study could be made of our situation in the twentieth century. What is striking is that vast numbers of both intelligent and unintelligent people still fit into the five religious categories. We shall be looking at the sixth basically Christian alternative later. In any case the renewed interest in eastern religions, and the exploring of monistic experiences through drugs and meditation, indicate that monism as well as atheism and ethicism are still very much with us as living religions.

Buddhism-Hurricane of the North-East

In this vertically divided Indian society the productive classes such as the Vaishyas, Sudras and the untouchables were longing for a Kshatriya rebellion to humble the Brahmin in the society. There rose up a great challenge ever made to the Varnashrama Dharma, not as a Kshatriya but as a non-Brahmin republican.

This "hurricane of the North-East," Buddhism, swept the whole of India for many centuries, and India could offer, for the first time, through this lighof Asia a philosophy and a way of life which has a universal application.

Siddhartha's revolutionary movement, though subdued after about six centuries, could effect the complete destruction of the three lower varnas, i.e. Kshatriya, Vaishya and Sudra. In their place emerged a number castes, predominantly with local characters.

All these "caste Hindus" are now called as Sudra, the lowest of the Sathur varnas.

After this Kshatriya revolt: Brahmins adopted a new strategy that of supporting, canonising any person from any caste to become the ruler, provided he respected the Brahmin as the spiritual, social and cultural master of society.

Now comes the ruler nor necessarily from the Kshatriya varna. To quote a few examples, the Nandas of Magadha were Barbers, the Mauryas were out-castes, the Guptas were Vaishyas and so forth. This strategy they maintained even when the rulers were non-Hindus, such as the Muslims or the Europeans.

In the beginning of the 19th century, the Christian missionaries were convinced that for the cultural growth of the people, many social and religious reforms were necessary, for example, the total abolition of caste. Rapid changes occurred following the establishment of British power in the area, "coupled with the slow erosion of certain traditional institutions" of the society and habits of the people. As the enthusiasm for English education increased in India, a steadily increasing number of young Indians fell a prey to the influence of the missionaries, and some cases of conversion or laxity in the observance of their own religion became more frequent.

The impact of English education, of Western ideas and of Christianity created a schism in the Hindu society in the 1820s, and it was symbolised by the formation of rival sections among the natives, one representing the liberal and the other the conservative elements.

Struggle to Win Fights On

Towards the close of the 19th century the South posed a great challenge to the domination of the Brahmins in society. This culminated in an association called the South India Liberal Federation, popularly known as the Justice Party. Yet a more powerful movement on these lines could be provided only by Periyar E.V. Ramasamy, whose fight against Varnashrama Dharma was two-fold. While the Justice Party opposed only the Brahmin domination in the society; the self-respect movement of Periyar questioned not only the Brahmin domination in society, but also waged a real war against the very caste system.

But for many reasons this "non-Brahmin movement" which can be adjudged as the greatest after the one by the great Siddhartha is yet to succeed to the extent of the latter.

The 20th century also witnessed a great rebellion from the North-West India for the first time after the Deva Ashura war of Rama-Ravana. Baba Saheb Dr. B.R. Ambedkar launched a great revolt against the Varnashrama system of the Indian society. Like the Buddha, Dr. Ambedkar too adopted a common base for all the untouchables, irrespective of their caste, creed, language or region.

This, for the first time, after the Buddha, made all the untouchables from Kashmir to Kanyakumari to unite under one banner, to voice and to agitate against the political, social, economic and cultural exploitation by the Brahmin caste.

It is interesting to note that Periyar's movement is second to that of the Buddha, and Ambedkar's movement is second to the legendary Ashura movement under Ravana. But with this difference: that where the Buddha and Ravana failed, "Periyar" and "Ambedkar" are striving had to win once for all.

Folk Life, Discrimination and Toleration

Before I proceed to examine Caste in detail, I wish to make a distinction central to ideas expressed in this paper: I distinguish Folk Life from organised forms of political life. This is not to say the two are not interrelated, but only asserts that they are distinct. The way discrimination and tolerance are looked at and practised in Folk Life, and the way they are looked at within the framework of the organised political system of a given society need not always be the same; often they are very different. Experience shows that frequently a particular form of discrimination against a particular group is created in the process of making a particular political system. The political system introduces the problem, leaving a need for solutions by way of changes to the legal system. The solutions may fall far short of the problem and seemingly permanent forms of discrimination may arise as a result. These seemingly permanent forms of conflict are then attributed to the Folk Life, as inherent conflicts that had always been present among the peoples of a particular locality.

It is also necessary to clarify that Folk Life does not mean a disorganised way of life. Folk Life has its own modes of organisation. At risk of generalising, it may be said that the chief characteristic of Folk Life is spontaneity of relationships among the Folk. The relationships are marked by something more than mere tolerance. Sharing, compassion and basic justice remain the overarching considerations in Folk Life. Nicolas Frederick Severin Grundtvig (1783-1872) recognised these qualities when he asserted that Folk Life is first and Christianity is second. To Christianity I add all religions and philosophies, particularly legal philosophies.

Discrimination results in varying degrees of suppression or killing of Folk Life. When in Boris Pasternak's Doctor Zhivago the hero declares the end of love in Russia, it is recognition of the death of Folk Life and the take-over of all aspects of life by the state. We see similar perceptions elsewhere in the works of Franz Kafka. In fact, the over-powering effect of the state on peoples is quite a common theme in modern times.

Study of Caste from the Point of View of Discrimination and Toleration: It is with these preliminary considerations that I approach Caste from the point of view of discrimination and toleration. In the Indian Caste system, the following features stand out:

(a) Caste was not present in India at all times.

(b) Caste is not based on race or ethnicity.

(c) A Caste is not a mere social group, like a class or religious group.

(d) The essential feature of Caste is its enclosed nature, from the moment of birth.

(e) Among the upper Castes, (Brahmins, Kshatriyas, Vaishyas,) Brahmins enjoy an incomparably advantageous position over the other two.

(f) Every form of social and political power is completely withdrawn from the lowest Castes (Sudras, Dalits).

(g) The overwhelming majority of people in India are of lower Castes.

(h) Caste discrimination, based on birth, violates all human rights norms on which UN instruments are founded.

(i) Rejection of equality prevents the possibility of associated living among the people. It thus blocks development of Folk Life. Politically, it makes the functioning of democracy impossible.

Caste was not present in India since time immemorial. There were many migrations and conflicts among various groups. Over a long period of time an homogenous culture developed and exogamy was normal. Later, with groups enclosing themselves, Caste and endogamy became the rule. Discrimination on the basis of group began during this time, and religious and judicial notions were developed to justify Caste.

Then came a collapse and revolt against Caste, leading to a virtual ousting of this system. The radicalism of Buddhism at this time was its fundamental rejection of Caste and acceptance of all persons on the basis of equality. The results included more widespread democratic practices, equality and freedom. They were accompanied by abandonment of religious and judicial norms justifying Caste and emergence of new ethical and juridical norms. I shall examine this era in greater depth momentarily.

After this period of sanity, India fell back into the Caste system again. The re-emergence of forces favouring the Caste system led to a protracted contest for supremacy between the two sides. Finally, the Caste system was reimposed, but this time practices of discrimination were even worse than before and draconian regulations were developed to ensure Caste segregation. The notion and practice of 'untouchability' was introduced. The period of colonialism and subsequent independence weakened legal aspects of Caste discrimination, but at economic and social levels discrimination has remained much the same.

The theological justification of Caste was found in Purusha Sukta of the Rig Veda, according to which Brahmins came from the mouth, Kshatriyas from the arms, Vaishyas from the thighs and Sudras from the feet of Brahma, the Creator. This fourfold division is called Chaturvarna, the literary translation of which is four Castes. The Brahmins were in the modern sense the intellectual class, having a monopoly over knowledge. They were also the priestly class, the most powerful and all dominating of the four. Kshatriyas were the soldier class and they alone were allowed to bear arms. Vaishyas were traders. The Sudras performed menial jobs. To this a fifth category of 'untouchables' (Dalits) was added later.

As the Brahmins were both the predominant and priestly class, their arguments took the form of theological positions and were called Dharma. Religious rules imposing various forms and rituals were also developed, and these went into minute details of life. Much later came the draconian Law of Manu, which comprehensively entrenched the rules of Caste enclosure.

Importantly, it was the Brahmins who introduced the idea of Chaturwarna to the West, asserting that the fourfold division did not involve any form of discrimination. They maintained it was only a division of labour. Prestigious scholars such as Coomaraswamy, well known to the West, accepted the Caste system merely as a division of labour and part of the Varnasharma and Sanatana Dharma. Mahatma Gandhi, who strongly condemned the present day manifestation of the Caste system, describing it as a leprosy, likewise defended the conceptual basis for Caste along these lines.

Tracing the origin of Caste to division of labour or similar functions is unsatisfactory in that like divisions exist in all societies but do not give rise to such rigid practices. Comparison of Caste to the European guild system is not useful for the same reason. Many misconceptions of Caste have originated due to writers trying to explain it to a European audience (most of whom may not have had a deep interest in the matter) by comparing it with experiences that their audience may understand. However, such explanations understate the discrimination suffered by those bearing the brunt of the Caste system.

It was left to the first generations of educated people among those who suffered under the Caste system to make a more comprehensive critique. Their analyses reflected those of the anti-Caste Buddhist movement centuries earlier. Dr. Brim Rao Ambedkar (1881-1956) became the undisputed leader of the Dalits and the pre-eminent exponent of their cause. Ambedkar left an examination of Caste that remains unchallenged even by his worst opponents. Himself a Dalit, Ambedkar knew personally the extremes to which Caste discrimination could touch the most rudimentary aspects of daily life: 'I would like to tell you some of the reminiscences of my childhood... One day, I remember, I was very thirsty. I was not allowed to touch the water tap. I told my master that I wanted to drink water. He called the peon and asked him to turn on the tap and I drank water. Whenever the peon was absent I had to go without water. Thirsty, I had to return home and then only I could quench my thirst.'

Ambedkar argued that Caste practice might have arisen when one social group enclosed itself from others. Exclusion and enclosure may have entailed advantages for this group. From this he argued that only the more socially powerful group would have both found benefit in such enclosure and also had the ability to isolate itself in this manner. Others followed, either by imitation of the more powerful social class or because they had no choice anyway. This is more plausible than any other theory put forward so far on the origins of Caste. Others have not even attempted to explain the unique nature of Caste and the inherent discrimination involved in the practice of Caste. In fact, the labour-function theory is used to explain Caste as inherently neutral (if not good) and to claim that any discrimination is only a result of abuse within the system. The Dalit movement has always proceeded from this position that the Caste system was discriminatory by origin. The extent of discrimination far exceeded anything that may occur within an otherwise non-discriminatory system. It follows that 'To the Untouchables, the problem of discrimination in order of seriousness is only next to the problem of recovering their manhood. The discrimination against the Untouchables is practised by the Hindus on a scale, the extent of which it is impossible for an outsider to imagine. There is no field of life in which the Untouchables and the Hindus come into competition and in which the former is not subject to discrimination.'

Thus, observed Ambedkar, Caste is a division not of labour but of labourers. The annihilation of Caste, he stated, is an undeniable pre-condition for democracy in India.

Every form of discrimination involves some type of enclosure. In Europe, lower classes were denied access to many social privileges by the aristocracy. Blacks in the United States and South Africa were also disenfranchised. The difference with Caste is that enclosure is complete, to the extent that direct contact between Castes is prohibited, in order to avoid 'pollution'. It means total segregation, whether in temples, at wells, on roads, in schools and most importantly, in marriage. Thus, while discrimination by Caste bears some similarity to that imposed by slavery and Apartheid, the Caste system is in many respects more dehumanising. The very term 'untouchable' means ones with whom no social contact of any sort should be held, under threat of punishment. It degrades beyond all comparison. Thus Caste was not a mere division of labour but the most extreme division of social and political power. The question of balancing interests between groups did not exist, for the simple reason that each Caste was a world unto itself.

Thus it was that Caste became entrenched practically, theologically, and jurisprudentially. In every respect, Caste rejects the notion of human equality and thus justified enclosure of each Caste within its own boundaries on the basis of graded inequality. In this set-up the idea of common good existed only within each Caste group.

The First Great Revolt against Chaturwarna

That there would have been much opposition to Chaturwarna philosophy and practices is natural, for it imposed barbarous conditions upon many. In fact, literature provides many examples of such resistance. However, one great revolt made history and for quite some time kept Indian society open, defeating forces supporting the enclosed Caste units. This was the social revolution led by Siddhartha Gautama Buddha. Buddha refused to recognise Caste distinction. He attacked the Chaturwarna philosophy both theoretically and practically, by creating a new type of a religious leadership, the Sangha. This movement, with begging bowl in hand, entered into communion with all sectors of society, including the lowest Castes.

Himself a born follower of Sanatana Dharma, Buddha tested its every tenet and found it false. In his later teaching he repudiated each of these tenets. He refused to recognise the belief in God or soul as a precondition for leading a good life; he rejected the authority of Vedas; he refused to recognise superiority based on birth; he opposed Vedic sacrifices. He repudiated the Caste system.

Buddha recognised the right of everyone to learn. He admitted persons belonging to any Caste into his following, admonishing all who became his disciples to abandon Caste. He allowed women into the Sangha, whereas the Brahmins forbade women even to read the Vedas, considering them as 'impure as falsehood itself'. His fundamentalist position was an all-round attack on enclosed social units and a call for more open social interactions. From rejection of the Vedas and Vedic sacrifices also grew his position on non-violence. Rejection of violence against all beings, insects, animals and others naturally implied opposition to the use of violence against human beings. The Caste system rested on the threat of violence by a higher Caste against a lower Caste. Without this threat, Caste enclosures could not last.

While all these positions can be considered radical, in my view Buddha's most fundamental attack on the Caste system was the creation of the Sangha. In it, Buddha created a substitute for the Brahmin. Yet these religious leaders differed from Brahmins in every aspect. The most extreme difference between the two was the begging bowl. It is interesting to note that the begging bowl was called bhiksha patra, which literally meant 'sharing bowl'. Likewise, the word bhikkhu, meaning 'member of the Sangha', is derived from bhik, of the root bhaj, meaning 'the wish to share'. Thus, one religious leadership sought enclosure, the other acted on a desire to share. To beg for food from anyone, including a Sudra, was indeed the very annihilation of Caste. One Indian scholar notes: 'What this means is difficult to explain to anyone who does not know that most Indians would rather go hungry, and many have preferred death by starvation to eating soiled food or that prepared by a person of a lower Caste.' The Sangha moved among all persons. Their position was not hereditary but one of choice. The choice was not for power but for sharing. The following poem by an early monk reflects the radical change of lifestyle that came as result of joining the Sangha:

I made a hut

From three palm leaves by the Ganges

Took a crematory pot

For an eating bowl,

Lifted my robe off a trash bin

Two rainy seasons passed and I

Spoke only one word

Clouds came again

But this time the darkness

Tore open

Taking a crematory pot as a food bowl, taking a robe off a trash bin; these were marks of renunciation, from the prestigious position of the highest Caste to identify with the lowest, the Sudras.

Like the Lutheran Reformation, Buddha's renaissance spread fast. The sheer frustration people would have had under the Chaturwarna system may have been the main reason for its advancement. Human nature inevitably revolts against enclosed systems and Folk Life makes use of every opportunity to rise again when it appears crushed.

Soon, it influenced even kings, among whom Emperor Ashoka remains the best known. Ashoka had been shaken by the violence of war. After more than two and a half years due consideration, he converted to Buddhism and helped to propagate it beyond the borders of India.

It has been written of his era that 'Buddhism of [Emperor Ashoka's] age was not merely a religious belief; it was in addition a social and intellectual movement at many levels, influencing many aspects of society. Obviously, any statesman worth the name would have had to come to terms with it.' Ashoka transformed Buddhist teaching into a philosophy explaining the responsibilities people owe to each other. Ashoka spread this system by edicts:

'These may be described as proclamations to the public at large. They explain the idea of Dhamma [Universal Law]. It was in this concept in the context of Mauryan India that the true achievement of Ashoka lay. He did not see Dhamma as piety resulting from good deeds inspired by formal religious beliefs, but as an attitude of social responsibility. In the past, historians have generally interpreted Ashoka's Dhamma almost as a synonym for Buddhism, suggesting thereby that Ashoka was concerned with making Buddhism the state religion. It is doubtful if this was his intention.

Dhamma was aimed at building up an attitude of mind in which social responsibility, the behaviour of one person towards another, was considered of great relevance. It was a plea for the recognition of the dignity of man, and for a humanistic spirit in the activities of society.' (My emphasis)

During this time, as the Caste system declined, ideas of common humanity, human dignity and responsibilities towards each other flourished in its place. As a result, the Caste situation changed dramatically. The dominant Caste, the Brahmins, became marginalised. During at least 140 years of the Mauryan Empire the Brahmins lost the state patronage they had held. As Ashoka forbade animal sacrifices, Brahmins also lost their main occupation as priests offering the sacrifices.

With the spread of Buddhism, the history of India became the struggle for supremacy between Buddhism and Brahminism. The fate of the Caste system in India depended on who had the upper hand in this struggle. In this context, something happened quite independently that decided the outcome in favour of Brahminism: the Muslim invasions of India.

Muslim suppression of Buddhism was ruthless. It was part of their struggle against idolatry. There are many historical narratives on the brutality with which Buddhism was suppressed. The greatest loss to Buddhism was the Sangha, who were either killed or fled to other lands such as Nepal and Tibet. As Buddhism was weakened, Brahmin attacks against the Buddhists increased, both physically and theologically. Sri Sankaracarya conducted a mass propaganda campaign in every part of India. Against Buddha's secularist position, worship of gods was restored. The dominance of the male and the priest was also restored. In short, the dominance of religion over Folk Life was re-established. The Caste system revived with greater harshness than before. Bereft of their Sangha, Buddhists soon preferred to be Muslims rather than live under their age-long oppressors, for Islam also rejected the Caste system. Thus there were many conversions to Islam from Buddhism.

While much more could be said on this reimposition of Brahminism and the Caste system, we may derive more profit from a reconsideration of the distinct moral principles offered by each of the two competing systems. The Buddhist view of human beings is that of equals. In contrast, inequality is a fundamental principle of Brahminism. It is based on the premise that Brahmins are the most important class and they are entitled to special privileges and immunities. Yet the Buddhist view goes further than mere equality; the Human is seen as part of the wider world of nature. As such the human does not have an absolute superiority over nature. The Brahmin view was that higher Castes, being so ordained by God, were superior not only to others but everything else likewise.

The views on toleration emerging from these two worldviews are polarised. One admits a feeling of fellowship only towards a particular group; the other the feeling of fellowship extends to all and cannot be abandoned at any cost. For one, 'the other' is partially or totally an enemy, but under the second view, the idea of total enmity is never acceptable. Under one view, one can (and in fact must) be indifferent to what happens to 'the other'; such indifference is not morally possible under the latter. Under one, differences can be absolute and under the other differences are only of relative importance. Under one, it is permissible to create and maintain absolute conflicts; under the other, conflicts (when they arise) are relative and transitory. When conflicts are made absolute, total war is possible and even unavoidable. But total war is never acceptable under the other view, where kalyana mitrata" beautiful friendship " with everyone is the underlying search in all relationships. Under one, basic, decent human relationships can be sacrificed for greater goals; but under the other, nothing is greater than these relationships. That is, as far as I understand it, the meaning of Folk Life.

Eliminating Discrimination, Reviving Toleration

Rejection of equality via Caste prevents the possibility of associated living among the people. It thus blocks development of Folk Life. Politically, it makes the functioning of democracy impossible.

Caste discrimination violates all human rights norms on which UN instruments are founded. In its application, Caste has led to sub-human treatment of a vast population. Presently, India's Dalits constitute around 17% of the population. With other minorities, such as tribal peoples, Sikhs and Muslims, minorities in India constitute roughly 85%; the overwhelming majority. To this day, the level of violence against Dalits and other 'lower' Castes is atrocious. Social degradation perpetuated under the Caste system has very few parallels in human history. Such treatment continues to this day. Discrimination is extended to all aspects of life: whether in employment, education, health, land holding, security, and all aspects of women's rights. The psychological effects on 'inferior' Castes constitute gross human rights abuse and a continuing cruelty.

On 26th of January 1950, the Constitution of India came into force. This Constitution accepted the principles of equality, fraternity and liberty. Jurisprudentially, the Constitution outlawed all enclosed units and philosophies that support such enclosures by implication. M.V. Pylee, a foremost authority on the Indian Constitution, remarked, '[The constitution] represents the political, economic and social ideals and aspirations of vast majority of the Indian people.' However, between this legal position and the reality of India there is a vast gap. The world's largest democracy has thus failed to develop beyond a mere formal democracy.

A Caste can exist only within a system of Castes. An enclosed unit called a Caste has no meaning if it does not exist in the midst of other enclosed units. The Caste system is one in which doors and windows to other Castes are closed. To open or to break the doors cannot be a decision of just one Caste. It has to be a decision by consensus. The breaking of Caste boundaries involves an exit as well an entrance. Whilst one Caste may make a decision to exit from its boundaries, entering into boundaries held by others requires their consent. When the most socially and politically powerful Castes want to remain enclosed, lower Castes' decisions to break open can have little effect. When higher Castes rules of internal discipline require strict observance of enclosure, revolts by lower Castes can make very little progress.

Emancipation lies in destroying Caste enclosure. In other words, making it open. Yet in India, after a few thousand years of enclosure practice, breaking open has proved near impossible, despite many gigantic efforts. It is perhaps not difficult to understand the inability of some leaders-those who are reliant on the support of the upper Castes-to take a strong position against Caste. One may recall that even during the early part of this century, the prominent white politicians in the United States could not take up the issue of discrimination against blacks strongly. The emergence of Martin Luther King and his ilk in the United States and Nelson Mandela of South Africa were a necessary part of the process dealing with discrimination in those countries. Ultimately, as understood by Dalits themselves, the annihilation of Caste is likewise a precondition for democracy in India. The solution to Caste discrimination does not lie in toleration among the Castes. It demands nothing less than the elimination of Caste itself, from within Caste itself.

Discrimination causes suffering, often very deep forms of inner suffering. People who are thus made to suffer withdraw. As result, they also refuse to cooperate. In such circumstances, if tolerance is to have any meaning, it must be sufficiently genuine and strong enough to restore cooperation. Thus discrimination and toleration both reflect the quality of compassion, mercy and justice. If there is a perception that these qualities are missing, the legitimacy of the social organisation and the political system as whole will be under challenge. If such legitimacy is finally lost, deep enmities arise, leading to violence. Violence can reach a point that people become indifferent to cruelty; cruelty they cause and cruelty they suffer. Such indifference kills folk relationships and communication. Ultimately, the test of active tolerance is its ability to genuinely revive the Folk Life in the face of suffering caused by discrimination.

Challenges to Brahminical Hegemony and Caste-rigidity

In the Upanishads, there is also recognition that conceptions of god could be quite varied, that Brahminical rituals were not essential to spiritual release, and that individuals might choose different deities or methods of worship. This secular outlook facilitated the growth of alternative viewpoints not only in the realm of religious practice but also on norms of how society ought to be structured. Social challenges to absolute monarchical rule and the immense power of the priestly class probably led to a crescendo during the Buddhist period when Brahmin hegemony received challenges from several quarters-from radical atheists such as the Lokayatas, from Jain agnostics, and heterodox Hindus and Buddhists who wanted to reconstruct society on a less discriminatory and more humane basis.

Although it would be wrong to romanticize the Buddhists as being completely against caste distinctions {since there is evidence that they accepted caste distinctions in society outside their sanghas (communes)}, Buddhists along with other social critics undoubtedly played a powerful role in ensuring that caste was not the sole or even the dominant factor in shaping Indian society of that period. This is borne out by how so many ruling clans arose from a non-Kshatriya (and also non-Brahmin) background. The Nandas, the Mauryas, the Kalingas and the Guptas are just some of the more illustrious of India's ruling dynasties that did not arise from a Kshatriya background.

Of course, once some of these clans established themselves as ruling dynasties, they took on the Kshatriya mantle, and over time, the radical changes that accompanied their ascent to power gave way to social conservatism and a decaying of the radical currents that had contributed to their rise to power.

It is also worth noting that the classical four varna division of Hindu society (as described in the Manusmriti) does not appear to have had much practical significance if one were to go by the accounts of the Greek chronicler, Megasthenes. In his accounts of Mauryan India. Megasthenes appears to list a seven fold social order in which he differentiates between the priest and the philosopher (who he ranked much above the priest, and who could have been a Brahmin, Jain or Buddhist) and also gives special attention to court bureaucrats such as record keepers, tax collectors and judicial officials. He also ascribed to the peasantry a higher status than might be inferred from the Manusmriti and noted with amazement how the peasantry was left unharmed during battles.

According to Megasthenes, philosophers-whether Brahmins or Jain/Buddhist monks also had obligations in terms of offering advice to the ruler in matters of public policy, agriculture, health and culture. Repeated failure to provide sound counsel could lead to a loss of privileges-even exile or death. Thus, although many Brahmins may have held on to their privileges by being shameless sycophants-others made significant contributions in the realm of science, philosophy and culture. Social mobility was possible since learning was not an exclusive preserve of the Brahmins and both the Buddhist and Jain sanghas admitted people from different social backgrounds and also admitted women. (Jyotsna Kamat points to a Karnataka inscription from 1187 AD that suggests that Jain nuns enjoyed the same amount of freedom as their male counterparts.) The more advanced sanghas enforced a separate quorum for women to ensure that a largely male gathering may not take decisions that did not meet with the approval of the women members of the sangha.

Over time, it appears that the sanghas degenerated, losing their intellectual vitality and egalitarian spirit allowing the Brahmins to gradually consolidate their power and influence in the Gangetic plain. But even as late as the 6th-7th C, Gupta-period inscriptions describing land grants in Bengal appear to corroborate Megasthenes' view of how Indian society was structured. Social rank of senior court administrators (who may have risen from different caste backgrounds) invariably exceeded the rank of ordinary village priests.

In Orissa, Rajasthan and parts of Central and Southern India, this pattern prevailed till even later. Moreover, as society headed towards caste-ossification, it was the court administrators who after acquiring hereditary caste status, became the most privileged agents in society. In some instances, these administrative castes simply merged with other privileged castes such as Brahmin or Kshatriya, or else they were treated as equivalent, and the historic distinctions between then became blurred or obscured.

In a sampling of Gupta period land grant decrees, it is intriguing that caste identities are omitted more often than explicitly included. Had caste been as important or dominant a social category, one might expect otherwise. Some of the most important figures appear to be officials involved in tax collection and land measurement. Various ranks of officials are mentioned without any explicit mention of their caste. Villagers are also frequently named without reference to their cast. Only occasionally, there are references to villagers who are also mentioned as being Brahmins. Some of the land grant records indicate that before land grants were made, certain categories of villagers-perhaps those considered more important-were consulted by the higher officials. Although Brahmins are mentioned in the list of those consulted, there are equal references to other categories of villagers such as kutumbins and mahattaras who may have been village officials or important landholders in the village.

Other references point to consultative committees that included the chief artisan, the chief scribe, the merchant and the guild-president of the town. It also appears that administrative changes led to the creation of new posts, the merger or elimination of older posts, and changes in ranks of various officials over time. An examination of the land grant decrees over a space of three centuries (5th-7th C Bengal) points to such changes and others-such as changes in procedures, or changes in the constitution of consultative committees, perhaps to reflect changing political alliances or changes in the economic status of different groups of townspeople and villagers.

In a land allotment plate from Paschimbagh (Bengal) Brahmins are mentioned as tax payers, and the status of ordinary Brahmins does not seem at all exceptional. For instance, it points to a teacher or a Vedic scholar as being entitled to 10 patakas of land, but other Brahmins were entitled to only 2 patakas-a share less than that of a Kayastha (record-keeper) or Vaidya (medical practitioner). Carpenters, smiths and artisans were also put far above other service communities in terms of their share of land. The Paschimbagh inscription also describes the grant of plots of land to florists, potters, carpenters, masons, blacksmiths and sweepers for serving a matha (monastery) indicating that when land was granted for a temple or monastery, priests were not the exclusive beneficiaries of land grants.

A study of land grants from 12th C Rajasthan (Pali) and Karnataka (Kalikatti) suggests that land grants had a limited life tenure even when initially decreed to be for life or for perpetuity. Beneficiaries of land grants were subject to transfers, and grants to a particular beneficiary were transferred to another beneficiary five or ten years later. It also appears that the beneficiaries were selected based on administrative rank rather than any particular caste-affiliation.

It is also not at all apparent that administrative rank was limited by birth. In Orissa, there is explicit evidence to the contrary. Ordinary peasants were able to rise up in the ranks of the military, and it is likely that a similar situation prevailed in the administrative ranks. Mayadhar Mansinha suggests that a combination of factors such as training, merit and personal determination played a role, (in addition to social standing and political connections) in determining rank and promotions. In Karnataka, there is evidence that some of the chief administrators were women.

Brahminical Ascendance

Nevertheless, the seeds for a more privileged role for the Brahmins were also being sown through the process of land grants to Brahmins. In some instances, thousands of Brahmins were granted rights to hitherto uncultivated land. In other cases, Brahmins were appointed as the local representatives of the state authorities in what are described as agrahara villages where Brahmins presided over small peasants, who in Bihar were mostly landless sharecoppers or bonded labourers. These agrahara villages were typically small villages and sattelites of bigger villages that included members of several castes and bigger land-holders. In Bihar, such agrahara villages proliferated and it is quite likely that in such agraharas oppressive social relations and some of the most egregious patterns of caste-centred discrimination and exploitation may have developed.

While early Gupta period records indicate the existence of rural consultative councils that mediated between the rulers and the artisans and peasants, it seems that such consultative councils became less important or were phased out with the growth of the agraharas. Thereafter, the Brahmins became the sole intermediaries between the village and the state, and over time, this may have enabled the Brahmins to exercise social and political hegemony over other inhabitants of the village. It also appears that the greatest incidence of the practice of untouchability occurs in conjunction with the growth in the power and authority of the Brahmins in such villages.

But these developments took time to spread elsewhere in India, first spreading to Bengal and eastern UP, and very gradually elsewhere in India. However, this pattern was not necessarily replicated in identical form throughout India and some parts of India virtually escaped this trend. In agrahara villages in other parts of India, Brahmins did take on the role of local administrators and tax collectors, but the status of the small peasantry was not always as miserable as in Bihar. The degree of exploitation and oppression appears to be related to the extent of alienation from land-ownership.

For example, evidence for Brahmin domination in Kalikatti, Southern Karnataka emerges after the 13th C. when villagers were instructed to pay taxes to the Brahmin assignees, leading to constant tensions and disputes, but without dramatic changes in the overall status of the tax-paying villagers.

Although Brahminization was an important factor in leading to caste ossification, it was not necessarily the sole or even the most important factor in the mix. The impact of the Islamic invasions, colonization by the British and ecological changes played an equally crucial if not decisive role in many instances.

For instance, in Orissa, the ossification of the bureaucracy and its conversion into a group of privileged and exclusive castes appears to take place after the 14th-15th C. when we begin to see a general decline in its overseas trade due to the silting up of its rivers. At the same time, we see the growth of Brahminical hegemony in the realm of religion and military defeats at the hands of the Mughal armies led by Raja Man Singh of Jaipur. All these factors may have played a role in destroying the vibrancy of Oriya society and encouraging caste conservatism.

Impact of the Islamic Invasions

Unfortunately, many social historians have studiously ignored the effect of such external factors in the shaping of social relations in India. But we know that the Islamic invasions led to monumental changes in the political and cultural life of the sub-continent and especially so in the Gangetic plain-so it would be exceedingly odd if the invasions had no impact on the social structure of Indian society. While some social analysts have tried to analyse Hindu society during the period of Islamic rule as though it had been untouched by the Islamic invasions and left to stagnate in a cocoon of its own making, others have succumbed to illusory simplifications such as Islam was an egalitarian faith whereas Hinduism had caste divisions.

Because Islam first arose in those parts of the world where settled agriculture was not possible-i.e.. in the desert sands of the Arabian peninsula-social divisions had not yet emerged in quite the same way that they had in long settled agricultural societies like India. For the warring nomadic tribes of the desert, Islam may have been a relatively progressive and unifying current that brought to an end fratricidal battles over water and trade rights; a very selective and superficial look at the Indian record might affirm such a view because in the midst of increasing social instability during the Sultanate period, some of the slave dynasties were able to propel a surprising level of upward social mobility. But in the hands of expansionist conquerors, Islam became more an instrument of devastation and terror rather than a vehicle for social equality or social justice.

Taken in its entirety, the period of Islamic rule in India cannot be seen as furthering social equity or social harmony in the subcontinent. As a faith-based ideological system Islam could only guarantee equality before "God" i.e. equality after death. But on earth, the plight of Muslim converts depended more on social realities, on political equations-than on the abstract and remote promise of equality offered by Islam.

During times of heavy political and economic oppression, the only option for the poor was complete and total submission to the will of "God" which in effect meant sacrificing all their autonomy in favour of the clergy, (who rarely challenged political authority), and more often than not, were largely beholden to the rulers who chose to support and promote them. When the clergy did resist political authority, it often tended towards social conservatism and reaction rather than social progress.

By and large, social inequities widened with the onset of Islamic rule in the sub-continent. Land revenue records clearly indicate that with few exceptions (as in Kashmir and Bengal for a time), Islamic rulers taxed the peasantry at significantly higher rates. If the average rate of taxation during the pre-Islamic period varied between 10% to a maximum of 20%-averaging around 15-16%, it had increased to 33% or even more under the Mughals. (Note that even the Manusmriti limited the tax rate on the peasantry to one-sixth-about 16%)

While all Islamic rulers may not have insisted on the discriminating jaziya, many of the earlier invaders insisted upon it, and more than one court chronicler of the Delhi Sultanate describes the violent means taken to suppress peasant rebellions and extract the high taxes from the crushed peasantry. Urban revolts were also not uncommon and the Arab chronicler Ibn Batuta mentions how such rebellions were suppressed with great cruelty. Punishment for those who rebelled could mean loss of adults (particularly young women) and children to slavery, massacres or forced evacuations of entire villages and small towns, pillage and destruction of places of learning, of temples and other symbols of cultural identification, and denial of job opportunities in the courts. In the early centuries of Islamic rule, the distrust of the locals was so intense that virtually all the important administrative positions were kept in the hands of foreigners.

Romila Thapar has pointed out that prior to the Islamic invasions, Hindu rulers also invaded or pillaged the temples of their rivals, especially since these temples were repositories of great wealth. She has also indicated that the management of some of these rich temples was extremely corrupt. Plunder of temple wealth was definitely a factor in the destruction of such temples during raids and attacks by Islamic invaders and conquerors. However, during the Islamic invasions, this practice accelerated both in frequency and intensity.

It should also be noted that not all temples were storehouses of great wealth or under the management of corrupt Brahminical trusts. The majority of temples had considerable cultural significance for the local populations and many were built and maintained by non-Brahminical cults. For instance, in Bundelkhand, Rajasthan, Madhya Pradesh and Orissa, there are a sizable number of surviving temples that not only escaped the path of the Islamic invaders, but were obviously left untouched in local battles between rival Hindu kings. There are even scattered remains from the Gupta period. But in the Gangetic plain, virtually nothing from the region's pre-Islamic past has survived. Clearly, there were important political dimensions to the destruction of Northern India's cultural wealth. One might speculate that the political subjugation of a reluctant and possibly even hostile population required the physical elimination of cultural symbols that instilled pride and self-confidence, and thus threatened the authority of the alien rulers.

In any case, the smashing of facial features, genitalia and breasts on sculpted figures has no parallel to earlier practices. There is also little evidence that those defeated in battle were killed or enslaved on the scale of what happened during the Islamic invasions.

For instance, the Afghanistan region (which once had a sizeable Hindu and Buddhist population) acquired the reputation of being a land where Hindus were slaughtered and hence took the name Hindu-Kush, and references to wanton destruction occur with boastful regularity in the records of the triumphant conquerors. However, in the Gangetic plain the Hindu population was essential in maintaining the tax base for the rulers and therefore, it was only necessary to break the autonomy of the Hindu population and crush their resistance to higher taxation. This was largely achieved through the almost complete destruction of older centres of culture and learning, burning of libraries such as in Nalanda and Vikramshila, the widespread conversion of Buddhists to Islam, and violent acts of reprisal against those who resisted.

One of the most deleterious effects of the Islamic invasions on social relations in India was the practice of slavery, which was introduced on a scale hitherto unseen in the subcontinent. Unlike the societies of the East, slavery appears to have played an important role almost throughout the history of the Western world and the Quran has passages that endorse the practice of slavery. During the Islamic period, in sub-Saharan Africa, slaves laboured in the salt mines and copper mines and served as a vital link in the trans-Saharan trade routes acting as porters where camels and donkeys could not go.

Scott Levi (Univ. of Wisconsin) points to judicial documents of medieval Samarqand (and other Central Asian sources) that disclose the presence there of many thousands of Indian slaves throughout the medieval period. A number of Indian sources make it clear that, from the early Ghaznavid raids to the Mughal period, hundreds of thousands (if not millions over the centuries) of men, women and children were marched over to the slave markets in Iran and Central Asia, i.e. beyond the northwest frontier of India, and out of the reach of their familial support systems.

Although state sanctioned slavery came to an end with the dawn of the Christian era in Europe, a slave-owning replica of ancient Rome arose in the American South, and slaves were employed throughout the Caribbean and South America. The Portuguese were notorious for their slave-markets in India. Even as slavery was banned in Europe, the European trading companies made huge profits from the slave trade. Slavery was not a practice confined to the Islamic parts of the world.

The practice of slavery probably led to the growth in the custom of Jauhar and Sati amongst the military castes. Prior to the Islamic invasions, there are very few records to indicate that such practices were widely followed. But the onslaught of the Islamic invaders had led to a complete breakdown in the implementation of war ethics. Whereas in earlier wars, it was required of both sides to protect the peasantry, to leave women, children and the elderly at peace, and there were injunctions against the enslavement of prisoners or of harming those who surrendered in battle-the invaders had few if any compunctions in unleashing all manner of torments on the defeated population. In such an environment, it is not surprising that for the proud Rajput societies, the act of jauhar, or mass suicide was a more honourable option.

It should be noted that such acts of mass or individual suicide are not unknown elsewhere in the world. Sometimes these acts were voluntary (as was usually emphasized in the Indian tradition), at other times they were entirely coerced. Amongst the Vikings, it was customary for a warrior's young concubines to join the funeral pyres of dead Viking warriors. In ancient Nubia (upper Sudan and lower Egypt) there are records of mass suicide upon the death of a warrior king and Nubian burials of warriors indicate practices quite similiar to Jauhar / Sati. There are also parallels in the Japanese tradition of Harakiri' (suicide for honour) or Sepukku amongst the Samurai-warrior nobles of Japan. Voluntary suicide of widows (although rare) also took place in China during the reign of the Qing dynasty. There are also records of the Celts and the Romans practicing human sacrifice. Amongst the Aztecs of the 15th C, the custom of human sacrifice of the defeated does not appear to have any voluntary character, and was seen as a legitimate rite in the celebration of a victory in war.

Western feminist indologists who see the practice of Sati as a unique form of gender oppression peculiar to India might note that in the Christian world, the scourge of witch-burning was a far more dangerous threat to the lives of women. The mere charge of being a "witch" could lead to public hanging, and the Salem-witch trials in America were part of a long chain of witch-burnings that took place throughout Christian Europe and carried over into New England

Nevertheless, Islamic rule in India did not prevail entirely without benefits for certain social classes. During periods of urban expansion and accelerating trade, opportunities for social mobility, particularly horizontal mobility opened up for the artisan classes, and mercantile classes enjoyed special benefits.

Trading communities probably benefited from the installation of Islamic rulers whose policies of lower taxes on trade, and state support of local traders and financiers was in their interest. Scott Levi suggests that from the end of the thirteenth century, and throughout much of the Delhi Sultanate period, the Muslim nobility were dependent upon heavily capitalized indigenous banking firms (identified in the Tarikh-i Firuz Shahi as 'Sahs' and 'Multanis'). These domestic financiers loaned seeds and other necessary inputs to peasants and village-artisans and manufacturers (such as textile weavers) in return for a share of the produce. The rest they bought in cash, and a part of that cash was then recovered by the state treasuries through taxation.

It should also be noted that, (by and large), Islamic rulers born and raised in India relied less on violence and sheer terror, but sought alliances with sections of the local population, especially with those amongst the Hindu elite who were willing to collaborate. Although some of these alliances were coerced, others led to tangible material benefits for the royal collaborators.

Alliances were forged through marriage, or simply from political convenience. Military alliances with Hindu rulers were crucial in maintaining the power of many Islamic rulers. After Akbar, the Mughals relied heavily on the Jaipur and Bikaner Rajputs, who in return were given rights to a share of the taxes extracted from the Gangetic plain. And although Hindus were numerically discriminated in jobs at the courts, by skillfully playing off different caste communities against one another, the Mughals were able to win over a section of the Hindus in maintaining their position of political preeminence.

Hence, it would be wrong to see the many centuries of Islamic rule in India purely from the prism of religious antagonisms. But it would be equally wrong to see the long period of rule by Islamic-identified rulers (even those that were born in India) as entirely benevolent or benign, or no different from the rule of earlier Hindu kings. Since most were heavier taxers, the distance between the ruling elites and the peasant and artisan masses tended to widen and there were other aspects of Islamic rule (particularly during the rule of the more oppressive Sultanates) that limited social mobility.

For many of the Islamic rulers, the Brahmin dominated agraharas were highly suited to efficient tax collection and the might of the Sultanates came down very heavily on social challenges that weakened the ability of the state to collect taxes. The fear of enslavement and the denial of equal access to job opportunities in the Sultanate courts led to Hindu society becoming extremely inward-looking in large parts of the plains. With opportunities for jobs in the administrative ranks shrinking, caste loyalties were in all likelihood strengthened, not weakened. Thus, rather than shake up the caste system as some might expect, Islamic rule (by foreign invaders who distrusted the locals) may have actually helped in its crystallization. Neither is there any evidence that Islamic rule helped end the practice of untouchability.

In fact, the problems of untouchability and caste-discrimination are especially notable in states like UP and Bihar where Islamic rule held complete sway for five centuries. In Sindh and Western Punjab, where almost the entire population was converted to Islam, it is important to observe that janitorial workers were never converted, and to this date remain a highly oppressed and discriminated group. There is also evidence that Muslims developed their own versions of caste. Romila Thapar points out how foreign-origin Muslims such as Syeds, Sheiks and Ashrafs kept themselves consciously apart from Muslims who came from artisan and peasant backgrounds. Language was another divider. In Bijapur district, the elite Muslims spoke Urdu whereas the ordinary Muslims spoke Kannada. Zarina Bhatty in an essay on "Social stratification among Muslims" describes caste differentiation amongst Ashraf and non-Ashraf Muslims and notions of impurity that closely parallel caste cleavages and attitudes in Hindu society. Sandra Mackey in the Caste/Class System in Iran describes patterns of social differentiation remarkably similiar to India's.

Over time, Islamic rule in India created a much stronger and more unified elite, which made it more difficult for the ordinary masses to resist regressive social changes, particularly in the realm of philosophical choice, religious pluralism, regional and local autonomy in matters of religion, gender equity, freedom of sexual expression and sexual choice. For instance, prior to the arrival of Islam, women enjoyed greater freedom of movement and dress. 11th C chronicler of Indian life, Al-Biruni expresses puzzlement at how the Hindu men (of Punjab) took the advice of the women "in all consultations and emergencies". But in a matter of few centuries, Islamic notions of gender separation and sexual prudery had infected Hindu households as well. A weaker version of the Purdah system and a more conservative dress code became the custom even in Hindu homes, especially so amongst those of the trading community that had frequent contacts with Muslims.

Although the Quran states that their ought to be no compulsion in matters of religion, the practice of Islam was often drastically different. In Mali, the Tunisian chronicler Ibn

Batuta noted that children who were neglectful in learning the Quran were put in chains until they had it memorized. Regarding India, he commented how newly converted peasants had a very lackadaisical attitude towards attending regular prayers and how the Imams had to cane non-attendees to force attendance. He also describes how he personally led a battle against the reluctance of women to cover their breasts in the Maldives.

In the Indian tradition, moral codes concerning dress were more in keeping with the natural environment. Clothes were light and simple, consistent with the generally hot climate. And in matters of religion, there was greater diversity, and much more personal choice. It was often up to the devotee to visit a temple at a time of his or her choosing. Which deity to worship involved an element of local choice and different jatis might worship different deities. Local versions of the epics such as the Ramayana and the Krishna-Leela were popularized and recent research points to hundreds of different versions in circulation. Unlike in Islam, pilgrimages were undertaken under less pressure and with greater individual volition. Al-Biruni also noted how the Hindus were remarkably flexible and willing to change customs and traditions they no longer felt to be relevant or essential. Although notions of Dharma played an important role in determining the boundaries for social conduct, these varied with time and were also adapted to suit the individual needs and preferences of different regions and localities.

Pluralism in Indian History

In religions that paid tremendous stress on "revealed truth" (such as Christianity or Islam) there have always been strong tendencies towards dogmatic rigidity. But even at the peak of their influence, India's Brahmins were never quite able to impose any comparable sort of rigid uniformity in the practice of Hinduism on a national (let alone, international) scale. In some localities, the lower castes did without the Brahmins entirely while elsewhere, especially in the South, or in Central India and Orissa-Brahmins often felt obliged to give due deference to dissenting and heterodox cults, and incorporated their belief systems into mainstream Hinduism.

T.K Venkatasubramaniam describes how in Tamil Nadu, Brahmins begin to play an important role in politics and society only after the 7th C., when the Pallavas began to challenge the authority of the previous ruling clans such as the Chera, Chola and Pandya. Because the Pallavas did not rise from an aristocratic background, they used the Brahmins to validate their right to rule through a combination of persuasion and coercion.

At that time, Tamil Nadu was a hotbed of a variety of non-Brahminical traditions, (such as Buddhist, Jain and many others)-hence, a synthesis of these different traditions took place between the 7th and the 11th centuries. Vajrayana Buddhism, Shaivite Tantrism and Hata-Yoga were amongst the trends that became integrated. The Bhakti tradition in which the devotee is held in a higher status than the Brahmin had it's impact as did the ideals of the Siddhis whose supreme ideal was freedom, perfect health and immortality-all to be gained on this earth through magic and yoga. The Kalamukas, Pasupatas and Kapalikas were popular practitioners of Yogic and Tantric cults-the latter helped assimilate the ecstatic tribal cults of earlier times. This was also the period when the androgyne forms of the Hindu gods (the Ardhanarishwara) became popularized.

The existence of these numerous cults was partly an expression of the struggle for social equality and freedom from exploitation, but for some, it was also a means for accessing greater social privileges. The Brahmins of Tamil Nadu (along with the rulers) attempted to manage these social tensions through co-option, philosophical accommodation and synthesis.

In Andhra, folk religions played a powerful role in mediating Brahminical influences, and a vibrant example of the deep penetration of folk influences in popular religion is to be seen in the sculpted array of folkloric panels in the temple of Srisailam (sponsored by the Vijayanagar rulers in the 14th-15th C.). In neighbouring Karnataka, the Bhakti ideal and Jain influences put their stamp on prevailing religious practices.

Religion in India thus developed in a much more organic fashion than is commonly realized, and it was never completely divorced from popular inputs. Both male and female deities drew followers, and while goddesses were sometimes displayed in demonic warrior roles, gods were sometimes displayed with feminine qualities. In the Yogini temples, all the deities were women and although today, there are only a handful of surviving Yogini temples, (mostly in Orissa and Madhya Pradesh) it is not unlikely that many more may have been in existence.

In the 8th-10th C Pratihara era temples, men and women were sculpted in identical heights and proportions-perhaps implying that male domination had not yet fully come to pass. Tantric ideas on sexual liberation found their way into the grand temples not only of Khajuraho and Konarak but also in temples in Rajasthan, the Jabalpur and Raipur regions, in Telengana and elsewhere in the South. Unlike Islam where entry into mosques was curtailed for women, and separate zenana areas were constructed, restraints on the entry of women in temples were not commonplace. Contrary to the suppression of female sexuality in the Semitic religious streams, temple architecture from the 11th-13th C appears to revel in the eroticism of both genders-and there are even displays of same-gender interaction. In this relatively liberal atmosphere, philosophy continued to flourish and while some tendencies drifted towards religious idealism, others emphasized the rational and worldly. The slow but steady record of scientific progress up to the 12th-13th C points to the toleration that atheist, agnostic and rational currents may have enjoyed in Indian society in contrast to the violence meted out towards "heretics" and disbelievers in medieval Europe and the Middle East. Religion in India developed in a relatively secular atmosphere where all manner of religious variations coexisted with the abstract and all-inclusive monotheism articulated in the Upanishads and later emulated in the various Bhakti streams of worship.

At the grassroots level, these relatively more liberal tendencies had their impact on the practice of Islam as well. Sufism, the worship of pirs (saints), the practice of the Urs were attempts at forging some sort of a compromise.

Romila Thapar points to peasant and artisan Muslims of Bijapur who continued to celebrate Hindu festivals. To this day, Muslim peasants of Northern Karnataka celebrate Islamic festivals with folk dances that have Hindu origins-quite unlike the orthodox practice of these festivals where singing and dancing might be frowned upon. Such hybrid Muslim communities exist elsewhere in India too.

But in the Madrasahs, (with few exceptions) conservatism and orthodoxy were the norm; attempts at providing a secular education never really took off, and over time this had a distinctly illiberal effect on how social relations matured in the sub-continent.

The Sikh Renaissance

However, an even greater blow to equitable social relations came during the period of British rule. Just prior to British rule, Mughal rule had virtually collapsed and power had gone into the hands of Sikh rulers in the North and the Maratha kings in much of Central and Southern India. The Sikhs had been at the forefront of powerful social reforms as they fought against the intolerable burden of high taxes imposed by the Mughals. Gender equality received particular attention from the early Sikh Gurus as did caste discrimination. During the time of Guru Gobind Singh-women not only participated as warriors but they also led some of the battles, and 40% of the spiritual leadership came from the ranks of women.

However once the Sikhs became rulers, the egalitarian currents in the Sikh tradition became successively dissipated. Upper caste converts to Sikhism retained their caste identification, and Gurudwaras became divided between those for the upper and lower castes. Nevertheless, the peasantry did win some concessions and the Gurudwaras institutionalized charitable practices on a scale unmatched in previous eras. Overall, the century that preceded colonization was a period of growing social ferment in India, but as British colonial rule tightened, it was to put a great damper on the pace of social reforms.

The British Colonial Era

Although some versions of Indian history ascribe to the early colonial administrators a penchant for social reform, it should be noted that the colonial "reformers" were at best aligning themselves with active indigenous reform currents.

They were not usually the initiators or great crusaders for social reform as is frequently portrayed.

In any case, after 1857, the cynical strategy of divide and conquer not only impacted relations between Hindus and Muslims, but also aggravated caste tensions. But even independently of conscious attempts by British administrators to inflame caste tensions, the ruination of the Indian economy alone led to a disastrous degradation in social relations.

The Zamindari system particularly disenfranchised the peasantry whose status dropped dramatically in comparison to those castes who were able to find a foothold in the new administration, or find some employment in the new colonial cities. The enormous burden of high taxes led to unprecedented levels of indebtedness and the privileging of the money-lending castes. The economic devastation caused by the Mahalwari system of taxation in the Awadh region led to higher levels of gender discrimination, and an increase in coercion in matters related to dowry. Differential access to modern education and jobs in the colonial administration increased the distance between the favoured castes-and the Indian masses.

The favoured castes naturally included Brahmins, Kshatriyas and Banias, but also other important administrative castes such as Kayasthas. Large land owning castes such as Mehtas and Reddis were also favoured, as were Marathas, Jatts and other castes who had risen during the decline of Mughal rule.

It was also the British who resurrected the Manusmriti and used it to frame the "Hindu Civil Code". Prior to colonization, the Manusmriti was nothing more than an obscure text, long-forgotten and rarely used to determine what was acceptable social practice. The Manusmriti came in very handy in social control. Because the numerical presence of the Britishers in India was not substantial, the Britishers had to rule largely by proxy. It was important that their agents did not face resistance or rebellion, even in the social realm. Owing to it's repressive and highly divisive character, the Manusmriti helped in preventing both individual and collective resistance to local authorities, who were typically upper caste and often Brahmin. That the Manusmriti represented an archaic and outdated social code didn't matter. It fit in very well with the British colonial project.

It was also convenient in providing ideological cover for repressive legal steps the British wanted to take anyway. For instance it didn't hurt that the Manusmriti advocated laws that legitimized gender discrimination or attacked same-gender relationships. Such attitudes were then equally prevalent in Europe and it made it easier to disenfranchise women in matters of inheritance or introduce legal injunctions against same-gender sexual relations (as was the case in Britain during the 18th C.).

ECONOMY AND THE CASTE

Transition between the Old and New Traditional Economies in India

Rosser and Rosser (1996, 1998, 1999) introduce the concept of the New Traditional Economy to the discussion and analysis of economic systems. This idea derives from the trichotomization between tradition, market, and command made by Karl Polanyi (1944). For Polanyi and his followers the traditional economy is embedded within a broader socio-cultural framework. They see the traditional economy associated with backward technology and pre-modern societies, with the rise of the market economy leading to a "disembedding" of the economy from its socio-cultural framework to come to dominate that framework rather than the other way around. This was the Old Traditional Economy.

In the New Traditional Economy there is an effort to re-embed a modern or modernizing economy within a traditional socio-cultural framework, usually associated with a religion, but to do so while maintaining or adopting modern technology. The most well-known example is that of the Islamic economies such as Iran where a reconstructed view of Islamic economics has been pursued that was developed initially in Pakistan (Maududi, 1975 [1947]) as part of the anti-colonialist struggle. Eventually this became part of the search for an independent identity separate from the competing ideologies of capitalism and socialism during the Cold War. But it is also seen as emerging in other socio-cultural frameworks as well.

India presents a special case with respect to this discussion. With the possible exception of much of rural, sub-Saharan Africa, it remains arguably the site of the most entrenched and extensive example of an actually existing Old Traditional Economy in the jajmani system associated with the Hindu caste system in rural India. This system persists despite markets being established in rural India for a long time and a period of emphasis on socialist ownership of industry and indicative central planning since India's independence in 1947 that is still largely in place and with the caste system being formally outlawed. Although rejecting elements of the system, Mohandas (Mahatma) Gandhi ("Father of Indian independence") defended the ideal of the rural Indian village economy with a pre-industrial technology, arguably an Old Traditionalist ideology. However the reality is that increasingly the forces of modernization are gradually breaking down the isolation of India's rural villages and integrating them into the broader market economy of India with its continuing elements of socialist central planning.

Thus, a consciously constructed ideology of Hindu economics has appeared that accepts modern technology more than Gandhi did and that seeks integration in the modern world economy even while attempting to re-embed the economy within the Hindu socio-cultural system, perhaps expressed earliest and most clearly in the work of Deendayal Upadhyaya (1965). Currently associated with the ruling Bharatiya Janata Party (BJP), this ideological movement can be described as New Traditionalist. Thus India, more sharply than other nations with New Traditionalist movements, has seen a transition from Old to New Traditionalism take place within a fairly short time period. The nature of this transition, both in economic thought and in its relation to the actual state of the Indian economy, is the subject of this paper.

Following this introduction, the second section reviews the comparison between the Old and New Traditionalist perspectives. The third examines this comparison in relation to the views of Gandhi and Upadhyaya in particular. The fourth considers the historical development of the Indian economic system and its prospects in light of this discussion. A concluding section follows.

Old and New Traditionalist Perspectives Compared

The concept of the traditional economy is largely due to Karl Polanyi, with his views about it evolving over time. In The Great Transformation (1944) he posited three kinds of traditional economy: household, reciprocal, and redistributive, with an implied story of historical evolution through these three. Later (1957) he modified his perspective to accept the more widely held view of economic anthropologists that the reciprocal form was historically the most primitive form (Stodder, 1995a,b). The paradigmatic example for such reciprocal exchange is the famous case of the Trobriand Islanders ritually trading kula within a broad socio-cultural framework, as studied by Malinowski (1922). The redistributive form is exemplified by the "Big Man" societies wherein a central leader collects and then redistributes goods. It has been argued that the ancient empires developed out of this form, and some see it as a precursor of the later command economic system.

The household system is more likely to arise in peasant economies with independent households. Such systems are likely to be more technologically advanced and more involved in market exchanges than the earlier reciprocal form. But, it is arguably a common characteristic of all traditional economic systems to emphasize the role of the household and of familistic groupism, with such a concern often extending beyond the immediate family to broader groups such as clans, or arguably castes as in India, or even a nation as a whole as has been argued for modern (and partly New Traditionalist) Japan (Murakami, 1984).

Few observers appear to advocate the Old Traditional economy as a system in any of its forms, at least fully. One does find Polanyi and others comparing such economies at least partly favourably with more market-oriented and dominated economies on the grounds of the stronger community orientation to be found in the traditional economy, and the Marxist tradition has long idealized the supposed "primitive communism" of early human societies. This point has certainly been emphasized in literature, especially Romantic poetry, with William Blake complaining of the "Satanic mills" of the industrial revolution in Britain. Indeed, it is easy to dismiss such arguments as merely representing a misplaced nostalgia or romanticization. But, it can be argued that if one allows a broader view of the literature then another set of works emerge that can be seen as taking such a view. These might include Islam's holy book, the Qur'an, and the Hind Swaraj by Mohandas Gandhi as will be argued further below. For these works the central issue is subordinating market forces to the strictures of ethical rules based on religion.

The great divide between the Old Traditional and New Traditional perspectives is over technology and accepting or advocating the adoption of modern technology. Accompanying this is the advocacy of a re-embedding of modern or modernizing economies within some traditional socio-cultural framework, usually based on some religion. Certainly Polanyi accepted the adoption of modern technology, but he appears to have seen the resolution of the problems of alienation and dislocation associated with modern market economies in their replacement by some form of socialism. In short, he accepted the idea that the appearance of modern technology, especially industrial technology, necessarily brings about the end of the traditional economy and its replacement by and subordination to either the market or command system.

As Rosser and Rosser (1996, 1998, 1999) argue, New Traditionalism has arisen largely out of advocates of various religions, especially in countries that faced actual or threatened political or economic domination from outside by the western industrialized powers. Most of the major world religions now have persons associated with them who can be seen as advocating to some degree or other a New Traditionalist perspective, including even various branches of Christianity and Judaism in the advanced market economies. In the case of Japan, the move arguably came with the Meiji Restoration of 1868 when the leadership chose to open up to outside influences in science and technology while seeking to preserve Japanese culture. This is symbolized by the phrase that was emphasized beginning then of Wa-kon Yo-sai, "Japanese spirit and Western ability." Such a shift would come later in other areas of the neo-Confucian zone (Hung-chao, 1989; Rozman, 1991; Zhang, 1999).

The important case of Islamic economics was a consciously constructed effort arising directly out of the anti-colonial struggle in the British Raj. The work of Maududi (1975 [1947]) combined a search for an Islamic identity in newly independent Pakistan within the modern world with studies of modern British economic thought whose influence was felt by thinkers in that area under the British colonial experience. Even today, a disproportionate number of leading Islamic economists have come from Pakistan originally (Siddiqui, 1980; Kuran, 1993; Nasr, 1994).

Curiously, it can be argued that the views of the Prophet Muhammed himself were New Traditionalist in that he did not oppose modern technology or science, per se. The same might be argued for the great medieval Islamic philosopher, Ibn Khaldun, who presented fairly sophisticated analyses of economic issues and questions (Issawi, 1987). But, of course neither of these had to deal with the kind of society that would arise with the emergence of modern industrial technology and the phenomenon of rapid technological and social change. This made them de facto and in comparison with the modern Islamic economists, theorists of the Old Traditional economic system.

Given this array of examples and cases it can be asked at this point if there is any substantial difference between the concept of the New Traditional economy and that of "national capitalism" (Rodrik, 2003) that has become especially popular since the collapse of the command socialist system. This view argues that although now almost all nations have adopted the market capitalist system, each does so in its own way with its own local institutional variations that reflect its own national cultural, political, and historical traditions, including those involving economic practices. Thus, the French economic system continues to exhibit elements of its long dirigiste tradition from Colbert (if not earlier intellectually), even as it no longer uses formal indicative planning (Kresl and Gallais, 2002); the German economic system continues to exhibit remnants of its unique Mitbestimmung system of industrial relations that arguably reflects traditions dating from the medieval guild system even as this has weakened with the slowdown of the German economy since its 1990 reunification (Smyser, 1992), and Sweden continues to have probably the most extensive welfare state system of any essentially market capitalist economy despite some cutbacks and reforms in the early 1990s, which arguably reflects a balance of individualism and communalism that dates from the Viking era (Freeman, Topel, and Swedenborg, 1997). Likewise, the familistic groupism of Japan discussed above can be seen as simply a holdover of elements of its feudal system.

However, in our view what distinguishes this viewpoint from ours is that in the case of the New Traditional economy there is a conscious effort to revive something that has been perceived to have been lost, and that what has been lost is part of a fully developed socio-cultural system, usually based on a religion. Ideologically the goal is to re-embed the modern economy within this system, even if this is ultimately a hopeless cause. Often, this perceived system has been artificially reconstructed, as with the example of modern Islamic economics, and arguably with the more extreme (and more recent) versions of Hindu economics as well. In contrast, the sorts of national variations described above in Western Europe do not involve efforts to revive some full blown traditional system. Rather they are simply institutional forms that have evolved in those economies fully as part of their modernity, but which nevertheless reflect elements of their past national uniqueness. They exist separately from any effort to reimpose a presumed former system ultimately based on a non-economic ideological structure.

Transition from Gandhi to Upadhyaya

Perhaps more than any other work, Mohandas Gandhi's Hind Swaraj of 1909 (Gandhi, 1958), written well before he became the leader of the Congress Movement in India (and "Father of Indian independence"), is a clear statement of support for the Old Traditional economy as an economic system. Indeed, the general public image of Gandhi's views on economics is based on this work, which takes a more extreme position than he evolved to later in his life. It calls for a particularly utopian economic model for India. Central to this work is the concept of swaraj, or "self-rule," achievable for Indians only by adhering to their traditional civilization. He saw this as corrupted by the influence of the British colonial rulers who broke down the autarkic autonomy of rural villages through introducing railroads, through their imposing of laws that undermined traditional customs, and through doctors who lowered the mortality rate thus triggering a population explosion that undermined the "Hindu equilibrium" (Lal, 1988-89, 1993), although it can be argued that the introduction of green revolution technologies into rural agriculture has more recently played this role. He opposed modern machinery, with villages to be self-sufficient in producing hand-spun cloth with spinning wheels, with the latter becoming the symbol of the Congress movement. The caste system and its system of reciprocal patron-client relations known as jajmani was to be preserved, although untouchability, the condition of being beneath all caste categories, was to be eliminated. Trade protectionism was strongly supported, a position that became a main feature of post-independence Indian economic policy.

However, a more complete overview of the evolution of Gandhi's views shows a moderation of some of these views as he came to feel the responsibility of leading the national independence movement. Dasgupta (1996) has documented this evolution by thoroughly surveying his numerous articles, interviews, letters, and speeches in Hindi, English, and his native Gujarati. A general theme that emerges is that although Gandhi favoured an ethical approach over that of mere utilitarian economics, he came to understand that moral values themselves may be in conflict, especially within the context of economic decisionmaking. This led him to a position of arguing that ethical rules that imply impractical economics may be invalid. Thus, by the end of his life, Gandhi's views on many economic issues came to be more nuanced with general positions modified by exceptions or qualifications derived from the hard practicalities of economic imperatives.

Thus, although the poorest should be materially uplifted, welfare is bad because it destroys work incentives and the rich should not be dispossessed. Although villages should be self-sufficient, they may import certain necessary items such as surgical equipment. Machinery may be allowed to produce certain necessary items, such as Singer sewing machines to be used in conjunction with spinning wheels. While supporting the rights of the oppressed (to be asserted nonviolently according to the doctrine of satyagraha or "truth-force"), he saw rights as tied to duties and opposed the UN Declaration of Human Rights. While opposing the killing of cows in accordance with traditional Hindu beliefs, he discussed ways to improve productivity in the leather goods and other animal parts industries.

While supporting cooperation between workers and capitalists and between tenants and landlords through his theory of "trusteeship," he supported nonviolent removal by tenants of landlords receiving special privileges from the British. While opposing contraceptives, he supported slowing population growth through the "rhythm method" of birth control. He proclaimed the equality of men and women and supported equal pay for equal work, while declaring it a woman's place to raise children. While the individual was the foundation of society, the good of the individual is the good of all. He called the law of supply and demand a "devilish" concept, yet he supported the use of the market and the ideas of efficiency and entrepreneurship (Dasgupta, 1996).

Furthermore, he declared himself to be a "socialist" and was the prime force behind the more strongly socialist Jawaharlal Nehru's coming to the leadership of the Congress movement, even as he rejected Marxist class struggle and differed with Nehru's pro-industrialization position. Given the ultimate complexity of his views it is unsurprising that today nearly all political movements look to Gandhi's writings as a source of support for their respective ideological positions, from pro-free market to socialist, and, of course, the new traditionalist Hindu nationalists of the BJP.

For the latter, as well as their predecessors in the Bharatiya Jana Sangh (BJS) party, how to deal with Gandhi and his legacy has been a profound problem. This is because historically he was the great opponent of their viewpoint of Hindu nationalism, supporting general religious tolerance and especially of the Muslims. The history of the Congress movement included a period when the Hindu nationalists dominated it, notably after Lord Curzon partitioned Bengal in

1905, leading to the formation of the Muslim League and a backlash by the Hindu nationalists. This period continued until Gandhi came to lead the movement around 1919 and imposed his more tolerant perspective (Frykenberg, 1993; Pattanaik, vol. 2, 1998).

It was only after they lost control of the Congress movement that the Hindu nationalists began to form their own separate organizations and political movements. Probably the most important of these was a technically purely cultural organization, the Rashtriya Swayamsevak Sangh (RSS) which exists today. It has formed the activist core of both the BJS and the current ruling BJP, with the current Prime Minister of India, Atal Bihari Vajpayee, having come out of it. The RSS has been banned three times in India's history: first after a Hindu nationalist assassinated Gandhi in 1948 for his tolerant views of religion, then during the period of direct rule by Indira Gandhi in the mid-1970s, and in 1992-93 after Hindu nationalists destroyed a mosque on a sacred Hindu site in Ayodha in northern India, thus triggering widespread communal riots.

Clearly there are serious difficulties for any Hindu nationalist in invoking the authority of Gandhi, not only his tolerance of Muslims and other minority religious groups in India, but his support of equal rights for untouchables and women. And of course there is the terrible legacy of Gandhi's assassination by a Hindu nationalist, a continuing embarrassment for them. Nevertheless, given his support of the caste system and his support of the traditional culture and economy of rural India, the Hindu nationalists have been strongly attracted to many of his views and have not only adopted them but have indeed loudly proclaimed his support of these positions. They have even invoked him regarding the issue of "reservations" of government jobs for members of lower castes, which they strongly oppose, noting that Gandhi supported equality of opportunity rather than equality of outcomes.

The key figure in reconciling Hindu nationalism and Gandhism was Deendayal Upadhyaya, most notably in his Integral Humanism (1965). Upadhyaya is especially important in being both a main founder of the BJS as well as being its leading ideologist, with the successor BJP also looking to him for guidance. He is the figure who took the more announced positions of Gandhi and transformed them into something more closely resembling New Traditionalism. Although he argued for a "third path" consonant with the ancient Hindu social order and supported Gandhian decentralization and self-sufficiency, he altered the view of technology to be that of swadeshi.

This still implied the idea of being "home-spun," but now was altered to allow for modern technology. In conjunction with ideas of several western-influenced economists, Upadhyaya emphasized the issue of what would now be called "appropriate technology," namely that it be consistent with the labour-intensive factor conditions of India. Also, he explicitly called for a "third way" between capitalism and communism, a position even more strongly stated by Vajpayee, the current Prime Minister, who led the BJS at the end of the 1960s (Lal, 1993, p. 419).

More recently a variety of Indian economists have followed up on Upadhyaya in trying to construct a "Hindu economics." Much of this effort consciously imitates the efforts of the New Traditionalist Islamic economists of Pakistan in attempting to explicitly reconcile modern economics concepts with traditional Hindu ideas taken from such ancient texts as the Rig Veda. One is Bokare (1993) who claims to subsume all previous economic thought in his system of thought. He supports a decentralized (Gandhian) order of "exploitationless" self-employment (socialism), with no taxes and no interest (Islamic economics), appropriate technology (Upadhyaya), and a general market context. Arguably this sort of effort reflects more an all-embracing incoherence than a genuine alternative economic system.

We should be clear about why Old Traditionalism simply cannot fill the bill for the Hindu nationalists. Even though much of the rural economy continues to fall into that category, Gandhi was right in noting the breakdown of the autarky of the rural villages with the spread of railroads. British-based legal codes broke down the authority of the old traditions, and the rise of population broke down the old economic equilibrium. More recently since Gandhi's time this latter has been further accelerated by the introduction of green revolution technologies into the countryside. Furthermore, this rise in population has resulted in large-scale migration to the cities where the more modern market and planned socialist sectors of the Indian economy hold sway, with urbanites more able to escape from the socioeconomic strictures of the caste system to some extent. This pattern repeats that which emerged in Europe initially in the late medieval period, but which accelerated dramatically with the Industrial Revolution, of peasants escaping from the feudalism of the countryside by joining the market economy of the cities. So, the drive for a New Traditional approach in India depends more on being relevant for those who live in the more modern economy of the urban areas than on being so for the still largely Old Traditional rural dwellers, even if this relevance is substantially to provide a nostalgic identity in a rapidly changing economic and social environment.

4

SYSTEMIC EVOLUTION OF THE INDIAN ECONOMY

Using the Polanyian trichotomization of tradition, market, and command, it can be argued that India possesses the most compexly mixed economic system in the world, with all three elements strongly present. We have already noted the ongoing presence throughout much of rural India of the caste system and its non-monetary set of reciprocal patron-client jajmani relations involving direct compensation in services and products (Lal, 1988). This is the deeply entrenched remnant of the Old Traditional economy, which has largely lost its economic hold in urban areas. We note here that although traditional Brahminic Hinduism has four broad castes: Brahmin priests, Kshatriya warriors, Vaishya merchants, and Sudra workers and farmers, the more detailed reality is a much finer gradation of many specific castes who constitute the elements of the specific jajmani economies in specific local areas of India.

At the same time, even as it was once one of the "ancient empires," India has from the depths of history been a major centre of international trade throughout the Indian Ocean. As far back as Mohenjodaro around 2500 BCE. there was trade with Mesopotamia and with Rome from the time of Emperor Tiberius out of the southeastern port of Arikamedu. Although the earliest exports were precious jewels, from the time of Tiberius forward cotton cloth would be India's prime export until the industry was severely reduced under the impact of the industrial revolution in Britain during British rule in the early 1800s (Tomlinson, 1993). Indeed, during 1200-1300s,

India was arguably the "hinge" of world trade (Abu-Lughod, 1989). There is evidence that prior to the British conquest in the 1700s, India may even have had a higher standard of living than Britain as attested by none other than India's conqueror, Robert Clive:

> *"On entering Murshidabad, the old capital of Bengal in 1757, Clive wrote: 'The city is extensive, populous and rich as the city of London, with this difference that there were individuals in the first possessing infinitely greater property than in the last city.' Similar words were used of Agra, Fatechpore, Lahore and many other Indian towns." (Goody, 1996, p. 113)*

Whatever the actual reality, it was widely perceived in India that the Indian cotton cloth industry was destroyed by British imperialism and trade policies, a fundamental underpinning of both Gandhi's swaraj ideology of self-sufficiency as well as of the protectionist trade policies adopted after independence by the Congress Party governments initially led by Gandhi's pro-socialist protegé, Nehru. Inspired by the Soviet example, Nehru introduced extensive central planning of the indicative variety (Mohan and Aggarwal, 1990; Byrd, 1990), and established new state-owned enterprises. These policies were carried much further by his daughter, Indira Gandhi, in the early 1970s when she carried out a wave of nationalizations and imposed a series of strict regulations on the remaining privately owned sector and on imports, an ultra-protectionist system known as the "License-Permit Raj" (Nayar, 1989).

Much of Indian economic policy since, both under her son, Rajiv Gandhi in the 1980s, and especially under a Congress government in 1991, has been to undo her legacy. This has included some lowering of tariffs and loosening of controls on foreign direct investment, some loosening of the various regulations on firm size and firm entry, sale of stock in state-owned enterprises, and various monetary and fiscal changes (Bhagwati, 1993; Joshi and Little, 1996; Ahluwalia, 2002). The GDP growth rate has risen since the early 1980s, despite a foreign exchange crisis in 1991 (Clark and Wolcott, 2003; Basu, 2004), and has been accompanied by the emergence of a high technology sector seen to be competing with high income countries such as the United States. However, along with this increased growth rate has come an apparent increase in income inequality, both regionally (Drèze and Sen, 1995, 1996) and between rural and urban areas (Datt and Ravallion, 2002).

Nevertheless, India retains much of its previous socialism, with indicative planning still in place, if weakened, with continuing state ownership of most firms previously owned by the central government (even though some state governments are engaged in full privatization programs), and the continuation of many regulations, especially in labour markets, and a still higher degree of trade protectionism than in all of India's trading partners (Ahluwalia, 2002). Thus it is that India is a deeply mixed economy with significant elements of all three of the principal systemic categories defined by Polanyi, with these elements altering their respective balance over time.

The position of the ideologically pro-New Traditionalism BJP in all of this is highly equivocal and complex and evolving. Prior to its gaining power at the national level in the mid-1990s, the BJP and its predecessor BJS only had governing experience at the state level. Generally the most prominent policies actually implemented were weakening the favoring of lower castes in state government hiring and imposing strict rules forbidding the killing of cows. After marketizing and opening to foreign trade and investment accelerated after 1991 under the Congress Party, state governments under the BJP opposed certain direct foreign investments that had been approved by the central government on cultural grounds, including by KFC and Coca-Cola. The most prominent such example case came in 1995 in the state of Maharashtra which contains India's largest city and financial capital, Mumbai (Bombay), when the local BJP-dominated government cancelled a contract by US.-based Enron to build new electricity generating facilities, a particularly severe need in much of India. This decision was later overturned by a federal court and the contract reinstated.

However, since achieving power at the national level, the BJP appears to have at least initially downplayed its Hindu nationalist ideology except for proceeding with building and testing nuclear weapons in confrontation with neighbouring Pakistan over Jammu-Kashmir and more generally competing with Pakistan over nuclear energy and space programs. Even so, and despite engaging in military conflict with Pakistan, Prime Minister Vajpayee visited Pakistan in a peace effort and such efforts have continued despite ups and downs in the Indo-Pakistani relationship. In power, the BJP has continued the opening and marketizing reforms initiated by the previous Congress government, although this has been demanded by the coalition partners in its government, most of them regionally based parties without whom the BJP would be unable to rule.

Despite this turn of policy, it remains the case that substantial factions within the BJP (especially those associated with the old RSS) oppose these policies and support a reimposition of protectionism and other more identifiably New Traditionalist policies. Some of these views have been manifested in such phenomena as the suppression of Christian missionaries in some parts of India, and other actions to assert the cultural supremacy of Hinduism within Indian society. This has accelerated more recently since riots between Hindus and Muslims broke out in Gujarat where the BJP-led state government supported a hard pro-Hindu line and was strongly reelected. In 2003, new efforts were made to impose restrictions at the national level on the killing of cows by the BJP, against the wishes of its coalition partners. The exact balance that the BJP-dominated government will establish between its marketizing reform policies, the maintenance of its socialist indicative planning, and its impulses towards New Traditionalism remain unclear. But, it is clearly the case that the remaining traditional element in Indian economic ideology and reality is increasingly of the New rather than of the Old variety. That particular transition is fully underway.

Summary and Conclusions: In India the transition between the Old and New Traditional economies, both ideologically and in fact, has been much closer and immediate than in other areas where New Traditionalist movements are important. In the Islamic world a much longer gap existed between the formulation of the Old Traditionalist doctrines in the medieval period and their replacement by the New

Traditionalist ones beginning in the mid-twentieth century after the experience of European colonialism. Similar observations can be made about most other such movements as well.

In the case of India, a substantial actually existing Old Traditional economy has persisted in the villages and countryside, although under pressures to change from modern transportation and agricultural technologies as well as the increasing influence of the official legal system. The writings of Mohandas Gandhi early in the twentieth century represent a strong advocacy of the Old Traditionalist perspective, albeit with some reformist elements such as equal rights for lower castes, women, and religious minorities that put him at odds with Hindu nationalists. Many of his ideas, such as trade protectionism and small village industries, came to have influence on post-independence economic policy, despite a strong emphasis on heavy industry by the socialist central planners under the direction of India's first Prime Minister, Jawaharlal Nehru. The combination of these socialist-oriented policies with the traditionalist legacy and a deeply entrenched market economy has left India as one of the most complexly mixed economies in the world.

Although they were tainted with the assassination of Gandhi in 1948, Hindu nationalists under the leadership of Deendayal Upadhyaya in the 1960s developed a New Traditionalist ideology that drew heavily on Gandhi's ideas. However, they accepted modern technology in "appropriate" forms while differing with Gandhi on such issues as religious tolerance. While ruling state governments, the Hindu nationalist parties have opposed programs favouring hiring of disadvantaged castes and have implemented such laws as forbidding the killing of cows. In the early 1990s, such state governments opposed foreign direct investments that were being allowed by a reforming central government. However, leading several central governments since the mid-1990s in coalition with parties favouring pro-market reforms, the Hindu nationalist BJP has increasingly shifted toward such policies, although continuing to push certain distinctive policies such as preventing the killing of cows.

Effectively its New Traditionalism in practice may amount to a gradualism that leaves the major elements of the highly mixed Indian economy in place. Such an outcome would be consistent with the long expressed admiration for a "third way" between capitalism and communism by the leaders of this movement in India, and by supporters of New Traditionalism more generally. Thus, the movement has made its transition from the old to the new, both ideologically and in policy terms as well.

Wisdom of Ancient India's Caste System: Division of Labour

I have been defending since 1997 the underlying wisdom of ancient India's caste system: division of labour. My defense has frustrated many India-bashers, who do not want to see any wisdom in any practice of ancient India. I have always believed that historically people moved from one caste to the other depending on the nature of their work vis-a-vis talent and skills. Those who wrote, read and interpreted law, for example, were called Brahmins, and those who defended boundaries were called Kshyatriyas, and so on.

The caste system in India was akin to professional distribution of labour of modern society. Michel Spence received a Nobel Memorial Prize on economics by telling that education is a credible (though imperfect) signal of productivity of an individual. Because of this credibility, the labour market pays consistently (though not 100% accurately) more to those with better education than the others. This observation/finding of "modern research" is nothing but wisdom underlying ancient India's caste system. My own published research deals with valuation of latent information imperfectly emitted through such signals.

Supplanting wisdom of India's caste system with birth right made our society weaker over time.

The rot in the caste system started when the elite (Brahmins and Kshatriyas) disallowed to their fold the talents-with writing, reading and interpretation skills or with prowess to defend boundaries-born to parents practising a different profession, e.g., that of Sudras.

Caste system in India became rotten because of allocation or reservation of resources based on birth. The son of a ruler became the king, the son of a Brahmin adviser remained so, and so on. When talent or merit-the driving wisdom of professional division of labour (caste system)-was trashed, the society weakened irreparably. A weakened society could be easily capitulated by external forces.

The "enlightened" invaders called Indians pagans or heathens to connote unenlightened people. The enlightened ancient Indian civilization became unenlightened due to the irrationality of reservation of national resources based on birth of people.

India is turning more unenlightened after independence. Children of politicians are anointed as heirs of fiefdoms of their fathers. The public is being forced to salute or face the oppression of the rulers, their kith, kin and cronies. To keep their thrones and power of subjugation of Indian masses, they are perpetuating reservations of national resources based on birth by abandoning merit and talent.

The unenlightened system of governance has been driving talents out of India. When productive people are hobbled or ejected out of society due to the unenlightened system of governance, exports fall below the level of imports needed for India's survival. This weakens the international exchange value of rupee and everyone becomes poorer as a result, thanks to unenlightened governance perpetuated by our politicians.

To import vital necessities, India is being forced to export its limited mineral resources (with the net proceeds distributed among rulers and their crony miners), which denudes landmass, deforests countryside, pollutes water supplies, and destroys environment and scorches the nation. It also forces Indian talents to work for external forces. This is modern capitulation of India by external forces due to the unenlightened system of governance.

The objective of quota reservation system and how to achieve it. There are three objectives of a quota reservation system in jobs, education and other economic opportunities:

1. Provide succour to the weaker sections of society.

2. Control or discipline masses in each quota category through quota usurpers.
3. Distribute the national pie among elite in each category.

Indian constitution writers had pleaded that objective 1 was noble and needed to restore social justice. It is immaterial whether they had objective 2 or 3 in mind in mind. Pandit Nehru wanted to accomplish objective 2 to extend his support for quotas, though he had initially argued that such quotas would not improve the plight of weaker sections.

We all know that quotas have achieved only objective 3. It is so plainly obvious that only objective 3 could be achieved through quotas in a democracy. If it was not obvious to constitution writers, then they were either (i) naive and incompetent or (ii) as bad schemers and manipulators as the politicians then and now. Our constitution writers, as badly as politicians, are squarely responsible for dividing and weakening our society for ever. This does not bode well for India.

If history repeats, India will be subjugated again if such divisive policies, as the ones based on religion and caste, are perpetuated. Pandit Nehru admitted the quota system because he was more interested in ruling by virtual dictatorship under the guise of democracy through language-based, caste-based, and religion-based "leaders." His system of governance has resulted in the Criminal Raj that we have today. It was designed to use the quota usurpers to subdue masses in each category, military style. But the result was a weakened India that was humiliated by China. Pandit Nehru may have felt that the Chinese deceived him. But he was deceived by his own myopic policies of dividing and weakening Indians to remain in power, just like the current rulers.

In military, caste based regiments function because of discipline in forces. But the military would likely function better (not worse) if the regiments were not based on caste and tribe. Now the rulers are conceiving of religion based regiments. This is really preposterous. There is no rational foundation for division of humanity based on religion and caste. This is why even the administration or allocation of resources based on such divisions, which are not rational, is irrational and cannot serve the long-run integrity or strength of society.

Due to the afore cited logics, CFD has been pleading with the President and Prime Ministers since 2002 to reform the quota system (if it must be continued) to allow only the families without a government job or with below median income to avail of the quotas. This is the only way to accomplish objective 1. No caste or tribe leader (mostly the elite in each category) will dare to object this rule because the masses in each category will end the career of the leader. But our Prime Ministers have iso far gnored CFD's advisory for a rational amendment to the constitution because they do not care to accomplish objective 1, like the constitution writers and past rulers. They care for votes of MPs and MLAs, not for strengthening society or raising welfare of masses. They continue to believe (falsely) that the MPs and MLAs in respective categories will subdue masses in those categories to get elected to keep rulers in power. They are deceiving themselves. Only by sterngthening society and enhancing welfare of masses through equal opportunities will the leaders have their prestige and power within India and globally.

Myopia, self-entrenchment and self-aggrandizement goals of our leaders are the biggest national security threats. Just read the New York Times article this week on Naxal movement in India.

Objective 2 cannot be accomplished in a democracy. Masses in each quota category will eventually revolt against the quota usurpers within the category. This is detrimental for stability and prosperity of society. Objective 3 is not sustainable because masses will eventually riot against the aggrandizing elite. The current quota system is thus suboptimal. This is why the quota laws of the constitution should be amended to reflect CFD's advisory to serve the integrity, stability and prosperity of the nation.

SOCIAL STRUCTURE IN BUDDHISM INDIA

The Clans and Nations

It is much the same with the clans. We have a good deal of information, which is, however, at the best only fragmentary, about three or four of them. Of the rest we have little more than the bare names.

More details are given, very naturally, of the Sakiya clan than of the others. The general position of their country is intimated by the distances given from other places. It must have been just on the border of Nepalese and English territory, as is now finally settled by the recent discoveries of the tope or burial-mound put up by the Sakiyas over the portion they retained of the relics from the Buddha's funeral pyre, and of Asoka's inscription, in situ, recording his visit to the Lumbini garden in which the Buddha was born. Which of the numerous ruins in the immediate vicinity of these discoveries are those of Kapilavastu, the chief town of the clan, and which are the remains of the other townships belonging to them, will be one of the questions to be solved by future exploration.

It was at the last-mentioned place that the mother of the Buddha was born. And the name of her father is expressly given as Añjana the Sakiyan. When, therefore, we find in much later records the statements that she was of Koliyan family; and that Prince Devadaha, after whom the town was so named, was a Koliyan chief, the explanation may well be that the Koliyans were a sort of subordinate subdivision of the Sakiya clan.

The existence of so considerable a number of market towns implies, in an agricultural community, a rather extensive territory. Buddhaghosa has preserved for us an old tradition that the Buddha had eighty thousand families of relatives on the father's side and the same on the mother's side. Allowing six or seven to a family, including the dependents, this would make a total of about a million persons in the Sakiya territory. And though the figure is purely traditional, and at best a round number (and not uninfluenced by the mystic value attached to it), it is, perhaps, not so very far from what we might expect.

The administrative and judicial business of the clan was carried out in public assembly, at which young and old were alike present, in their common Mote Hall (santhagara) at Kapilavastu. It was at such a parliament, or palaver, that King Pasenadi's proposition was discussed. When Ambalaha goes to

Kapilavastu on business, he goes to the Mote Hall where the Sakiyas were then in session. And it is to the Mote Hall of the Mallas that Ananda goes to announce the death of the Buddha, they being then in session there to consider that very matter.

A single chief-how, and for what period chosen, we do not know-was elected as office-holder, presiding over the sessions, and, if no sessions were sitting, over the State. He bore the title of raja, which must have meant something like the Roman consul, or the Greek archon. We hear nowhere of such a triumvirate as bore corresponding office among the Licchavis, nor of such acts of kingly sovereignty as are ascribed to the real kings mentioned above. But we hear at one time that Bhaddiya, a young cousin of the Buddha's, was the raja; and in another passage, Suddhodana, the Buddha's father (who is elsewhere spoken of as a simple citizen, Suddhodana the Sakiyan), is called the raja.

A new Mote Hall, built at Kapilavastu, was finished whilst the Buddha was staying at the Nigrodharama (the pleasaunce under the Banyan Grove) in the Great Wood (the Mahavana) near by. There was a residence there, provided by the community, for recluses of all schools. Gautama was asked to inaugurate the new hall, and he did so by a series of ethical discourses, lasting through the night, delivered by himself, Ananda, and Moggallana. They are preserved for us in full at M. 1. 353, foll., and S. 4. 182, foll.

Besides this Mote Hall at the principal town we hear of others at some of the other towns above referred to. And no doubt all the more important places had such a hall, or pavilion, covered with a roof, but with no walls, in which to conduct their business. And the local affairs of each village were carried on in open assembly of the householders, held in the groves which, then as now, formed so distinctive a feature of each village in the long and level alluvial plain. It was no doubt in this plain, stretching about fifty miles from east to west, and thirty or forty miles to the southward from the foot of Himalaya Hills, that the majority of the clan were resident.

The clan subsisted on the produce of their rice-fields and their cattle. The villages were grouped round the rice-fields, and the cattle wandered through the outlying forest, over which the peasantry, all Sakiyas by birth, had rights of common. There were artisans, probably not Sakiyas, in each village; and men of certain special trades of a higher standing; the carpenters, smiths, and potters for instance, had villages of their own. So also had the Brahmins, whose services were in request at every domestic event. Khomadussa, for instance, was a Brahmin settlement. There were a few shops in the bazaars, but we do not hear of any merchants and bankers such as are mentioned as dwelling at the great capitals of the adjoining kingdoms. The villages were separated one from another by forest jungle, the remains of the Great Wood (the Maha Vana), portions of which are so frequently mentioned as still surviving throughout the clanships, and which must originally (not so very long, probably, before the time under discussion) have stretched over practically the whole level country between the foot of the mountains and the Great River, the Ganges. After the destruction of the clans by the neighbouring monarchies this jungle again spread over the country. From the fourth century onwards, down to our own days, the forest covered over the remains of the ancient civilisation.

This jungle was infested from time to time by robbers, sometimes runaway slaves. But we hear of no crime, and there was not probably very much, in the villages themselves-each of them a tiny self-governed republic. The Koliyan central authorities were served by a special body of peons, or police, distinguished, as by a kind of uniform, from which they took their name, by a special headdress. These particular men had a bad reputation for extortion and violence. The Mallas had similar officials, and it is not improbable that each of the clans had a somewhat similar set of subordinate servants.

A late tradition tells us how the criminal law was administered in the adjoining powerful confederate clan of the Vajjians, by a succession of regularly appointed officers,-"Justices, lawyers, rehearsers of the law-maxims, the council of representatives of the eight clans, the general, the vice-consul, and the consul himself." Each of these could acquit the accused. But if they considered him guilty, each had to refer the case to the next in order above them, the consul finally awarding the penalty according to the Book of Precedents. We hear of no such intermediate officials in the smaller clans; and even among the Vajjians (who, by the by, are all called "rajas" in this passage), it is not likely that so complicated a procedure was actually followed. But a book of legal precedents is referred to elsewhere, and tables of the law also. It is therefore not improbable that written notes on the subject were actually in use.

The names of other clans, besides the Sakiyas, are:

1. The Bhaggas of Sumsumara Hill.
2. The Buhs of Allakappa.
3. Kalamas of Kesaputta.
4. The Koliyas of Rama-gama.
5. The Mallas of Kusinara.
6. The Mallas of Pava.
7. The Moriyas of Pipphalivana.
8. The Videhas of Mithila.
9. The Licchavis of Vesali.

There are several other names of tribes of which it is not yet known whether they were clans or under monarchical government. We have only one instance of any tribe, once under a monarchy, reverting to the independent state. And whenever the supreme power in a clan became hereditary, the result seems always to have been an absolute monarchy, without legal limitations of any kind.

The political divisions of India at or shortly before the time when Buddhism arose are well exemplified by the stock list of the Sixteen Great Countries, the Sixteen Powers, which is found in several places in the books. It is interesting to notice that the names are names, not of countries, but of peoples, as we might say Italians or Turks. This shows that the main idea in the minds of those who drew up, or used, this old list was still tribal and not geographical. The list is as follows: 1. Anga, 2. Magadha, 3. Kasi, 4. Kosala, 5. Vajji, 6. Malla, 7. Ceti, 8. Vamsa, 9. Kuru, 10. Pañcala, 11. Maccha, 12. Surasena, 13. Assaka, 14. Avanti, 15. Gandhara, 16. Kamboja

1. The Angas dwelt in the country to the east of Magadha, having their capital at Champa, near the modern Bhagalpur. Its boundaries are unknown. In the Buddha's

time it was subject to Magadha, and we never hear of its having regained independence. But in former times it was independent, and there are traditions of wars between these neighbouring countries. The Anga raja in the Buddha's time was simply a wealthy nobleman, and we only know of him as the grantor of a pension to a particular Brahmin.

2. The Magadhas, as is well known, occupied the district now called Behar. It was probably then bounded to the north by the Ganges, to the east by the river Champa, on the south by the Vindhya Mountains, and on the west by the river Sona. In the Buddha's time (that is, inclusive of Anga) it is said to have had eighty thousand villages and to have been three hundred leagues (about twenty-three hundred miles) in circumference.
3. The Kasis are of course the people settled in the district round Benares. In the time of the Buddha this famous old kingdom of the Bharatas had fallen to so low a political level that the revenues of the township had become a bone of con-tension between Kosala and Magadha, and the kingdom itself was incorporated into Kosala. Its mention in this list is historically important, as we must conclude that the memory of it as an independent state was still fresh in men's minds. This is confirmed by the very frequent mention of it as such in the Jatakas, where it is said to have been over two thousand miles in circuit. But it never regained independence; and its boundaries are unknown.
4. The Kosalas were the ruling clan in the kingdom whose capital was Savatthi, in what is now Nepal, seventy miles north-west of the modern Gorakhpur. It included Benares and Saketa; and probably had the Ganges for its southern boundary, the Gandhak for its eastern boundary, and the mountains for its northern boundary. The Sakiyas already acknowledged, in the seventh century BC, the suzerainty of Kosala.

It was the rapid rise of this kingdom of Kosala, and the inevitable struggle in the immediate future between it and Magadha, which was the leading point in the politics of the Buddha's time. These hardy mountaineers had swept into their net all the tribes between the mountains and the Ganges. Their progress was arrested on the east by the free clans. And the struggle between Kosala and Magadha for the paramount power in all India was, in fact, probably decided when the powerful confederation of the Licchavis became arrayed on the side of Magadha. Several successful invasions of Kasi by the Kosalans under their kings, Vanka, Dabbasena, and Kansa, are referred to a date before the Buddha's time. And the final conquest would seem to be ascribed to Kansa, as the epithet "Conqueror of Benares" is a standing addition to his name.

5. The Vajjians included eight confederate clans, of whom the Licchavis and the Videhans were the most important. It is very interesting to notice that while tradition makes Videha a kingdom in earlier times, it describes it in the Buddha's time as a republic. Its size, as a separate kingdom, is said to have been three hundred leagues (about twenty-three hundred miles) in circumference. Its capital, Mithila, was about thirty-five miles north-west from Vesali, the capital of the Licchavis. There it was that the great King Janaka ruled a little while before the rise of Buddhism. And it is probable that the modern town of Janak-pur preserves in its name a memory of this famous Rajput scholar and philosopher of olden time.
6. The Mallas of Kusinara and Pava were also independent clans, whose territory, if we may trust the Chinese pilgrims, was on the mountain slopes to the east of the Sakiya land, and to the north of the Vajjian confederation. But some would place it south of the Sakiyas and east of the Vajjians.
7. The Cetis were probably the same tribe as that called Cedi in older documents, and had two distinct settlements. One, probably the older, was in the mountains, in what is now called Nepal. The other, probably a later colony, was near Kosambi to the east and has been even confused with the land of the Vamsa, from which this list makes them distinct.

8. Vamsa is the country of the Vacchas, of which Kosambi, properly only the name of the capital, is the more familiar name. It lay immediately to the north of Avanti, and along the banks of the Jumna.
9. The Kurus occupied the country of which Indraprastha, close to the modern Delhi, was the capital; and had the Panchalas to the east, and the Matsyas to the south. Tradition gives the kingdom a circumference of two thousand miles. They had very little political importance in the Buddha's time. It was at Kammassa-dhamma in the Kuru country that several of the most important Suttantas-the Maha Satipalahana, for instance, and the Maha Nidana-were delivered. And Ramahapala was a Kuru noble.
10. The two Pañcalas occupied the country to the east of the Kurus, between the mountains and the Ganges. Their capitals were Kampilla and Kanoj.
11. The Macchas, or Matsyas, were to the south of the Kurus and west of the Jumna, which separated them from the Southern Pañcalas.
12. The Surasenas, whose capital was Madhura, were immediately south-west of the Macchas, and west of the Jumna.
13. The Assakas had, in the Buddha's time, a settlement on the banks of the Godhavari. Their capital was Potana, or Potali. The country is mentioned with Avanti in the same way as Anga is with Magadha, and its position on this list, between Surasena and Avanti, makes it probable that, when the list was drawn up, its position was immediately north-west of Avanti. In that case the settlement on the Godhavari was a later colony; and this is confirmed by the fact that there is no mention of Potana (or Potali) there. The name of the tribe is also ambiguous. Sanskrit authors speak both of Asmaka and of Asvaka. Each of these would be Assaka, both in the local vernacular and in Pali. And either there were two distinct tribes so called, or the Sanskrit form Asvaka is a wrong reading, or a blunder in the Sanskritisation of Assaka.

14. Avanti, the capital of which was Ujjeni, was ruled over by King Carva Pajjota (Pajjota the Fierce). The country, much of which is rich land, had been colonised or conquered by Aryan tribes who came down the Indian valley, and turned west from the Gulf of Kach. It was called Avanti at least as late as the second century AD, but from the seventh or eighth century onwards it was called Malava.
15. Gandhara, modern Kandahar, was the district of Eastern Afghanistan, and it probably included the north-west of the Panjab. Its capital was Takkasila. The King of Gandhara in the Buddha's time, Pukkusati, is said to have sent an embassy and a letter to King Bimbisara of Magadha.
16. Kamboja was the adjoining country in the extreme north-west, with Dvaraka as its capital.

From the political point of view this list is curious. Some names we should expect to find-Sivi, for instance, and Madda and Sovira, and Udyana and Virata-are not there. The Mallas and the Cetis occupy a position much more important than they actually held in the early years of Buddhism. Vesali, soon to become a "Magadha town," is still independent. And Anga and Kasi, then incorporated in neighbouring kingdoms, arc apparently looked upon as of equal rank with the others. It is evident that this was an old list, corresponding to a state of things existent some time before, and handed on by tradition in the Buddhist schools. But this only adds to its interest and importance.

Geographically also the list is very suggestive. No place south of Avanti (about 23° N.) occurs in it; and it is only at one place that the list goes even so far to the south as that. Not only is the whole of South India and Ceylon ignored in it, but there is also no mention of Orissa, of Bengal east of the Ganges, or even of the Dekkan. The horizon of those who drew up the list is strictly bounded on the north by the Himalayas, and on the south (except at this one point) by the Vindhya range, on the west by the mountains beyond the Indus, and on the east by the Ganges as it turns to the south.

The books in which the list has been preserved have preserved also abundant evidence of a further stage of political movement. And in geographical knowledge they look at things from an advanced point of view. They know a very little farther south at the one point where the old list goes farthest in that direction.

The expression Dakkhinapatha which occurs in an isolated passage in one of our oldest documents cannot indeed possibly mean the whole country comprised in our modern phrase the Dekkan. But it is used, in the very passage in question, as descriptive of a remote settlement or colony on the banks of the upper Godhavari. The expression does not occur in any one of the Four Nikayas. When it appears again, in a later stage, it seems still to refer only, in a vague way, to the same limited district, on the banks of the Godhavari. And it is coupled with Avanti, the Avanti of the ancient list.

The expression, in its form, is curious. It means "the Southern Road," a strange name to apply to any fixed locality. Already in a Vedic hymn though it is one of the latest, we hear of a banished man going along the "path of the South." No doubt at different times different points on that path had been reached. In the Buddha's time the most southerly town is given (at S. N. 1011) as Patilahana, the place afterwards called Paithana, and Baithana by the Greeks (73° 2 E. by 21° 42' N.). And the extreme southerly point reached at all is the hermitage on the Godhavari, about 20° N. One place still farther south may possibly be referred to incidentally as known in the Buddha's time. A teacher of olden time named Tagara-sikhin, is several times mentioned. Sikhin is otherwise known as a name, and the distinctive epithet Tagara may possibly be local, and mean "of Tagara," the modern Ter, 76° 12' E. by 18°, 19' N. But the point is very doubtful, the place is not mentioned elsewhere, and I think another explanation of the name is more likely.

Besides this extension in the Dekkan, the Nikayas speak also of sea voyages out of sight of land and they mention the Kalinga forest, and the settlement on the coast there, with its capital Dantapura. The Vinaya has a probable reference to Bharu-kaccha, and the Udana one to Supparaka. These points, taken together (and no doubt others can be traced), show a marked advance in geographical knowledge. But it is suggestive to notice that the advance is limited, and that there is still no reference whatever either to South India or to Ceylon, which play so great a part in the story of the Ramayana.

These geographical considerations are of very considerable importance for the history of later Vedic and early Sanskrit literature. They go far to confirm Professor Bhandarkar's recent views as to the wholesale recasting of Brahmin literature in the Gupta period. If Apastamba, for instance, as Hofrath Dr. Bühler thought, and Hiranya-Kesin, wrote in the south, below the Godhavari, then they must be later than the books whose evidence we have been considering.

The consideration of this question has been hindered by a generally accepted hypothesis which does not fit the facts. It is supposed that the course of Aryan migration lay along the valleys of the Ganges and the Jumna. It cannot have been so simple. We must postulate at least two other lines of equal importance-one down the Indus, round the Gulf of Cutch, and so up to Avanti; and another along the foot of the mountains from Kashmir, by way of Kosala, to the Sakiya country, and so on through Tirhut to Magadha and Anga. There is a great deal more evidence available, both in literature and in the conclusions to be drawn from language, as to tribal migration in India than has yet been collected or analysed. Mr. Grierson, for instance, has only just recently pointed out the important fact that, even now, the dialects of Rajasthan have a close resemblance to the dialects spoken along the Himalayas not only in Nepal but as far west, at least, as Chamba. This would tend to show that their ancestors must have been living close together when they began their wanderings to the east and the south respectively. Both started from the Northern Panjab, and probably neither migration followed the Ganges route.

These children of hillmen tended to cleave to the hills; and, like mountaineers all the world over, were generally distinguished by a sturdy independence, both in politics and religion. Widely separated, they were always sympathetic; and any forward movement, such as Buddhism, readily found supporters among them.

Another point on which this geographical evidence throws light is the date of the colonisation of Ceylon. That cannot have taken place in any considerable degree before the period in which the Nikayas were composed. We know it had become a well-established fact at the time of Asoka. It must have happened, therefore, between these two dates; and no doubt nearer to the earlier of the two. The Ceylon chronicles, therefore, in dating the first colony in the very year of the Buddha's death (a wrong synchronism which is the cause of much confusion in their early chronology) must be in error.

It would be of great assistance on several questions if we could form some conclusion as to the number of inhabitants in Northern India in the seventh century, BC; though any such conclusion would necessarily be of the vaguest description. To judge from the small numbers of the great cities, and from the wide extent of forest and wilderness, mentioned in the books, it cannot have been very-large. Perhaps the whole territory may have contained fifteen to twenty millions. In the fourth century, BC, the confederation formed to oppose Alexander was able to muster an army of four hundred thousand. And in the third century, BC, Megasthenes describes the army of Magadha as then consisting, in peace time, of two hundred thousand foot, three hundred elephants, and ten thousand chariots.

The following is a list of the principal cities existing in India in the seventh century BC

Ayojjha (from which the Anglo-Indian word Oudh is derived) was a town in Kosala on the river Sarayu. The city owes all its fame to the fact that the author of the Ramayana makes it the capital at the date of the events in his story. It is not even mentioned in the Mahabharata; and was quite unimportant in the Buddha's time. There is another Ayojjha in the extreme west; and a third is said (wrongly, I think) to have been situate on the Ganges.

Baranasi (Benares) on the north bank of the Ganges, at the junction between it and the river Barana. The city proper included the land between the Barana and a stream called the Asi, as its name suggests. Its extent, including the suburbs, is often stated to have been, at the time when it was the capital of an independent kingdom (that is, some time before the rise of Buddhism) twelve leagues, or about eighty-five miles. Seeing that Megasthenes gives the circuit of the walls of Pataliputta, where he himself lived, as 220 stadia (or about twenty-five miles), this tradition as to the size of the city, or rather county, Benares at the height of its prosperity seems by no means devoid of credit. Its Town Hall was then no longer used as a parliament chamber for the transaction of public business. Public discussions on religious and philosophical questions were carried on in it.

Champa, on the river of the same name, was the ancient capital of Anga. Its site has been identified by Cunningham with the modern villages of similar names twenty-four miles east of Bhagalpur; and is stated to have been sixty leagues from Mithila. It was celebrated for its beautiful lake, named after Queen Gaggara, who had it excavated. On its banks was a grove of Champaka trees, well known for the fragrant odour of their beautiful white flowers. And there, in the Buddha's time, wandering teachers were wont to lodge. The Indian colonists in Cochin China named one of the most important of their settlements after this famous old town. And the Champa in Anga was again, in its turn, so named after the still older Champa in Kashmir.

Kampilla, the capital of the Northern Pañcalas. It was on the northern bank of the Ganges, about long. 79° W., but its exact site has not yet been decided with certainty.

Kosambi, the capital of the Vatsas or Vamsas. It was on the Jumna, and thirty leagues, say 230 miles, by river from Benares. It was the most important entrepót for both goods and passengers coming to Kosala and Magadha from the south and west. In the Sutta Nipata (1010-1013) the whole route is given from a place south of Ujjen, through Koshambi to Kusinara, with the stopping-places on the way. The route from Koshambi to Rajagaha was down the river. In the Buddha's time there were already four distinct establishments of his Order in the suburbs of Koshambi-the Badarika, Kukkuna, and Ghosita Parks, and the Mango Grove of Pavariya.] The Buddha was often there, at one or other of these residences; and many of his discourses there have been handed down in the books.

Madhura, on the Jumna, the capital of the Surasenas. It is tempting to identify it with the site of the modern Mathura, in spite of the difference in spelling. Very ancient remains have been found there. The king of Madhura in the Buddha's time bore the title of Avanti-putto, and was therefore related to the royal family at Ujjeni. Madhura was visited by the Buddha, and was the residence of Maha Kaccana, one of his most influential disciples, to whom tradition attributes the first grammatical treatment of the Pali language, and after whom the oldest Pali grammar is accordingly named. As Madhura is mentioned in the Milinda (331) as one of the most famous places in India, whereas in the Buddha's time it is barely mentioned, the time of its greatest growth must have been between these dates. It was sufficiently famous for the other Madhura, in Tinnevelly, first mentioned in the Mahavansa, to be named after it. A third Madhura, in the extreme north, is mentioned at Jat. 4. 79, and Peta Vatthu Vamana, 111.

Mithila, the capital of Videha, and the capital therefore of the kings Janaka and Makhadeva, was in the district now called Tirhut. Its size is frequently given as seven leagues, about fifty miles, in circumference.

Rajagaha, the capital of Magadha, the modern Rajgir. There were two distinct towns; the older one, a hill fortress, more properly Giribbaja, was very ancient, and is said to have been laid out by Maha Govinda the architect. The later town, at the foot of the hills, was built by Bimbisara, the contemporary of the Buddha, and is Rajagaha proper. It was at the height of its prosperity during, and immediately after, the Buddha's time. But it was abandoned by Sisunaga, who transferred the capital to Vesali; his son Kakasoka transferring it to Pataliputta, near the site of the modern Patna.

The fortifications of both Giribbaja and Rajagaha are still extant, 4½ and 3 miles respectively in circumference; the most southerly point of the walls of Giribbaja, the "Mountain Stronghold," being one mile north of the most northerly point of the walls of the new town of Rajagaha, the "King's House." The stone walls of Giribbaja are the oldest extant stone buildings in India.

Roruka, or in later times Roruva, the capital of Sovira, from which the modern name Surat is derived, was an important centre of the coasting trade. Caravans arrived there from all parts of India, even from Magadha. As Ophir is spelt by Josephus and in the Septuagint Sophir, and the names of the ivory, apes, and peacocks imported thence into Palestine are Indian names, it is not improbable that Roruka was the seaport to which the authors of the Hebrew chronicles supposed that Solomon's vessels had traded. For though the more precise name of the port was Roruka, we know from such expressions as that used in the Milinda, p. 29, that the Indians talked about sailing to Sovira. The exact site has not yet been rediscovered, but it was almost certainly on the Gulf of Kach, somewhere near the modern Kharragoa. When its prosperity declined, its place was taken by Bharukaccha, the modern Bharoch, or by Supparaka, both on the opposite, the southern, side of the Kathiawad peninsula.

Sagala. There were three cities of this name. But the two in the far East were doubtless named after the famous Sagala in the extreme north-west, which offered so brave a resistance to Alexander, and where King Milanda afterwards reigned. It lay about 32° N. by 74° E., and was the capital of the Maddas. Cunningham thought he had found the ruins of it; but no excavations have been carried out, and the exact site is still therefore uncertain.

Saketa, the site of which has been indentified with the ruins, as yet unexplored, at Sujan Kot, on the Sai River, in the Unao district of the modern province of Audh. In ancient times it was an important city in Kosala, and sometimes the capital. In the Buddha's time the capital was Savatthi. Saketa is often supposed to be the same as Ayojjha (Oudh), but both cities are mentioned as existing in the Buddha's time. They were possibly adjoining, like London and Westminster. But it is Saketa, and not Ayojjha, that is called one of the six great cities of India. The Añjana Wood near by Saketa is the place at which many of the Buddhist Suttas are said to have been spoken. The distance from Saketa northwards, to Savatthi was six leagues, about forty-five miles, and could be covered in one day with seven relays of horses. But there was a broad river on the way, only to be crossed by ferry; and there are constant references to the dangers of the journey on foot.

Savatthi, or Sravasti, was the capital of Northern Kosala, the residence of King Pasenadi, and one of the six great cities in India during the lifetime of the Buddha. Archaeologists differ as to its position; and the decision of this vexed point is one of the first importance for the early history of India, as there must be many inscriptions there. It was six leagues north of Saketa, forty-five leagues north-west of Rajagaha, more than one hundred north-east of Supparaka, thirty leagues from Sankassa and on the bank of the Achiravati.

Ujjeni, the capital of Avanti, the Greek Ozene, about 77° E. and 23° N. There Kaccana, one of the leading disciples of the Buddha, and also Asoka's son Mahinda, the famous apostle to Ceylon, were born. In later times there was a famous monastery there called the Southern Mount; and in earlier times the capital had been Mahissati. Vedisa, where the famous Bhilsa Topes were lately found, and Erakaccha, another well-known site, were in the vicinity. Vedisa was fifty leagues from Pataliputta.

This was the capital of the Licchavi clan, already closely related by marriage to the kings of Magadha, and the ancestors of the kings of Nepal, of the Mauryas, and of the dynasty of the Guptas. It was the headquarters of the powerful Vajjian confederacy, afterwards defeated, but not broken up, by Ajatasattu. It was the only great city in all the territories of the free clans who formed so important a factor in the social and political life of the sixth century BC It must have been a great and flourishing place.

But though different guesses have been made as to its site, no one of them has yet been proved to be true by excavation. It was somewhere in Tirhut; and just three leagues, or, say, twenty-five miles, north of the Ganges, reckoned from a spot on the bank of that river, five leagues, say thirty-eight miles, from Rajagaha. Behind it lay the Great Forest, the Mahavana, which stretched northwards to the Himalayas. In that wood a hermitage had been built by the community for the Buddha, and there many of his discourses were delivered. And in an adjoining suburb, the founder of the Jains, who was closely related to some of the leading chiefs, was born. We hear of its three walls, each of them a gavuta, a cow's call, distant from the next; and of the 7707 rajas, that is Licchavi chiefs, who dwelt there; and of the sacred pool in which they received their consecration. There were many shrines of pre-Buddhistic worship in and around the city, and the discovery and excavation of the site is most desirable.

The same may indeed be said of all these ancient cities. Not one of them has been properly excavated. The archeeology of India is, at present, an almost unworked field.

The Village

In the Buddha's time and in that portion of North India where the Buddhist influence was most early felt-that is to say in the districts including and adjoining those now called the United Provinces and Behar-the social conditions were, on the whole, simple. But there are several points of great interest on which they differed from those of the same districts now, and from those of related tribes in Europe then.

Divergent theories have been propounded to explain these differences. The influence of food and climate is assigned a paramount importance. Vegetarian diet is supposed to explain the physical and mental degeneracy proved by the presumed absence of political movements and ardent patriotism. Or the enervating and tropical heat of the sultry plains is supposed to explain at once the want of political vigour and the bad philosophy. Or the overwhelming mental effect of the mighty powers of nature-the vivid storms of thunder and lightning, the irresistible rays of the scorching sun, the depressing majesty of the great mountains-are called upon as a sufficient explanation of the inferiority of the Indian peoples. Or the contact with aboriginal tribes in a semi-savage state of development, the frequent intermarriages, and the consequent adoption of foolish and harmful superstitions, are put forward as the reasons for whatever we find strange in their life and thought.

It may be doubted whether our knowledge of the state of things in the seventh century BC, either on the shores of the Mediterranean on the one hand, or in the Ganges Valley on the other, is sufficiently clear and precise to justify our taking for granted the then inferiority of the Indians. In some respects it would seem to be the other way. In intellectual vigour, at least, the Indians were not wanting. That Europeans should believe, as a matter of course, in the vast superiority of Europeans, not only now, but always, is psychologically interesting. It is so like the opinion of the ancient Greeks about barbarians, and of the modern Chinese about foreigners. But the reasons given are vague, and will scarcely bear examination. I recollect hearing Professor Buhler at the Oriental Congress in Paris, in 1897, when the argument of climate was adduced, entering an emphatic caution. As Inspector of Schools in India for many years, he knew the climate well; and observed that exaggerated estimates of its baneful influence had been most often advanced by those who had never been in India. Those who had lived there knew the great amount of energy and work, both physical and intellectual, that was not only possible, but habitual, to both Europeans and the natives of India. I can fully confirm this. The climate has its positive advantages. All the other most ancient civilisations (in Egypt for instance, in Mesopotamia, and in China) grew up, under somewhat similar outward conditions, in warm and fertile river valleys. And climate varies greatly even in India. We must not forget that the Sakiya country, at least, in which Buddhism arose, stretchcd up into the lower slopes of the Himalayas. And in the seventh century BC the most powerful kingdom was the Northern Kosala, whose capital lay under the hills, and whose power mainly depended on the mountaineers drawn from its vicinity.

It is probable that economic conditions and social institutions were a more important factor in Indian life than geographical position. Now the social structure of India was based upon the village. We do not as yet know all the details of its organisation; and no doubt different villages, in different districts, varied one from another in the customs of land-tenure and in the rights of individual householders as against the community.

It is a common error, vitiating all conclusions as to the early history of India, to suppose that the tribes with whom the Aryans, in their gradual conquest of India, came into contact, were savages. Some were so. There were hill tribes, gypsies, bands of hunters in the woods. But there were also settled communities with highly developed social organisation, wealthy enough to excite the cupidity of the invaders, and in many cases too much addicted to the activities of peace to be able to offer, whenever it came to a fight, a prolonged resistance. But they were strong enough to retain, in some cases, a qualified independence, and in others to impose upon the new nation that issued from the struggle many of their own ideas, many of the details of their own institutions.

And in many cases it never came to a struggle at all. The country was immense. Compared with its wide expanse the tribes and clans were few. Often separated one from the other by broad rivers and impenetrable forest, there must have been ample opportunity for independent growth, and for the interaction of peaceful contact.

These circumstances will explain the divergency in the village arrangements. But in some respects they were all similar. We nowhere hear of isolated houses. The houses were all together, in a group, separated only by narrow lanes. Immediately adjoining was the sacred grove of trees of the primeval forest, left standing when the forest clearing had been made. Beyond this was the wide expanse of cultivated field, usually rice-field. And each village had grazing ground for the cattle, and a considerable stretch of jungle, where the villagers had common rights of waste and wood.

The cattle belonged severally to the householders of the village. But no one had separate pasture. After the crop was cut the cattle roamed over the field. When the crops were growing they were sent all together, under the charge of a herdsman, hired by the village collectively, to the village grazing grounds beyond the field. The herdsman was an important personage, and is described as "knowing the general appearance of each one of his charge and the marks upon it, skilled to remove flies' eggs from their hide and to make sores heal over, accustomed to keep a good fire going with smoke to keep the gnats away, knowing where the fords are and the drinking places, clever in choosing pasture, leaving milk in the udders, and with a proper respect for the leaders of the herd."

The fields were all cultivated at the same time, the irrigation channels being laid by the community, and the supply of water regulated by rule, under the supervision of the headman. No individual or corporate proprietor needed to fence his portion of the fields. There was a common fence; and the whole field, with its rows of boundaries, which were also the water channels, bore the appearance of the patched robe of a member of the Buddhist Order. As a general rule the great field was divided into plots corresponding in number to that of the heads of houses in the villages; and each family took the produce of its share. But there was no such proprietary right, as against the community, as we are accustomed to in England. We hear of no instance of a shareholder selling or mortgaging his share of the village field to an outsider; and it was impossible for him to do so, at least without the consent of the village council. We have three instances of sales of land in the books. But in one case it was forest land cleared by the proprietor or his ancestors. A very old text apparently implies that a piece of ground was given as a sacrificial fee. But it is at once added that the earth itself said, and Mother Earth was a most dread divinity,-"No mortal must give me away!"

Neither had any individual the right of bequest, even to the extent of deciding the shares of his own family. All such matters were settled by custom, by the general sense of the community as to what was right and proper. And the general sense did not recognise the right of primogeniture. Very often a family, on the death of a householder, would go on as before under the superintendence of the eldest son. If the property were divided, the land was equally divided among the sons. And though the eldest son received an extra share (differing in different places and times) in the personal property, that also was otherwise divided equally. We find in the earliest law book, that of Gautama, a statement that the youngest son also, as in the analogous English law of gavelkind, received an extra share; but in the later law books this disappears. The women, too, had their personal property, chiefly jewellery and clothes; and the daughters inherited from the mother. They had no need of a separate share of the land, as they had the advantage of the produce falling to the share of their husbands and brothers.

No individual could acquire, either by purchase or inheritance, any exclusive right in any portion of the common grassland or woodland. Great importance was attached to these rights of pasture and forestry. The priests claimed to be able, as one result of performing a particular sacrifice (with six hundred victims!), to ensure that a wide tract of such land should be provided. And it is often made a special point, in describing the grant of a village to a priest, that it contained such common. What happened in such a case was that the king granted, not the land (he had no property in the land), but the tithe due, by custom, to the government as yearly tax. The peasantry were ousted from no one of their rights. Their position was indeed improved. For, paying only the same tax as before, they thus acquired the protection of a strong influence, which would not fail, on occasion, to be exerted on their behalf.

Not that they were usually without some such protection. It was through the village headman that all government business was carried on, and he had both opportunity and power to represent their case to the higher officials. From the fact that the appointment of this officer is not claimed for the king until the later law books it is almost certain that, in earlier times, the appointment was either hereditary, or conferred by the village council itself.

This village headman had, no doubt, to prepare the road, and provide food, on the occasion of a royal person or high official visiting his village. But we find no mention of corvée, forced labour (raja-kariya) at this period. And even in the law books which refer to a later date, this is mentioned as a service due from artisans and mechanics, and not from villagers.

On the other hand villagers are described as uniting, of their own accord, to build Mote-halls and Rest-houses and reservoirs, to mend the roads between their own and adjacent villages, and even to lay out parks. And it is interesting to find that women are proud to bear a part in such works of public utility.

The economic conditions in such villages were simple. None of the householders could have been what would now be called rich. On the other hand there was a sufficiency for their simple needs, there was security, there was independence. There were no landlords, and no paupers. There was little if any crime. What crime there was in the country (of which later) was nearly all outside the villages. When the central power was strong enough, as it usually was, to put down dacoity, the people, to quote the quaint words of an old Suttanta, "pleased one with another and happy, dancing their children in their hands, dwelt with open doors."

The only serious inroad upon that happiness seems to have been famine resulting from drought. It is true that Megasthenes, long ambassador at the court of Magadha, says that, owing to irrigation, famines were quite unknown. But we have too many references to times of scarcity, and that, too, in the very districts adjacent to Patna where Megasthenes lived, to accept his statement as accurate for the time we are discussing. As those references refer, however, to a date two centuries earlier, it is possible (but not, I think, very probable) that things, in this respect, had improved in the interval between the times referred to in our records, and that of Megasthenes. We shall see below, in the chapter on Chandragupta, that his statements often require correction. And this is, more probably, merely another instance of a similar kind.

It was under some such economic conditions as these that the great bulk-say at least 70-80 per cent.-of the people lived. In the books, ancient and modern, a few of the remaining few are so much more constantly mentioned (precisely because they differ from the mass, and the mass is taken for granted as understood) that the impression given to the reader fs apt to be entirely misleading. These others-priests and kings, outcasts and jugglers, soldiers, citizens, and mendicant thinkers-played their part, and an important part. But the peoples of India, then much more even than now, were, first and foremost, village folk. In the whole vast territory from Kandahar nearly to Calcutta, and from the Himalayas southwards to the Run of Kach, we find mentioned barely a score of towns of any considerable size. It will have been seen, however, that the mass of the people, the villagers, occupied a social grade quite different from, and far above, our village folk. They held it degradation, to which only dire misfortune would drive them, to work for hire. They were proud of their standing, their family, and their village. And they were governed by headmen of their own class and village, very probably selected by themselves, in accordance with their own customs and ideals.

Social Grades

Perhaps the most important of these in their own eyes were the customs as to the holding and distribution of lands and property. But those as to religion on the one hand, and as to connubium and commensality on the other, had probably a greater effect on their real well-being and national progress.

We have learnt in recent years that among primitive peoples all over the world there exist restrictions as to the connubium (the right of intermarriage), and as to commensality (the right of eating together). Customs of endogamy and exogamy, that is, of choosing a husband or wife outside a limited circle of relationship, and inside a wider circle, were universal. A man, for instance, may not marry in his own family, he may marry within his own clan, he may not marry outside the clan. Among different tribes the limits drawn were subject to different customs, were not the same in detail. But the limits were always there. There were customs of eating together at sacred tribal feasts from which foreigners were excluded; customs of not eating together with persons outside certain limits of relationship, except under special circumstances; customs by which an outsider could, by eating with men of a tribe, acquire certain rights of relationship with that tribe. Here again the details differ. But the existence of such restrictions as to commensality was once universal.

In India also in the seventh century BC such customs were prevalent, and prevalent in widely different forms among the different tribes,-Aryan, Dravidian, Kolarian, and others,-which made up the mixed population. We have unfortunately only Aryan records. And they, of course, take all the customs for granted, being addressed to people who knew all about them. We have therefore to depend on hints; and the hints given have not, as yet, been all collected and sifted. But a considerable number, and those of great importance, have been already observed; so that we are able to draw out some principal points in a sketch that requires future filling in.

The basis of the social distinctions was relationship; or, as the Aryans, proud of their lighter colour, put it colour. Their books constantly repeat a phrase as being common amongst the people,-and it was certainly common at least among the Aryan sections of the people,-which divided all the world, as they knew it, into four social grades, called Colours. At the head were the Kshatriyas, the nobles, who claimed descent from the leaders of the Aryan tribes in their invasion of the continent.

They were most particular as to the purity of their descent through seven generations, both on the father's and the mother's side; and are described as "fair in colour, fine in presence, stately to behold." Then came the Brahmins, claiming descent from the sacrificing priests, and though the majority of them followed then other pursuits, they were equally with the nobles distinguished by high birth and clear complexion. Below these were the peasantry, the people, the Vaishyas or Vessas. And last of all came the Sudras, which included the bulk of the people of non-Aryan descent, who worked for hire, were engaged in handicraft or service, and were darker in colour.

In a general way this classification corresponded to the actual facts of life. But there were insensible gradations within the borders of each of the four Colours, and the borders themselves were both variable and undefined.

And this enumeration of the populace was not complete. Below all four, that is below the Sudras, we have mention of other "low tribes" and "low trades"-hina-jatiyo and hina-sippani. Among the first we are told of workers in rushes, bird-catchers, and cart-makers-aboriginal tribesmen who were hereditary craftsmen in these three ways. Among the latter-mat-makers, barbers, potters, weavers, and leather-workers-it is implied that there was no hard and fast line, determined by birth. People could, and did, change their vocations by adopting one or other of these "low trades." Thus at Jat. 5. 290, foll., a love-lorn Kshatriya works successively (without any dishonour or penalty) as a potter, basket-maker, reed-worker, garland-maker, and cook. Also at Jat. 6. 372, a sethi works as a tailor and as a potter, and still retains the respect of his high-born relations.

Finally we hear in both Jain and Buddhist books of aboriginal tribes, Chandalas and Pukkusas, who were more despised even than these low tribes and trades.

Besides the above, who were all freemen, there were also slaves: individuals had been captured in predatory raids and reduced to slavery, or had been deprived of their freedom as a judicial punishment; or had submitted to slavery of their own accord.

Children born to such slaves were also slaves; and the emancipation of slaves is often referred to. But we hear nothing of such later developments of slavery as rendered the Greek mines, the Roman latifundia, or the plantations of Christian slave-owners, scenes of misery and oppression. For the most part the slaves were household servants, and not badly treated; and their numbers seem to have been insignificant.

Such were the divisions of the people. The three upper classes had originally been one; for the nobles and priests were merely those members of the third class, the Vessas, who had raised themselves into a higher social rank. And though more difficult probably than it had been, it was still possible for analogous changes to take place. Poor men could become nobles, and both could become Brahmins. We have numerous instances in the books, some of them unconsciously preserved even in the later priestly books which are otherwise under the spell of the caste theory. And though each case is then referred to as if it were exceptional, the fact no less remains that the line between the "Colours" was not yet strictly drawn. The members of the higher Colours were not even all of them white. Some, no doubt, of the Kshatriyas were descended from the chiefs and nobles of the Dravidian and Kolarian tribes who had preserved, by conquest or by treaty, their independence or their social rank. And others of the same tribes were, from time to time, acquiring political importance, and with it an entry into a higher social grade.

That there was altogether a much freer possibility of change among the social ranks than is usually supposed is shown by the following instances of occupation]:

1. A Kshatriya, a king's son, apprentices himself successively, in pursuance of a love affair, to a potter,

a basket-maker, a florist, and a cook, without a word being added as to loss of caste when his action becomes known.

2. Another prince resigns his share in the kingdom in favour of his sister, and turns trader.
3. A third prince goes to live with a merchant and earns his living "by his hands."
4. A noble takes service, for a salary, as an archer.
5. A Brahmin takes to trade to make money to give away.
6. Two other Brahmins live by trade without any such excuse.
7. A Brahmin takes the post of an assistant to an archer, who had himself been previously a weaver.

8, 9. Brahmins live as hunters and trappers.

10. A Brahmin is a wheelwright.

Brahmins are also frequently mentioned as engaged in agriculture, and as hiring themselves out as cowherds and even goatherds. These are all instances from the Jatakas. And a fortiori-unless it be maintained that Buddhism brought about a great change in this respect-the statt of things must have been even more lax at the time when Buddhism arose.

The customs of connubium were by no means co-extensive with the four Colours, They depended among the Aryans on a quite different idea, that of the group of agnates (the Gotta); and among the other people either on the tribe, or on the village. No instance is known of the two parties to a marriage belonging by birth to the same village.

On the other hand, there were numerous instances of irregular unions. And in some cases the offspring of such unions took rank even as nobles (Kshatriyas) or as Brahmins.

As to customs of eating or not eating together, the books contain only a few hints. We have clear instances of a Brahmin eating with a Kshatriya, another of a Brahmin eating the food of a Chandala, and repenting of doing so.

The whole episode of the marriage of the Sakiya maiden to Pasenadi, King of Kosala, turns on the belief that a Kshatriya will not eat, even with his own daughter, if she be slave-born. And we hear of sending people to Coventry (as we should say) for breach of such customs. Thus at J. 4. 388, Brahmins are deprived, by their brother Brahmins, of their status as Brahmins, for drinking water mixed with the rice water a Chandala had used. And in an older document, one of the Dialogues, we are told how this was done. Three Brahmins "for some offence or other, outlaw a Brahmin, shaving him and cutting him dead by pouring ashes over him, thus banishing him from the land and from the township."

And the passage goes on to state that if Kshatriyas had done this to a Kshatriya the Brahmins would still admit him to connubium, and allow him to eat with them at their sacred feasts.

It then adds that "whosoever are in bondage to the notions of birth or of lineage, or to the pride of social position or connection by marriage, they are far from the best wisdom and righteousness." We see, therefore, that the whole passage is tinged with Buddhist views. But it is none the less good evidence that at the time when it was written such customs, and such pride of birth, were recognised as a factor in the social life of the people.

Again at Jat. 5. 280, we have, as the central incident of a popular story, the detail, given quite as a matter of course, that a Brahmin takes, as his only wife, the discarded consort of a Kshatriya. The people laugh at him, it is true, but not because he is acting in any way unworthy of its social standing, only because he is old and ugly.

There are also numerous instances, even in the priestly manuals of custom, of unions between men and women of all degrees of social importance.

These are not only between men of rank and girls of a lower social grade, but also between men of a lower, and women of a higher, position; and we ought not to be in the least surprised to find such cases mentioned in the books.

Even without them we should know, from the existing facts, what must have happened. It is generally admitted that there are now no pure Aryans left in India. Had the actual custom been as strict as the Brahmin theory this would not be so. Just as in England we find Iberians, Kelts, Angles, Saxons, Danes, and Normans now fused, in spite of theoretical restrictions on intermarriage, into one nation, so in Northern India the ancient distinctions, Aryan, Kolarian, and Dravidian, cannot, at the time of the rise of Buddhism, any longer be recognised. Long before the priestly theory of caste had been brought into any sort of working order, a fusion, sufficient at least to obliterate completely the old landmarks, was an accomplished fact; and the modern divisions, though race has also its share in them, use different names, and are based on different ideas.

We may remark incidentally that there can have been no such physical repulsion as obtains between the advanced and savage races of to-day-a repulsion arising partly from great difference in customs and in intellectual culture, but still more largely dependent on difference of colour.

On the other hand, though the fact of frequent intermarriage is undoubted; though the great chasm between the proudest Kshatriya on the one hand and the lowest Chandala on the other was bridged over by a number of almost imperceptible stages, and the boundaries between these stages were constantly being overstepped, still there were also real obstacles to unequal unions.

Though the lines of demarcation were not yet drawn hard and fast, we still have to suppose, not a state of society where there were no lines of demarcation at all, but a constant struggle between attracting and repelling forces.

It will sound most amazing to those familiar with Brahmin pretensions (either in modern times in India, or in priestly books such as Manu and the epics) to hear Brahmins spoken of as "low-born." Yet that precisely is an epithet applied to them in comparison with the kings and nobles. And it ought to open our eyes as to their relative importance in these early times.

The fact is that the claim of the priests to social superiority had nowhere in North India been then, as yet, accepted by the people. Even such books of the priests themselves as are pre-Buddhistic imply this earlier, and not the later, state of things with which we are so much familiar. They claim for the northwestern, as distinct from the easterly, provinces a most strict adherence to ancient custom. The ideal land is, to them, that of the Kurus and Panchalas, not that of the Kasis and Kosalas. But nowhere do they put forward in their earlier books those arrogant claims, as against the Kshatriyas, which are a distinctive feature of the later literature. The kings are their patrons to whom they look up, from whom they hope to receive approval and rewards. And it was not till the time we are now discussing that they put forward claims, which we find still vigorously disputed by all Kshatriyas-and by no means only by those of noble birth (a small minority of the whole) who happen also to be Buddhists.

We find, for instance, that the Jain books take it throughout as a matter of course, that the priests, as regards social standing, are below the nobles.

This was the natural relation between the two, as we find throughout the world. Certain priests, in India as elsewhere, had very high social rank-Pokkharasadi and Sonadana for instance. They were somewhat like the great abbots and bishops in our Middle Ages. But as a class, and as a whole, the priests looked up to the nobles, and were considered to be socially beneath them.

Restrictions as to marriage and as to eating together, such as then existed in North India, existed also everywhere throughout the world, among peoples of a similar stage of culture. They are, it is true, the key to the origin of the later Indian caste system. But that system involves much more than these restrictions.

And it is no more accurate to speak of caste at the Buddha's time in India, than it would be to speak of it as an established institution, at the same time, in Italy or Greece. There is no word even for caste. The words often wrongly rendered by that modern expression (itself derived from a Portuguese word) have something to do with the question, but do not mean caste.

The Colours (Varna) were not castes. No one of them had any of the distinctive marks of a caste, as the term is now used, and as it always has been used since it was first introduced by Europeans, and there was neither connubium nor commensality between the members of each.

Jati is "birth"; and pride of birth may have had to do with the subsequent building up of caste prejudices; but it exists in Europe today, and is an idea very different from that of caste. Kula is "family" or "clan" according to the context. And though the medieval caste system had much to do with families and clans, it is only misleading to confuse terms which are so essentially different, or to read back a medieval idea into these ancient documents. The caste system, in any proper or exact use of the term, did not exist till long afterwards.

5

ECONOMIC CONDITIONS IN INDIAN CASTES

INTRODUCTON

There has been as yet no attempt to reconstruct a picture of the economic conditions at any period in the early history of India. Professor Zimmer, Dr. Fick, and Professor Hopkins have dealt incidentally with some of the points on the basis respectively of the Vedas, the Jatakas, and the Epics. But generally speaking the books on India have been so exclusively concerned with questions of religion and philosphy, of literature and language, that we seem apt to forget that the very necessities of life, here as elsewhere, must have led the people to occupy their time very much, not to say mostly, with other matters than those, with the earning of their daily bread, with the accumulation and distribution of wealth. The following remarks will be chiefly based on Mrs. Rhys-Davids's articles on this important subject in the Economic Journal, for 1901, and in the Journal of the Royal Asiatic Society, for 1901.

When the King of Magadha, the famous (and infamous) Ajatasattu, made his only call upon the Buddha, he is said to have put a puzzle to the teacher to test him-a puzzle characteristic of the King's state of mind. It is this:

> *"What in the world is the good of your renunciation, of joining an Order like yours? Other people (and here he gives a list), by following ordinary crafts, get something out of them. They can make themselves comfortable in this world, and keep their families in*

comfort. Can you, Sir, declare to me any such immediate fruit, visible in this world, of the life of a recluse?"

The list referred to is suggestive. In the view of the King the best examples of such crafts were the following: 1. Elephant-riders. 2. Cavalry. 3. Charioteers. 4. Archers. 5-13. Nine different grades of army folk. 14. Slaves. 15. Cooks. 16. Barbers. 17. Bath-attendants. 18. Confectioners. 19. Garland-makers. 20. Washermen. 21. Weavers. 22. Basket-makers. 23. Potters. 24. Clerks. 25. Accountants.

These are just the sort of people employed about a camp or a palace. King-like, the King considers chiefly those who minister to a king, and are dependent upon him. In the answer he is most politely reminded of the peasant, of the tax-payer, on whom both he and his depended. And it is evident enough from other passages that the King's list is far from exhaustive. There is mention, in other documents of the same age, of guilds of work-people; and the number of these guilds is often given afterwards as eighteen. Four of these are mentioned by name. But a list of the whole eighteen has unfortunately not yet been found. It would probably have included the following:

1. The workers in wood. They were not only carpenters and cabinet-makers, but also wheel-wrights; and the builders of houses, and of ships, and of vehicles of all sorts (863).
2. The workers in metal. They made any iron implements-weapons of all kinds, ploughshares, axes, hoes, saws, and knives. But they also did finer work-made needles, for instance, of great lightness and sharpness, or gold and (less often) silver work of great delicacy and beauty (864).
3. The workers in stone. They made flights of steps, leading up into a house or down into a reservoir; faced the reservoir; laid foundations for the woodwork of which the upper part of the houses was built; carved pillars and bas-reliefs; and even did finer work such as making a crystal bowl, or a stone coffer (864). Beautiful examples of these two last were found in the Sakiya Tope.
4. The weavers. They not only made the cloths which the people wrapped round themselves as dress, but manufactured fine muslin for export, and worked costly

and dainty fabrics of silk cloth and fur into rugs, blankets, coverlets, and carpets.

5. Leather workers, who made the numerous sorts of foot-covering and sandals worn by the people mostly in cold weather; and also the embroidered and costly articles of the same kind mentioned in the books (865).
6. Potters, who made all sorts of dishes and bowls for domestic use; and often hawked their goods about for sale.
7. Ivory workers, who made a number of small articles in ivory for ordinary use, and also costly carvings and ornaments such as those for which India is still famous (864).
8. Dyers, who coloured the clothes made by the weavers (864).
9. Jewellers, some of whose handiwork has survived, and is also so often represented in bas-reliefs that we know fairly well the shape and size of the ornaments they made.
10. The fisher folk. They fished only in the rivers. There is no mention of sea-fishing known to me.
11. The butchers, whose shops and slaughterhouses are several times mentioned (873).
12. Hunters and trappers, mentioned in various passages as bringing the animal and vegetable products of the woods, and also venison and game, for sale on carts into the city (873). It is doubtful whether they were formed into guilds. But their industry was certainly a very important one. The large stretches of forest, open to all, separating most of the settlements; the absence of any custom of breeding cattle for the meat-market; the large demand for ivory, fur, sinews, creepers, and all the other produce of the woods; and the congeniality of the occupation, all tended to encourage the hunters. And there is no reason to suppose that the very ancient instinct of the chase was confined to the so-called savages. The kings and nobles also, whether Aryan by blood or not, seem to have taken pleasure in it, quite apart from the economic question

of food supply. But men of good birth followed it as a trade; and when Brahmins did so (868) they are represented as doing so for profit.

13. The cooks and confectioners, a numerous class, probably formed a guild. But there is no passage saying that they did.
14. The barbers and shampooers had their guilds. They dealt in perfumes, and were especially skilled in arranging the elaborate turbans worn by the wealthier classes.
15. The garland-makers and flower-sellers (866).
16. Sailors, occupied for the most part in the traffic up and down the great rivers, but also going to sea. In some of our earliest documents we hear of sea voyages out of sight of land; and in the later documents, such as the Jatakas, the mention of such voyages is frequent (872). So the earlier documents speak of voyages lasting six months made in ships (nava, perhaps, "boats") which could be drawn up on shore in the winter, And later texts, of about the third century BC, speak of voyages down the Ganges from Benares to the mouth of the river and thence across the Indian Ocean to the opposite coast of Burma; and even from Bharukaccha (the modern Baroch) round Cape Comorin to the same destination (871). It is clear, therefore, that during the whole of this period the occupation of sailor was neither unfrequent nor unimportant.
17. The rush-workers and basket-makers (868).
18. Painters (865). They were mostly house-painters. The woodwork of the houses was often covered with fine chunam plaster and decorated with painting. But they also painted frescoes. These passages tell us of pleasure-houses, adorned with painted figures and patterns, belonging to the kings of Magadha and Kosala; and such frescoes were no doubt similar in character to, but of course in an earlier style than, the well-known ancient frescoes of the seventh and eighth centuries AD on the Ajanta Caves, and of the fifth century on the Sigiri Rock in Ceylon.

It is doubtful with regard to two or three in this list whether they were organised in guilds (seniyo, puga). But it is certain that these were among the most important branches of handicraft apart from agriculture; and most of them had, no doubt, their guilds not unlike the medieval guilds in Europe. It is through their guilds that the king summons the people on important occasions (865). The Aldermen or Presidents (pamukha) of such guilds are sometimes described as quite important persons, wealthy, favourites at the court. The guilds are said to have had powers of arbitration between the members of the guild and their wives. And disputes between one guild and another were in the jurisdiction of the maha-sethi, the Lord High Treasurer, who acted as a sort of chief Alderman over the Aldermen of the guilds (865).

Besides the peasantry and the handicraftsmen there were merchants who conveyed their goods either up and down the great rivers, or along the coasts in boats; or right across country in carts travelling in caravans. These caravans, long lines of small two-wheeled carts, each drawn by two bullocks, were a distinctive feature of the times. There were no made roads and no bridges. The carts struggled along, slowly, through the forests, along the tracks from village to village kept open by the peasants. The pace never exceeded two miles an hour. Smaller streams were crossed by gullies leading down to fords, the larger ones by cart ferries. There were taxes and octroi duties at each different country entered (875); and a heavy item in the cost was the hire of volunteer police who let themselves out in bands to protect caravans against robbers on the way (866). The cost of such carriage must have been great; so great that only the more costly goods could bear it.

The enormous traffic of today in the carriage of passengers, food-stuffs, and fuel was non-existent. Silks, muslins, the finer sorts of cloth and cutlery and armour, brocades, embroideries and rugs, perfumes and drugs, ivory and ivory work, jewellery and gold (seldom silver),-these were the main articles in which the merchant dealt.

The older system of traffic by barter had entirely passed away never to return. The later system of a currency of standard and token coins issued and regulated by government authority had not yet arisen. Transactions were carried on, values estimated, and bargains struck in terms of the kahapana, a square copper coin weighing about 146 grains, and guaranteed as to weight and fineness by punch-marks made by private individuals. Whether these punch-marks are the tokens of merchants, or of guilds, or simply of the bullion dealer, is not certain (874).

No silver coins were used (877). There were half and quarter kahapanas, and probably no other sort. The references to gold coins are late and doubtful; and no such coins have been found. Some thin gold films with punch marks on them were found in the Sakiya Tope, but these are too flimsy to have been used in circulation as coins (878).

It is interesting to notice that Alexander, when in India, struck a half kahapana copper piece, square (in imitation of the Indian money), and not round like the Greek coins of the time. It is only in later times that we hear (as for instance in Manu, 8. 401) of any market price being fixed by government regulation. In the sixth century BC there is only an official called the Valuer, whose duty it was to settle the prices of goods ordered for the palace-which is a very different thing (875). And there are many instances, incidentally given, of the prices of commodities fixed, at different times and places, by the haggling of the market (875). These are all collected together in the article referred to (at pp. 882, foll.); and the general result seems to be that though the kahapana would be worth, at the present value of copper, only five sixths of a penny, its purchasing power then was about equivalent to the purchasing power of a shilling now.

Besides the coins, there was a very considerable use of instruments of credit. The great merchants in the few large towns gave letters of credit on one another. And there is constant reference to promissory notes (879). The rates of interest are unfortunately never stated. But interest itself is mentioned very early; and the law books give the rate of interest current at a somewhat later date for loans on personal security as about eighteen per cent. per annum (881).

There were no banking facilities. Money was hoarded either in the house, or buried in jars in the ground, or deposited with a friend, a written record of the transaction being kept (881).

The details of prices above referred to enable us to draw some conclusion as to the spending power of the poor, of the man of the middle classes, and of the wealthy merchants and nobles respectively. Of want, as known in our great cities, there is no evidence. It is put down as the direst misfortune known that a free man had to work for hire. And there was plenty of land to be had for the trouble of clearing it, not far from the settled districts.

On the other hand, the number of those who could be considered wealthy from the standards of those times (and of course still more so from our own) was very limited. We hear of about a score of monarchs, whose wealth consisted mainly of the land tax, supplemented by other dues and perquisites; of a considerable number of wealthy nobles, and some priests, to whom grants had been made of the tithe arising out of certain parishes or counties or who had inherited similar rights from their forefathers; of about a dozen millionaire merchants in Takkasila, Savatthi, Benares, Rajagaha, Vesali, Koshambi, and the seaports (882), and of a considerable number of lesser merchants and middlemen, all in the few towns. But these were the exceptions. There were no landlords. And the great mass of the people were well-to-do peasantry, or handicraftsmen, mostly with land of their own, both classes ruled over by local headmen of their own selection.

Before closing this summary of the most important economic conditions in Northern India in the sixth century BC it may be well to bring together the few notices we have in the books about the trade routes. There is nothing about them in the pre-Buddhistic literature. In the oldest Pali books we have accounts of the journeys of the wandering teachers; and as, especially for longer journeys, they will generally have followed already established routes, this is incidental evidence of such as were then in use by traders. Later on, we have accounts of routes actually followed by merchants, either on boats, or with their caravans of bullock carts. We can thus draw up provisionally the following list:

1. North to South-west. Savatthi to Patilahana (Paithan) and back. The principal stopping places are given

(beginning from the south) as Mahissati, Ujjeni, Gonaddha, Vedisa, Koshambi, and Saketa.

2. North to South-east. Savatthi to Rajagaha. It is curious that the route between these two ancient cities is never, so far as I know, direct, but always along the foot of the mountains to a point north of Vesali, and only then turning south to the Ganges. By taking this circuitous road the rivers were crossed at places close to the hills where the fords were more easy to pass. But political considerations may also have had their weight in the original choice of this route, still followed when they were no longer of much weight. The stopping places were (beginning at Savatthi), Setavya, Kapilavastu, Kusinara, Pava, Hatthi-gama, Veshali, Pataliputra, and Nalanda. The road probably went on to Gaya, and there met another route from the coast, possibly at Tamralipti, to Benares.
3. East to West. The main route was along the great rivers, along which boats plied for hire. We even hear of express boats. Upwards the rivers were used along the Ganges as far west as Sahajati, and along the Jumna as far west as Koshambi. Downwards, in later times at least, the boats went right down to the mouths of the Ganges, and thence either across or along the coast to Burma. In the early books we hear only of the traffic downward as far as Magadha, that is, to take the farthest point, Champa. Upwards it went thence to Koshambi, where it met the traffic from the south (Route 1), and was continued by cart to the south-west and north-west.

Besides the above we are told of traders going from Videha to Gandhara, from Magadha to Sovira, from Bharukaccha round the coast to Burma, from Benares down the river to its mouth and thence on to Burma, from Champa to the same destination. In crossing the desert west of Rajputana the caravans are said to travel only in the night, and to be guided by a "land-pilot," who, just as one does on the ocean, kept the right route by observing the stars. The whole description of this journey is too vividly accurate to life to be an invention. So we may accept it as evidence not only that there was a trade route over the desert, but also that pilots, guiding ships or caravans by the stars only, were well known.

In the solitary instance of a trading journey to Babylon (Baveru) we are told that it was by sea, but the port of departure is not mentioned. There is one story, the worldwide story of the Sirens, who are located in Tambapanai-dipa, a sort of fairy land, which is probably meant for Ceylon. Lanka does not occur. Traffic with China is first mentioned in the Milinda.

POSITION OF WOMEN IN CASTE SYSTEM

Hindu Family Dharma

Hindu value system placed very high degree of importance to morality where a woman does not accept the seed form anyone other than her husband. We are talking of normal circumstances of life. We speak of rules not exceptions!

Family Structure and Allocation of Powers and Responsibilities: Each family would have a head known as Karta whose decision would be final in case of family disputes and disagreements. This authority would be vested in the Karta with the responsibility to be just and fair to all in the family, and not to base crucial decisions on personal preferences. In all his visible judgments and decisions, he would be expected to demonstrate justice and fairness.

Children of the family would grow up 'learning to value' these qualities of justice and fairness. This process of living through just and fair dealings, would inculcate those qualities in them, through the course of their growing up process.

This was a living reality of Hindu social life.

This was a living reality of Hindu social life or else, different visitors from different nations over different centuries would not have mentioned so consistently of this quality among Hindus.

Now, it is quite true that during the two thousand years which precede the time of Mahmud of Ghazni, Bhaarat Varsh has had but few foreign visitors, and few foreign critics; still it is extremely strange that whenever, either in Greek, or in Chinese, or in Persian, or in Arab writings, we meet any attempts at describing the distinguishing features in the national character of the Bhartiyas (*Hindus), regard for truth and justice should always be mentioned first. Max Muller, p 50

Hindu Joint Family Structure of Earlier Times and its Strengths: Returning to the Hindu family structure of earlier days, Karta would normally be the able-bodied able-minded eldest male member of the family. Position of authority and responsibility would be distributed in a hierarchical manner in the sense that elder the member greater the authority coupled with greater responsibility. Younger members would be groomed on the same pattern to learn to assume the authority as well as discharge corresponding responsibility, as they would grow up in the hierarchy.

The respect for the elders would be an unwritten law, and it would be expected of all to observe it without any reservation. With that elders would have the equal amount of responsibility to stay worthy of such respect by their thoughts and actions. This would be the balancing factor for maintaining necessary equilibrium in the family.

Adult male members of the family would have the responsibility of earning for the family to meet its needs, and to provide shelter and protection to the female members and children of the family. Female members would have the responsibility of taking care of the in-house needs of male members of family, and raising the kids in line with the culture and traditions of the family. Elder female members of the family would have the responsibility of grooming up the younger female members of the family in the desired direction.

Each new generation would learn the family values from their mothers and grandmothers, and in this manner the female members of the family would play the crucial role through the formative years of growing children. Spirituality would be an essential part of the family values, and women folk would be the custodian and deliverer of these values to each next generation through their growing up process.

Single spouse system and fidelity would be the norm. Exceptions would be found in the context of political marriages where a king would offer his daughter to another king and thus, the two ruling families would unite and not be threat to each other. Such marriages would primarily be conducted for maintaining power-balance and political equilibrium. These would be exceptions not rule, and we have references to many kings having only one wife.

How Hindu family structure changed so drastically that now we hardly see any evidence of our earlier system.

The whole system, however, changed after brutal onslaught of Islam and its direct interference in Hindu way of family life through forced conversions and forced marriages of Hindu girls and Hindu women into Muslim powerful families. This is when family values started deteriorating substantially though it did preserve a lot of it, as we can see from the testimonies of Sir Thomas Munro as presented below, even after thousand years of inhumane oppression that Max Muller called an inferno and wondered "how any nation could have survived such an inferno without being turned into devils themselves."

If a good system of agriculture, unrivalled manufacturing skill, a capacity to produce whatever can contribute to either convenience or luxury, schools established in every village for teaching, reading, writing, and arithmetic, the general practice of hospitality and charity amongst each other, and above all, a treatment of the female sex full of confidence, respect, and delicacy, are among the signs which denote a civilized people-then the Hindus are not inferior to the nations of Europe, and if civilization is to become an article of trade between England and Bhaarat Varsh, I am convinced that England will gain by the import cargo. Sir Thomas Munro, quoted in Mill's History, vol. i. p. 371, re-quoted by Max Muller, p 57 p 231

The True Culprits have remained unidentified all along.

There was so much of beauty left even until early 19th century that the eminent Governor of the then Madras Presidency wrote:

If civilization is to become an article of trade between England and Bhaarat Varsh, I am convinced that England will gain by the import cargo.

This would mean that real downfall has occurred during past 170 years. All factors remaining constant the only variable has been Christian English education system forcibly imposed on the Hindus by systematic elimination of ancient Hindu education system [documentary evidence in Hidden face of Christianity].

Hindu Family Values were totally transformed by the Christian English Education system, which was predominantly guided by the values propagated by Jesus Christ in the Christian Bible.

Oxford Dictionary p 1249, p 792, p 1143 New Testament is the second part of the Christian Bible; Gospel is the record of Christ's life and teachings in the first four books of the New Testament; St. Matthew was an Apostle, and the author of the first Gospel; p 1099 St. Luke was an evangelist, and the author of the third Gospel; p 1928, p 77 St. Thomas was an Apostle; Each of the twelve chief disciples of Jesus Christ is an Apostle.

Christian Bible New Testament Matthew 10:34 Think not that I am come to send peace on earth: I came not to send peace, but a sword. 10:35 For I am come to set a man at variance against his father, and the daughter against the mother, and the daughter in law against her mother in law. 10:36 And a man's foe shall be they of his own household. 10:37 He that loveth father or mother more than me is not worthy of me. 12: 30 He that is not with me is against me.

Christian Bible New Testament Luke 12:51 Suppose ye that I am come to give peace on earth? I tell you, Nay; but rather division: 12:52 For from henceforth there shall be five in one house divided, three against two, and two against three. 12:53 The father shall be divided against the son, and the son against the father; the mother against the daughter, and the daughter against the mother; the mother in law against her daughter in law, and the daughter in law against her mother in law. 14:26 If any man come to me, and hate not his father, and mother, and wife, and children, and brethren, and sisters, yea, and his own life also, he cannot be my disciple. [Nay a negative answer Oxford Dictionary p 1237]

Gospel of Thomas 16 Jesus said: Perhaps men think that I came to cast peace on the world; and they do not know that I came to cast division upon earth, fire, sword, war. For five will be in a house; there will be three against two and two against three, the father against the son and the son against the father. And they will stand because they are single ones. 56 Jesus said:

He who will not hate his father and his mother cannot be my disciple. And he who will not hate his brothers and sisters, and carry his cross as I have, will not become worthy of me.

[Gospel of Thomas as quoted in The Myth of Saint Thomas and Mylapore Shiva Temple, p 76 n]

To understand Jesus's agenda, as documented in the pages of Christian Bible, you may want to study Christianity in a different Light. Christian missionary educators taught the Hindus for past six generations and media experts created the image in the minds of the Hindus that ancient Hindu Joint Family structure was essentially an evil social structure.

This paved the way for promoting Split Family structure which has now been refined to such levels that gradually Single Parent system is becoming the norm in the Christian World that we mistakenly identify as Western world, and aping them faithfully we too are rapidly following their footsteps.

Marriages under Hindu Joint Family System

Marriage was one of the most significant aspects of Family Dharm. Marriage was not considered simply as union of two bodies. Marriage was a significant social event. It was union of two families and family traditions.

Marriages were decided with great care. Several aspects were considered. Not only boy and girl were important, but their parents were also important; so were family lineage, parental characters, parental nature, their values, their traditions, their health, their history and so many things.

Today boy and girl argue, why we need to look at parents, and what character and values they represent; we do not have to marry parents, we have to marry each other. Fine as it sounds, and nice as it feels, we tend to forget 'science' that we are so proud of, which has started understanding a little bit of the relevance of genes in human behavioural pattern. The hereditary attributes play their role in the long run and we find these lovebirds start splitting after a while.

Few years ago, I looked at divorce rates in North America exceeding 50%, while these statistics did not tell us the full story, for they covered only those who were legally married, and such couples often find separation and divorce process pretty demanding, considering future of children involved and therefore, not all broken marriages result in legal divorce.

A very large segment of married couple in North America (I speak of Canada, and assume it would be same in USA) are those called common-law where the boy and girl live together like husband and wife, have children, file tax returns as common-law spouses, for most purposes they are like married couple except they are not legally married.

Most of them are youngsters who have not yet planned children, and these marriages break fairly easy as compared to legal marriages, for all they need is to split, and start living separate. These are high ratio cases. Thus, if we were to take these into account, then total divorces (where divorce would mean essentially all failed marriages), would probably exceed 75%.

What a great system it is that does not stand the test of time, that does not stand the test of success in the desired venture that fails and fails, and finally gets reduced to multiple experiments with life! This, we call modern social structure, and we gloat at its supposedly advanced nature.

There is lot to learn from the systems of olden days that we look down upon thinking we have progressed! Have we? Except that we satisfy our ego by consoling ourselves with such inflated self-estimates!

The Secret of Stable Hindu marriages of yesteryears ~ a meticulous system of mathematics applied to human lives.

We may have occasionally heard about extraordinary accomplishments of Hindu mathematics. The Christian World, however, prefers to attribute them to the Greeks and (pre-Islamic) Arabs who basically imported the knowledge from the Hindus and then popularized with the people of Europe.

The foundation of Family Dharm was on the premises of the institution of marriage. Arranged marriages demonstrated great stability and reflected high success rate.

This was ensured by a meticulous system of mathematics applied to human lives. Based on time and place of birth of a human being, it could calculate with fair amount of accuracy the life span of the individual. This helped match-making in a manner that one of the spouses does not have to live very long without the other.

The system could calculate the ego development of the marrying partners. This helped match-making with due caution to conflicting egos between the boy and the girl in consideration.

The system could calculate with fair amount of accuracy the degree of magnetic control or amenability either spouse will have on the other. This helped match-making with a view to harmony between the two.

The system could calculate with considerable accuracy the sexual compatibility between the boy and girl in question. This helped match-making with regard to this very essential factor in a satisfying marriage.

The system considered sexual compatibility in physical as well as emotional context. It may be difficult for modern people to visualize that a mathematical system could be capable of ascertaining such details without reference to medical and psychological systems.

Well, that difficulty in perception is natural because modern education system has not tried to evolve mathematical modules applied to human lives. It has not tried so because the modern Christian education system is based on an inflated ego that it has nothing to learn from ancient Hindu systems. More significantly, the modern education system is based on knowledge base of the Christian World, which would not want to entertain the thought that Hindu world could have had better developed modules for social, economical, judicial and other processes.

Returning to the mathematical system we have been referring to, it had developed the capability of determining the psychological dispositions of the intended couple. This helped in (a) ascertaining mental qualities and (b) estimating likely affection for each other, this being very significant element in matchmaking. Then the system calculated the temperament and character of the couple concerned where compatibility of temperament was looked at for a satisfactory marriage union.

Finally, system looked at nervous energy indicating the physiological and to certain extent hereditary factors. This helped matchmaking with a view to the children that would be borne of such couple, for a marriage was not meant only for the present generation but also for the future generation of the society to come.

All these factors could be translated into mathematical module because the Creation and maintenance of this Universe itself works on a mathematical module of high precision. The method was widely followed and its results have shown over thousands of years of its application.

In modern times its use has dwindled, for an image has been successfully created that whatever modern Christian education system does not teach us is essentially superstitious. The result of our modernity has already started showing on our present day family structure.

The technique was not an end in itself.

Here, you need to understand another fundamental relating to this Creation. That is: nothing is stand alone in isolation to the exclusion of everything else. Do not think that any one aspect of esoteric knowledge would suffice for you to understand the entire gamut of complexities involved in the process of Creation.

Simply put you need to understand that the module I spoke of ~ applied mathematics to human lives ~ is not stand alone. Its well understood application does ensure substantially a stable married life but in itself, it is not the only means to that end.

Election of the right partner at the initial stage by application of that mathematical module can ensure a stable beginning and a stable journey but then that needs to be complemented with some other equally significant modules relevant to human lives. You cannot ignore other modules and expect the entire fruit by sticking to only one. There are several aspects of esoteric knowledge that have not only remained limited within the boundaries of Science but graduated beyond to the State of Art where they have become relevant to human lives in manners that you may not begin to think because your Christian English educators have systematically buried them over the past two centuries. I am not going to discuss them here but I will return with them someday.

In today's circumstances this clarification is all the more necessary because it is the age of quick fix where every one tends to look for an allopathic medicine for every headache ~ a pill that would instantly relieve you of the headache not bothering to fix the root problem.

Besides, the close association with and total dependence on Christian English education system for six generations has made us not only forget those essentials but also treat them as meaningless superstitions because an ignorant education system can give you no better knowledge ~ a culture that cares not to understand Mother Nature but only attempts to conquer it like all arrogant fools do can give you no better understanding of matters that truly affect your lives. All they do is whole lot of trial and errors and give them impressive names like psychiatry and various derivatives of those kinds which are nothing but a huge money making racket in the name of scientific education.

How we lost all that.

Christian British systematically destroyed ancient Hindu education system.

They withdrew all governmental support to any form of education that remotely related to Hindu system. Through Christian English education system they filled the minds of Hindu children that all of Hindu system of knowledge was nothing but superstition. Through six generations of Christian English education you have learned to think of them as superstition. Superstition is something that you believe in blindly. Aren't you doing the same thing? Didn't you believe blindly what those ignorant Christian British educators told you. Neither did they examine the validity of Hindu branches of knowledge, nor did you examine them. And, you blindly believed them all to be superstition. This belief of yours ~ isn't it a superstition by itself?

They killed our knowledge base, they let it get lost. If few kept it alive through generations without adequate support system and if they lost most of it, you call them quacks. Who is responsible for the degeneration of Hindu knowledge base? Are these whom you call quacks? Or, are those who methodically wiped it out over the period of time?

Sati was Started for Preserving Caste

With the much discussed subject, now in India, about a so called "sati" of Charanshah, in village Satpura in Uttar Pradesh, some information about this evil in Hindu social system, may be not only informative but also educative to the masses who wish to build a new India on new values.

Condition of Widows in Ancient India

In India, the condition of women in general, was made more dreadful than that of a slave, but the lot of widows was always very hard and they were forced to lead a horrible life of torture, disfigurement, tonsure and deprivation, with an enforced strict ban on remarriage. They were compelled to undergo sex with other men for procreation under the system of Niyoga. As if this was not enough, a peculiar system existed in India, whereby widows were burnt alive on the funeral pyre of their dead husbands. The practice existed among the higher castes mainly, though it was given a honourable and prestigious outlook among the masses by various means adopted by the Brahmins.

Why this system started in India? It was for maintaining the caste, which was very important for the welfare of those, who are benefited by it. And as the caste system grew more rigid, the sati become more strict. Notable example is Bengal, where it was enforced more strictly because of "Kulin system", where any of the hundreds of disgruntled young wives could easily poison the old man.

Position of Women

Ms. Shakuntala Rao Shastri, in her "Women in Sacred Laws" very aptly describes the pitiable condition of women before the Britishers came to India:

> *"True it is that anyone who has witnessed the pathetic condition of women in India at the dawn of British rule cannot but be shocked at it: the enforced child marriage, the exposure of female children, putting to death female children by throwing them at the junction of the Ganges and the sea, the violence used to make women follow the Sati rite and thus end their miserable existence, the*

shameful treatment accorded to a widow, the (in)famous kulinism which made marriage a profession rather than a sacrament, made woman not only an object of pity but many a woman sighed in the secret recess for her heart and wished that she had never been born a woman in this unfortunate country." [Shastri Shakuntala Rao, "Women in Sacred Laws" p. 171]

The situation described by the learned Vedic Scholar is at the time of dawn of British occupation, but since how long it was in existence? The reply is that this was the situation since the fall of Buddhism around tenth century AD. That the women enjoyed high position in Buddhist period can be judged by a mere glance at the Buddhist law being practiced in India before tenth century AD and which is practiced in all the Buddhist countries even now.

Today after passing of Ambedkar's Hindu Code, piece meal, the Hindu Laws of Marriage, Adoption, Succession, and other related Laws have been changed to a great extent. But prior to 1956, the Old Hindu Brahmanic Law was in force, under which the condition of women was pitiable. To get some idea of how these laws were made more and more cruel is seen if one considers that original law of India was Buddhist Law. BUDDHIST LAW WAS THE NATIONAL LAW OF INDIA, BECAUSE FROM THE HISTORICAL PERIOD, THE RELIGION OF INDIA WAS BUDDHISM. IT WAS THE MAIN STREAM. The Brahmins succeeded in causing the fall of Buddhism, at the cost of women and Shudras. They had to bear the brunt of all evils, to maintain the supremacy of the Brahmins.

Epigraphic Evidences of Sati

Ms. Shakuntala Rao Shastri describes the "Memorial stelae". They are small stone uprights sculptured with figures and inscriptions, and are called Devli, and are found in abundance in Rajputana. They are erected in commemoration of women immolating themselves on funeral pyres of their husbands. The earliest one found in Jodhpur state at Gatiyala is dated 890 AD. The earliest of these stelae is found in Eran in Sagar District in M.P. and is dated 510 A. D. Thus the practice of Sati was coming to vogue in sixth century AD. [Shastri Shakuntala Rao, Ibid. p. 130]

The Annals of Kashmir by Kallahna of 12th century, mentions some instances where, in addition to wife / wives others like concubines, slaves, mother nurse, friends and followers also practiced Anumaran. Earliest mentioned was in 902 King Samkaravarman, in 1081 King Ananta, in 1161 King Malla, and the last one mentioned was in 12th century of King Sussala. [Shastri Shakuntala Rao, Ibid. p.130]

Not only it was practiced in North, West and Central India, the examples of Inscriptions from Epigraphica Carnataka show that the custom existed in South India also. Anumarana was practiced after deaths of various kings like-in 1130 AD Kadamba King Tailapa, Ganga King Nitimarga, and Satyavakya Kongunivarman Lord of Nandagiri, both of whom lived in 915 AD, in 1220 AD King Ballala, and in 1180 King Bammarasa. [Ibid. p. 132 ff.]

When a Tomar King in Gujrath died, his 90,000 queens were requested not to commit sati. They consulted their Kula-brahmana, who advised them to commit sati as Veda verse 18/877 mentions "Agne" and not "Agre", just for the sake of golden coins, thus condemning these 90,000 women to flames. 3000 queens committed sati with king of Vijaynagar. On conquest of Jaselmere by Muslims, 24 thousand queens committed sati. Old cremation place has got inscriptions mentioning names of those committing sati. 112 queens of king Amarsing of Bundi, 88 queens of Keshosing, Jagirdar of Dharampur, 78 queens of Surendrasing of Palitana. Some social reformists tried to prevent sati of 95 queens of Bharatpur, but they had to commit sati. [Francis D'Souza, Loksatta, 3.12.99]

Why Sati was Started: Thus we find that excepting the solitary instance mentioned by Diodoras, which occured in a foreign land, and the persons involved were perhaps from foreign tribes settled in India during those times, the practice started from the time of decline and uitimate fall of Buddhism after seventh century. Still we find Banabhatta (7th century) in the court of Harshavardhana and later Medhatithi (9th century) condemning the practice.

The more important question is why this system started, developed and why it attained such a high respect. Sati custom in India has to be considered in combination with other customs of Child girl marriage with an elderly man and prohibition of widows to remarry. All these customs were imposed by the Brahmins in order to prevent transgression of caste rules. This was explained by Dr. Ambedkar as early as in 1919, ["Castes in India", W&S. vol. I, p. 5 ff.] while dealing with genesis and mechanism of Castes. The following are the salient points from it.

Endogamy is the only characteristic peculiar to caste. No civilized society in today's world shows more survivals of primitive times than Indian society. One such primitive practice is of exogamy long given up by the world but is still favoured in India. Though there are no clans in India, clan system is savoured, as there is prohibition on not only "sapinda" marriages but also on "sagotra" marriages among the Hindus. The various gotras and other totemic organizations have always been exogamus. When endogamy was superimposed over sagotra exogamy, a caste was formed.

To preserve and maintain this caste, inter caste marriages were banned. In case of death of a spouse, the other spouse was likely to marry outside the caste. To prevent this happening various means were adopted. These are:

1. Sati or burning of a widow on the funeral pyre of her deceased husband.
2. Enforced widowhood by which she is forced not to marry and
3. Girl marriage with an aged man.

All the medieval Brahmanic texts eulogize these customs in very glamourous language but give no reasons for them. Dr. Ambedkar, who calls all this eulogy as a sugar coating of the barbarous pill, gives the reasons:

> *"... Sati, enforced widowhood and girl marriage are customs that were primarily intended to solve the problem of the surplus man and surplus woman in a caste and to maintain its endogamy. Strict endogamy could not be preserved without these customs, while caste without endogamy is a fake." [Ibid., p.14]*

The Brahmins enclosed themselves into a caste, thus forcing others to be the other caste. This was divided and further subdivided into multiple non-Brahmin castes and the institution of castes spread through the length and breadth of India. This spread was due to the tendency of imitation of Brahmins by the others. As these customs were very harsh and barbarous, the imitation was imperfect and we find that nearer a caste is to Brahmins more strictly it insisted on observance of these customs. Example of Kulinism in Bengal, which also was a movement to preserve the Caste and ensure supremacy of Brahmins, is discussed elsewhere. That the reason, these customs had to be enforced strictly in Bengal following Kulinism, was to prevent any one among the hundreds of dissatisfied wives of a kulin man from easily poisoning him, could be easily appreciated.

6

HISTORY OF SOCIAL RELATIONS IN INDIA

INTRODUCTION

No aspect of Indian history has excited more controversy than India's history of social relations. Western indologists and Western-influenced Indian intellectuals have seized upon caste divisions, untouchability, religious obscurantism, and practices of dowry and sati as distinctive evidence of India's perennial backwardness. For many Indologists, these social ills have literally come to define India-and have become almost the exclusive focus of their writings on India. During the colonial period, it served the interests of the British (and their European cohorts) to exaggerate the democratic character of their own societies while diminishing any socially redeeming features of society in India (and other colonized nations). Social divisions and inequities were a convenient tool in the arsenal of the colonizers. On the one hand, tremendous tactical gains could be achieved by playing off one community against the other. On the other hand, there were also enormous psychological benefits in creating the impression that India was a land rife with uniquely abhorrent social practices that only an enlightened foreigner could attempt to reform. India's social ills were discussed with a contemptuous cynicism and often with a willful intent to instill a sense of deep shame and inferiority.

Strong elements of such colonial imagery continue to dominate the landscape of Western Indology. A liberal, dynamic West embracing universal human values is posed against an obdurate and unchanging East clinging to odious social values and customs.

It is little wonder, therefore, that India's intellectuals have been unable to either fully understand the historic dynamics and context which gave life to these social practices or find effective solutions for their cure. Many historians and social activists appear to have tacitly accepted the notion that caste divisions in society are a uniquely Indian feature and that Indian society has been largely unchanged since the writing of the Manusmriti which provides formal sanction to such social inequities.

But caste-like divisions are neither uniquely Indian nor has Indian society been as socially stagnant as commonly believed. In all non-egalitarian societies where wealth and political power were unequally distributed, some form of social inequity appeared and often meant hereditary privileges for the elite and legally (or socially) sanctioned discrimination against those considered lower down in the social hierarchy.

In fact, caste-like divisions are to be found in the history of most nations-whether in the American continent, or in Africa, Europe or elsewhere in Asia. In some societies, caste-like divisions were relatively simple, in others more complex. For instance, in Eastern Africa some agricultural societies were divided between land-owning and landless tribes (or clans) that eventually took on caste-like characteristics. Priests and warriors enjoyed special privileges in the 15th C. Aztec society of Mexico as did the Samurais (warrior nobles) and priests of medieval Japan. Notions of purity and defilement were also quite similar in Japanese society and members of society who carried out "unclean" tasks were treated as social outcasts-just as in India.

Amongst the most stratified of the ancient civilizations was the Roman Civilization where in addition to state-sanctioned slavery, there were all manner of caste-like inequities coded into law. Even in the Christian era, European feudalism provided all manner of hereditary privileges for the knights and landed barons (somewhat akin to India's Rajputs and Thakurs) and amongst the royalty, arranged marriages and dowry were just as common as in India. Discrimination against the artisans was also commonplace throughout Europe, and as late as the 19th century-artisans in Germany had to go through a separate court system to seek legal redress. They were not permitted to appeal to courts that dealt with the affairs of the nobility and the landed gentry. (For instance, Beethoven wrote numerous letters to German judicial authorities pleading that he not be treated as a second-class citizen-that as Germany's pre-eminent composer he deserved better treatment.)

A common pattern that seems to emerge from a study of several such ancient and medieval societies is that priests and warriors typically formed an elite class in most medieval societies and social privileges varied according to social rank; in settled agriculture based societies, this was usually closely related to ownership of land.

For instance, we find no evidence of caste-like discrimination in societies where land was collectively owned and jointly cultivated, or where goods and services were exchanged within the village on the basis of barter, and there was no premium assigned to any particular type of work. All services and all forms of human labour were valued equally. Such village communes may have once existed throughout India and some appear to have survived until quite recently-especially in the hills, (such as in parts of Himachal and the North East, including Assam and Tripura), but also in Orissa and parts of Central India. In such societies, we also see little evidence of gender discrimination.

In India, caste and gender discrimination appear to become more pronounced with the advent of hereditary and authoritarian ruling dynasties, a powerful state bureaucracy, the growth of selective property rights, and the domination of Brahmins over the rural poor in agrahara villages. But this process was neither linear nor always irreversible. As old ruling dynasties were overthrown, previously existing caste equations and caste hierarchies were also challenged and modified.

In many parts of India this process may have taken several centuries to crystallize and caste rigidity may be a much more recent phenomenon than has been commonly portrayed. The impression that caste divisions were always strictly enforced, or that there were no challenges to caste rigidity does not seem to square with a dispassionate examination of the Indian historical record.

It should also be emphasized that caste-distinctions were not the only way, or even the most egregious way in which social inequities manifested themselves in older societies. In ancient Greece and Rome, the institution of slavery was at least as cruel a practice, if not worse. (It is therefore quite ironic how the slave-owning Greek states are revered by Western intellectuals as the world's first "democratic" societies but ancient India is denigrated for it's incomprehensible social ills.)

Levels and degree of caste discrimination in India have varied with time and there has been both upward and downward mobility of castes and social groups. Going by the strictures outlined in the Manusmriti, one might conclude that caste distinctions were set in stone, rigidly enforced and the possibilities of caste mobility completely circumscribed. But a closer examination of the historical record suggests otherwise.

Already in the Upanishadic period there were tensions between Brahmins and Kshatriyas, and there are explicit parables in the Upanishadic texts illustrating how an enlightened Kshatriya was able to exceed a Brahmin in spiritual wisdom and philosophical knowledge. In the Mahabharatha, there are references to a Brahmin warrior suggesting that caste categories were not entirely inflexible.

There is also criticism of parasitism amongst Brahmins in some of the texts from the Upanishadic period, and social commentators emphasized how those who reneged on their social obligations were undeserving of their caste privileges.

This is an important point because it suggests that there was an implied social contract that involved both privileges and social obligations. The monarch might have enjoyed immense power and prestige, and exacted numerous rights over the common people, but also had the obligation to defend the people-to protect them from invaders, to dispense justice in an unprejudiced manner and assist in the development and preservation of irrigation facilities and roads. Failure to meet such expectations could and did lead to revolts, and dynasties rose and fell within a matter of few generations.

Closing Comment: It is okay for a person-having no one to extend to him objective or satisfactory help and guidance in the matters relating to spiritual fulfilment, prayer and the place to pray-to choose a mode of worship suited to his needs and resources. Incidentally, worthless worships, myths / tales, hate-mongering and evil/corrupt deeds are detrimental to spirituality / faith. It is also worth noting that all-men, women, believers, nonbelievers and others-have the same rights and freedoms and they all deserve equal protection and consideration under a law that is constantly evolving with time and according to the need of the society.

Thus, a contemporary civil legal code-progressive and reflective of the peoples and times-seems preferable to a law that may be perceived as antiquated, dictatorial, discriminatory, cultist or religious. The notion that a group / nation run by decree will be foremost in freedoms and human rights is misguided. A diverse, pluralistic and progressive society subjected to an autocratic or religious law / rule can quickly drift into a puritanical, singular and regressive system as the dissenting people either run away from it or totally succumb to the ruling dogma to ensure their own safety. Thus, the sectarian territorialization or vision of the world must cease, and any regime adverse to progressiveness should be shunned.

In addition, the practices of casteism (social stratification in terms of vocation or caste), animal abuse, child labour, gender discrimination, dowry, veil (e.g. the body and face covering apparel) etc. must stop. It is also in the interest of humanity to rise above various tenets and practices and, while not ignoring the local issues, tackle serious global problems: rapidly deteriorating environment, depleting natural resources, disappearing flora and fauna, and overpopulation-already indicating a population exceeding the reasonable limit of about five billion people worldwide.

VEDAS AND THE CASTE

The 'Varna' popularly known as the 'Caste system' is perhaps the most explosive topics in Hinduism, which so often gives handle to Non-Hindus to bash Hinduism. Popular misconceptions say that the Vedic religion encourages division of human beings based on one's birth. As a result, some people have been kept backward and uneducated while others have abused this misconceptions and misinformation for personal gains. Much of this misconception can be attributed to the use of the words 'Varna' and 'Jati' interchangeably. A closer analysis will reveal just how wrong these misconceptions are.

Caste: "The word caste is not a word that is indigenous to India. It originates in the Portuguese word casta which means race, breed, race or lineage. However, during the 19th century, the term caste increasingly took on the connotations of the word race. Thus, from the very beginning of western contact with the subcontinent European constructions have been imposed on Indian systems and institutions. The caste system had been a fascination of the British since their arrival in India.

Coming from a society that was divided by class, the British attempted to equate the caste system to the class system. As late as 1937 Professor T. C. Hodson stated that: "Class and caste stand to each other in the relation of family to species. The general classification is by classes, the detailed one by castes. The former represents the external, the latter the internal view of the social organization." The difficulty with definitions such as this is that class is based on political and economic factors, caste is not. Caste was seen as the essence of Indian society, the system through which it was possible to classify all of the various groups of indigenous people according to their ability, as reflected by caste, to be of service to the British. It was not until 1872 that a planned comprehensive census was attempted. This was done under the direction of Henry Beverely, Inspector General of Registration in Bengal. The census went well beyond counting heads or even enquiring into sex ratios or general living conditions. Among the many questions were enquiries regarding nationality, race, tribe, religion and caste." (from The Indian Caste System and the British, by Kevin Hobson).

Varna: The root word for Varna is 'Vri' which means one's occupation. The Varna Dharma was based on division of labour.

This division was solely based on the attitude of an individual and his/her propensity for performing certain duties according to Gunas (qualities). There are three Gunas-Sattva (white), Rajas (red), and Tamas (black).

Jati: The Root word for 'jati' is 'jan', which means Birth.

The Issue: The issue of Varna Dharma is highly misunderstood. There are many issues and reasons for the decline of Varna Dharma. A key point in the Varna Dharma is the definition and Gunas associated with various classes of Varnas. This paper deals with following two main issues;

- Definition and duties of the Varna Dharma
- Basis of division-Gunas or birth

Supremacy of Vedas

First part in the understanding of Varna Dharma is to accept supremacy of Vedas in all the Hindu scriptures. As Swami Vivekananda said "The Vedas are our only authority, thus says the Shukla Yajur Veda (XXVI, 2). The Smritis, Puranas, Tantras-all these are acceptable as far as they agree the Vedas; and wherever they are contradictory, they are to be rejected as unreliable".

Even Manu Smriti declares that the Vedas are the supreme authority. The knowledge of the sacred law is prescribed for those who are not given to the acquisition of wealth and to the gratification of their desires; to those who seek the knowledge of the sacred law the supreme authority the revelation (Sruti).

What Constitutes Vedic Knowledge

The second part in the understanding of Varna Dharma is what constitutes Vedic knowledge.

Nirukta says on this topic; "He, who reads the Vedas even with proper accents, but does not know their meanings, is like a tree weighed down by its fruit, branches, leaves and flowers, or like a beast of burden carrying on its back grain which it can not eat. But he, who understands their meanings and acts up to their teachings by avoiding sin and leading a virtuous life, enjoys perfect happiness in this world, and eternal bliss hereafter in consequence thereof", Nirukta 1, 18.

Once supremacy of Vedas and the meanings of Vedic education are understood, all the doubts about Varna Dharma will evaporate. There is no division in Vedic knowledge. The division is in our ignorance.

Origin of Varnas

The first reference to the origin of Varna Dharma comes from the Rig Veda and subsequently explained in the Gita and Smritis (e.g. Manu, Prashar etc.).

Rig Veda: The Purusa Sukta has the first reference to the origin of four groups.

The Brahmana (spiritual wisdom and splendour) was His Mouth; the Kshatriya (administrative and military prowess) His Arms became. His Thighs the Vaishya (commercial and business enterprise) was; of His Feet the Sudra (productive and sustaining force) was born. (by Swami Krishnananda The Divine Life Society Sivananda Ashram, Rishikesh, India)

Gita: The Gita elaborates on the origin of Varnas. "The fourfold order was created by Me according to the divisions of quality (Guna) and work (karma); though I am its creator, know Me to be incapable of action or change." (from The Bhagavad Gita by S. Radhakrishnan)

Definition and Duties of Varnas

Brahman (the Supreme Reality) is not known to those who are possessed of avarice, delusion, fear, egotism, lust, anger, and sin or possessed of (unable to bear) heat and cold, hunger and thirst, or mental resolve and indecision, or pride of birth in a Brahmin (priest) family, or vanity in having read a mass of books on Mukti (liberation or salvation).

Gita: "There is no being on earth, or again in heaven among the gods, that is liberated from the three qualities (Sattva, Rajas, and Tamas) born of Nature." "Of Brahmans, Kshatriyas and Vaishyas, as also the Sudras, O Arjuna, the duties are distributed according to the qualities born of their own nature."

> *"Serenity, self-restraint, austerity, purity, forgiveness and also uprightness, knowledge, realization and belief in God are the duties of the Brahmans, born of their own nature."*

"Prowess, splendour, firmness, dexterity and also not fleeing from battle, generosity and lordliness are the duties of Kshatriyas, born of their own nature."

"Agriculture, cattle-rearing and trade are the duties of the Vaishya merchant class), born of their own nature; and action consisting of service is the duty of the Sudras, born of their own nature." (All meanings from Srimad Bhagavad Gita by Swami Chinmayananda)

Varna by Birth: The next issue in the Varna system is to understand the order and how to belong to one Varna. Is it by birth or by 'guna'.

Channdogaya Upanishad: The following story (Channdogaya Upanishad, 4.1.4) reveals that Brahminhood does not depend on birth but on character and Gunas.

"Satyakama, the son of Jabala, addressed his mother and said "I wish to become a brahmacharin, mother. Of what family am I?" She said to him: I do not know, my child, of what family thou art. In my youth, when I had to move about much as a servant, I conceived thee. So I do not know of what family thou art. I am Jabala by name. Thou art Satyakama. Say that thouart Satyakama Jabala."

He going to Gautama, the son of Haridrumat, said to him: I wish to become a brahmacharin with thee, Sire. May I come to you?

He said to him, "Of what family art thou, my friend?"

He replied: "I do not know, Sire, of what family I am. I asked my mother, and she answered: "In my youth, when I had to move about much as a servant, I conceived thee. So I do not know of what family thou art. I am Jabala by name. Thou art Satyakama.' I am therefore Satyakama Jabala, Sire."

He said to him" "No one but a true Brahmin would speak out. Go and fetch fuel, I shall initiate thee. Thou has not swerved from the truth."

Vajra Suchikopanishad: I now proceed to declare the vajrasuuchi-the weapon that is the destroyer of ignorance-which condemns the ignorant and praises the man of divine vision.

There are four castes-the Brahman, the Kshatriya, the vaishya, and the shudra. Even the smritis declare in accordance with the words of the Vedas that the Brahman alone is the most important of them.

Then this needs to be examined. What is meant by the Brahman ? Is it a jiva ? Is it a body ? Is it a class ? It is Gyana ? Is it karma ? Or is it a doer of Dharma ?

To begin with: is jiva the Brahman ? No. Since the jiva is the same in the many past and future bodies (of all persons), and since the jiva is the same in all of the many bodies obtained through the force of karma, there jiva is not the Brahman. Then is the body the Brahman ? No. Since the body, as it is made up of the five elements, is the same for all people down to chandalas, etc., since old age and death, dharma and adharma are found to be common to them all, since there is no absolute distinction that the Brahmans are white-coloured, the Kshatriyas red, the vaishyas yellow, and the shudras dark, and since in burning the corpse of his father, etc., the stain of the murder of a Brahman, etc., will accrue to the son, etc., therefore the body is not the Brahman. Then is a class the Brahman ? No. Since many rishis have sprung from other castes and orders of creation-Rishyashringa was born of deer; kaushika, of kusha grass; jaambuka of a jackal; Valmiki of valmika (an ant-hill); Vyasa of a fisherman's daughter; Gautama, of the posteriors of a hare; Vashishtha of Urvasi (a celestial nymph in the court of Indra); and agastya of a water-pot; thus have we heard. Of these, many rishis outside the caste have stood first among the teachers of divine wisdom; therefore a class is not the Brahman.

Is Gyana the Brahman ? No. Since there were many Kshatriyas and others well versed in the cognition of divine Truth, therefore Gyana is not the Brahman.

Then is karma the Brahman ? No. Since the prarabdha, sanchita, aagami karmas are the same for all beings, and since all people perform their actions impelled by karma, therefore karma is not the Brahman.

Then is the doer of dharma (virtuous actions) the Brahman ? No. Since there are many Kshatriyas, etc., who are givers of gold, therefore a doer of virtuous actions is not the Brahman.

Who indeed then is Brahman ? Whoever he may be, he who has directly realised his aatmaa and who is directly cognizant, like the myrobalan in his palm, of his aatmaa, that is without a second, that is devoid of class and actions, that is free from the faults of the six stains (hunger, thirst, grief, confusion, old age, and death) and the six changes (birth, existence etc.), that is of the nature of truth, knowledge, bliss and eternity, that is without any change in itself, that is the substratum of all the kalpas, that exists penetrating all things that pervades everything within and without as aakaash, that is of nature of undivided bliss, that cannot be reasoned about and that is known only by direct cognition. He who by the reason of having obtained his wishes is devoid of the faults of thirst after worldly objects and passions, who is the possessor of the qualifications beginning with saama (dama, uparati, titikshaa, samadhana, sraddha), who is free from emotion, malice, thirst after worldly objects, desire, delusion, etc., whose mind is untouched by pride, egoism, etc., who possesses all these qualities and means-he only is the Brahman. Such is the opinion of the veda, the smritis, the itihasa, and the puranas. Otherwise one cannot obtain the status of a Brahman. One should meditate on his aatma as sachchidananda, and the non-dual Brahman. Yea, one should meditate on his aatma as the sachchidananda Brahman. Such is the Upanishad.

Right to Study Vedas

Contrary to existing view everyone irrespective of caste or sex, has right to read the Veda or hear it read.

Yajur Veda: "As I have given this Word (i.e. the four Vedas) which is the word of salvation for all making-Brahmans, Kshatriyas, Vaishyas, Sudras, women, servants, aye, even the lowest of the low, so shoul you all do, i.e. teach and preach Veda. Let all men therefore read and recite, teach, and preach the Veda and thereby acquire true knowledge, practice virtue, shun vice, and consequently being freed from all sorrow and pain, enjoy true happiness." 26,2 (translated from Sayarth Prakash, Ch 3, page 78).

Atharva Veda: "Just as boys acquire sound knowledge and culture by the practice of Brahmacharya and then marry girls of their own choice, who are young, well educated, loving and of like temperament, so should a girl practice Brahmacharya, study the Veda and other sciences and there by perfect her knowledge, refine her character, give her hand to a man of her own choice, who is young, learned and loving." (Xl, xvi, 3, 18.)

Brahma-Sutras: "Apasudradhikaranam: Topic 9 (Sutras 34-38) The right of the Sudras to the study of Vedas discussed Sugasya tadanadarasravanat tadadravanat suchyate hi I.3.34 (97) Suk: grief; Asya: his; Tat: that, namely that grief; Anadarasravanat: from hearing his (the Rishi's) disrespectful speech; Tada: then; Adravanat: because of going to him i.e, to Raikva; Suchyate: is referred to; Hi: because. (King Janasruti) was in grief on hearing some contemptuous words used about him by the sage in the form of a swan; owing to his approaching Raikva, overwhelming with that grief, Raikva called him Sudra; for it (the grief) is pointed at by Raikva.

The Purvapakshin says: The Sudras also have got bodies and desires. Hence they are also entitled. Raikva refers to Janasruti who wishes to learn from him by the name of Sudra. "Fie, necklace and carriage be thine, O Sudra, together with the cows" Chh. Up. IV-2 & 3.

But when he appears a second time, Raikva accepts his presents and teaches him. Smriti speaks of Vidura and others who were born from Sudra mothers as possessing highest knowledge. Therefore the Sudra has a claim to Brahma Vidya or knowledge of Brahman. This Sutra refutes the view and denies the right to the study of the Vedas for Sudra. The word 'Sudra' does not denote a Sudra by birth which is its conventional meaning, because Janasruti was a Kshatriya king. Here we will have to take the etymological meaning of the word which is, "He rushed into grief (Sukam abhi dudrava) or as "grief rushed on him" or as "he in his grief rushed to Raikva". The following Sutra also intimates that he was a Kshatriya.

Kshatriyatva: the state of his being a Kshatriya; Avagateh: on account of being known or understood; Cha: and; Uttaratra: latter on in a subsequent part of the text; Chaitrarathena: with Chaitraratha; Lingat: because of the indicatory sign or the inferential mark.

And because the Kshatriyahood (of Janasruti) is known from the inferential mark (supplied by his being mentioned) later on with Chaitraratha (who was a Kshatriya himself).

An argument in support of Sutra 34 is given. Janasruti is mentioned with the Kshatriya Chaitraratha Abhipratarin in connection with the same Vidya. Hence we can infer that Janasruti also was a Kshatriya because, as a rule, equals are mentioned together with equals. Hence the Sudras are not qualified for the knowledge of Brahman.

Samskaraparamarsat tadabhavabhilapacca (I.3.36) (99) Samskara: the purificatory ceremonies, the investiture with sacred thread; Paramarsat: because of the reference; Tat: that ceremony; Abhava: absence; Abhilapat: because of the declaration; Cha: and. Because purificatory ceremonies are mentioned (in the case of the twice-born) and their absence is declared (in the case of the Sudra).

The discussion on the privilege of Brahma Vidya on the part of Sudras is continued. In different places of the Vidyas the Upanayana ceremony is referred to. The Upanayana ceremony is declared by the scriptures to be a necessary condition for the study of all kinds of knowledge or Vidya. We read in Prasna Up. I-1 "Devoted to Brahman, firm in Brahman, seeking for the highest Brahman they, carrying fuel in their hands, approached the venerable Pippalada, thinking that he would teach them all that." Upanayana ceremony is meant for the higher castes. With reference to the Sudras on the other hand, the absence of ceremonies is frequently mentioned in the scriptures. "In the Sudra there is not any sin by eating prohibited food, and he is not fit for any ceremony" Manu X-12-6. A Sudra by birth cannot have Upanayana and other Samskaras without which the Vedas cannot be studied. Hence the Sudras are not entitled to the study of the Vedas. The next Sutra further strengthens the view that a Sudra can have no Samskara.

And on account of the prohibition in Smriti of (the Sudras) hearing, studying and understanding (the Veda) and performing Vedic rites (they are not entitled to the knowledge of Brahman).

Note: Sutras 34-38 of Brahma-Sutras disqualify the Sudras for the Knowledge of Brahman (Supreme Reality) through the study of the Vedas. But it is possible for them to attain that Knowledge through the Puranas and the epics (Ramayana and the Mahabharata)."

"Wherever it is declared (in the books of Rishis) that the Sudras are debarred from the study of the Veda, the prohibition simply amounts to this that he, that does not learn anything even after a good deal of teaching, being ignorant and destitute of understanding, is called a Sudra. It is useless for him to learn and for others to teach him any longer." Satyarth Prakash, chapter 3, 78.

Inter Movement in Varna

Can people by their actions move from one Varna to another? The answer is YES, which is another argument in favour of Varna not based on birth.

Gita: "By following his qualities of work, every man can become perfect. Now please hear from Me how this can be done. (By A. C Bhaktivedanta Swami Prabhupada)."

From Whom is the evolution of all beings, by Whom all this is pervaded, worshipping Him with one's own duty, man attains Perfection. (by Swami Chinmayananda)

Better is one's own duty (though) destitute of merits, than the duty of another wellperformed. He who does the duty ordained by his own nature incurs no sin. (by Swami Chinmayananda)

One should not give up the work suited to one's nature, O Son of Kunti (Arjuna), though it may be defective, for all enterprises are clouded by defects as fire by smoke. (The Bhagavadgita by S. Radhakrishnan).

Apastamba Sutras: "A low Class man may, by leading a virtuous life, rise to the level of a higher Class man and should be ranked as such. In like manner a high Class man can by leading a sinful life, sink down to the level of a Class lower than his, and should be considered as such." (Translation from Stayarth Prakash, chapter 4, page 100)

Manu Smriti

The scriptures are quoted out of context as if they are stand alone political statements. Manu Smriti is not very entertaining for Sudras is true, only when not understood properly. People take pride in quoting from Manu Smriti to show their knowledge and understanding, and also to put down Varna Dharma. A careful reading will give a different picture. Manu Smriti is very infamous for treatment of Sudras by popular belief. There are shlokas in Manu Smriti that debars a Sudra from learning any Vedic knowledge when read in isolation and not as one part of a scripture. The maximum damage to Varna Dharma was caused by piece meal acquisition and application of knowledge. Manu Smriti deals with all the four Varnas and not only Sudras. The first issue with Manu Smriti is what Vedic knowledge is and what different Varnas are.

Definitions and Duties of Varna: "The study of true sciences, the practice of Brahmacharya, the performance of Homa, the acceptance of truth and rejection of untruth, the dissemination of true knowledge, leading a virtuous life as enjoined by the Veda, the performance of seasonal Homa, the reproduction of good children, faithful discharge of the Five Great Daily Duties, and doing such other good works as are productive of beneficial results to the community, such as developing technical arts, association with the good and the learned, truthfulness in word, deed and thought, and devotion to public good and like, all these things go to make a Brahma. To Brahmans he assigned teaching and studying (the Veda), sacrificing for their own benefit and for others, giving and accepting (of alms).

Inter Movement of Varnas: "As the son of a Sudra may attain the rank of a Brahmin if he were to possess his qualifications, character and accomplishments, and as the son of a Brahmin may become a Sudra, if he sinks to his level in his character, inclinations and manners, even so must it be with him who springs from a Kshatriya; even so with him who is born of a Vaishya. In other words, a person should be ranked with the Class whose qualifications, accomplishments, and character he possesses.

> *"A Dwija as well his children who, instead of studying the Veda, wastes his time in doing other things soon goes down to the level of a Shudra." Manu Smriti 2, 168*

"A twice-born man who, not having studied the Veda, applies himself to other (and worldly study), soon falls, even while living, to the condition of a Sudra and his descendants (after him)." Manu Smriti 2, 168.

Special Treatment for Brahmans!: It is true that not very complementary and rude things were said about Sudras in Manu Smriti. But as shown in Manu Smriti (discussed in the definition section) that the position of Brahmin's was full of responsibility and not privileges. In (a case of) theft the guilt of a Sudra shall be eightfold, that of a Vaishya sixteen fold, that of a Kshatriya two-and-thirty fold, 8,337

That of a Brahmana sixty-fourfold, or quite a hundredfold, or (even) twice four-and-sixtyfold; (each of them) knowing the nature of the offence. 8,338 Guna or Birth-The Deciding Factor.

"A Brahmana who departs from the rule of conduct, does not reap the fruit of the Veda, but he who duly follows it, will obtain the full reward. (Manu Smriti 1,109)."

"Declares out Manu: Take the jewel of a woman for your wife, though she be of inferior descent. Learn supreme knowledge with service even from the man of low birth; and even from the Chandala, learn by serving him the way to salvation."

Is Breakdown in Varna Unexpected?

Prashar Smriti: Smriti created by sage Parashar and known by his name as 'Parashar Smriti, is the most benevolent for the modern Kali Yuga. Parashar has himself said:

Krite Tu Manavo Dharmastretayaam Gautamo Smritah ||

Dwapare Shankhalikhitaa Kalau Parasharah Smritah ||

Meaning-Manu Smriti was most relevant in Satya Yuga. In Treta, Smriti created by Gautam had most relevance whereas in Dwapar, Shankh's Smriti was mostly recognized. But in Kali Yuga, it is Parashar Smriti that by and large shows the way to the ignorant people.

Sri Ramacharitamanasa: Sri Ramacharitamanasa, Uttar-kanda, verses 97-98, explains very clearly that what happened and happening to Varna Dharma.

"No one follows the duties of one's own caste, and the four Dharms or stages of life also disappear. Every man and woman takes delight in revolting against the Vedas. The Brahmans sell the Vedas; the kings bleed their subjects; no one respects the injunction of the Vedas.

The right course for every individual is that which one takes a fancy to; a man of erudition is he who plays the braggart. Whoever launches spurious undertakings and is given over to hypocrisy, him does everyone call a saint. He alone is clever, who robs another of his wealth; he who puts up false appearances is an ardent follower of established usage. He who is given to lying and is clever at joking is spoken of as a man of parts in the Kali age. He alone who is a reprobate and has abandoned the path of the Vedas is a man of wisdom and dispassion in the Kali age. He alone who has grown big nails and long locks of matted hair is a renowned ascetic in the Kali age. (1-4)"

What went Wrong?: Swami Dayanand Saraswati (founder of Arya Samaj) has discussed this issue (downfall of Varna Dharma) very nicely in Satyarth Prakash and it states as:

"When the Brahmans became destitute of knowledge, there could be no talk of the ignorance of the Kshatriyas, Vaishyas and Shudras. Even the ancient practice of the study of the Vedas and other Shastras with their meanings died away. The Brahmans only learnt the Vedas by note-just enough to enable them to earn their livelihood. Even that much they did teach to the Kshatriyas, and others.

As the ignorant became the teachers of the people, deceitfulness, fraud, hypocrisy, and irreligion began to increase among them. The Brahmans thought that they should make some arrangement for their livelihood. They held a council among themselves and agreed to preach to the Kshatriyas and others: "We alone are the object of worship to you. You could never enter Heaven or obtain salvation except by serving us. Should you not serve us, you shall fall into an awful Hell."

The Vedas, and the Shastras written by the Vedic sages and seers have declared men of learning and as Brahmans and worthy of respect; but here they, who were ignorant, lascivious, deceitful, licentious, lazy and irreligious, declared themselves as Brahmans and worthy of homage. But how could the sterling virtues of the righteous, learned and truth-loving Brahmans be found in them. When the Kshatriyas and others became absolutely destitute of Sanskrit learning, whatever cock and bull stories the Brahmans concocted, the simpletons believed. They ensnared all in their net of hypocrisy, brought them under thorough control and began to teach:-"Whatever a Brahman declares is as infallible as words falling from Divine lips."

Conclusions: The most important issue in the understanding of Varna Dharma is to understand the definitions of the various Varnas as explained in Hindu scriptures. The rules of the groups prescribe the duties to society. The duties for various Varnas were based on the 'guna' of an individual and were dependent on the capacities of individuals. Therefore the division of labour, which broadly falls into 'the four orders of human beings' is based upon "guna and karma" of each individual.

> *"The complete definition of the Varna not only removes our present misunderstanding but also provides us with some data to understand its true significance. Not by mere birth is man a Brahmana (Brahmin); by cultivating good intentions and noble thoughts alone can we ever aspire to Brahmana-hood; nor can we pose as Brahmana merely because of our external physical marks, or bodily actions in the outer world. The definition insists that he alone is a Brahmana, whose thoughts are as much Sattvik, as his actions are. A Kshatriya is one who is Rajasik in his thoughts and actions. A Sudra is not only one whose thoughts are Tamasik, but he who lives a life of low endeavours, for satisfying his base animal passions and flesh-appetites. The scientific attitude in which this definition has been declared, is clear from the exhaustive implications of the statement: "According to the differentiation of 'guna' and 'karma'."*

As discussed earlier, there was no exclusion of any Varna to read Vedic Knowledge in the Veda. Later on restriction were put on people because of with Tamsic Guna. There was a structured and step-wise approach to learning which everyone was supposed to follow.

All Dwij's were following that system of learning. No Vedic knowledge was given even to Dwij's who do not follow the process of learning. With time this (not learning Vedas) became a rule in the society which led to consolidation of Vedic knowledge in very few peoples hand. If a tumbler is full of dirt, grease and other impurities, then it is an unfit receptacle for holding pure water. The mind is the container and if it is filled with Tamasic qualities, then it is an unfit receptacle for receiving pure spiritual knowledge.

> *"It is written in Chhandogya Upanishad that Gragee and other women of yore have read the Veda, and even Janshruti, a Sudra by birth, has studied the Veda under Raikyamuni" Satyarth Prakash, chapter 11.*

Brahma Sutras and Manu Smriti discuss that Sudras can not study Veda. But the important issue is to know who Sudra is. Why he can not study the Vedas. As explained in the section on "Inter-movement in Varna Dharma" section, when Sudra can become a Brahman then he has all the right to study the Veda. The restriction placed on the study of Vedas is because of absence of the process (character, capability, and/or prerequisite) to study the Vedas.

The issue is not whether Varna Dharma is based on birth or not, nor whether Brahmans are higher Varna than any other. These may be important but not sufficient. If Sudras are not Sudra by birth then Brahmans are not Brahmans by birth alone too. This must be an important aspect in the equation in any meaningful discussion about Varna Dharma.

There was no pecking order (higher or lower) in the society according to scriptures. Individuals were identified by their knowledge. The reverence given to a person in society (based on his knowledge) was a responsibility and not a privilege. All men are not equally wise or equally intelligent. Each one is trying to grapple with problems of life with whatever degree of wisdom each possesses. Hinduism provides for the highly evolved as well as those not so evolved or least evolved and even those not at all evolved in distinct categories of Brahimn, Kshatriya, Vaishya and Sudra with distinct Svadharma (assigned duties) suited to their individual state of evolution.

Realisation is not dependent on birth or book-learning as has been repeatedly demonstrated in the lives of saints, from the very earliest times to our own day (Comments by Swami Madhavananda, Advaita Ashrama).

> *"Who are Rishis? Vatsyayana says, He who has attained through proper means the direct realization of Dharma, he alone can be a Rishi even if he is a Mlechcha by birth"*

Many great Rishis were born in lower castes (e.g.) Vashishtha was the son of a prostitute; VYASA was born of a fisher woman; PARASARA's mother was a chandala; Nammalwar was a Sudra. Similarly Valmiki, Vishvamitra, Agastya were Brahmins inspite of their non-Brahmin origin. Swami Vivekananda is one of the most revered Hindu worldwide and was a non Brahmin. All these Hindus prove that birth was not a major player in attaining Brahminhood. It is the intellectual and spiritual level that differentiates people.

Swami Sivananda (The Divine Life Society, Rishikesh), in his commentary on Gita,Ch.18, verses 41,and 45 says: "Mankind is organised into the four castes and each man`s life is divided into four stages, according to the nature of the Gunas and the degree of growth or evolution. This is the division of labour for which each caste is fitted according to its own nature.

The duty prescribed is your sole support, each devoted to his own duty in accordance with his own nature or caste, and the highest service you can render to the Supreme is to carry it out wholeheartedly, without expectation of fruits, with the attitude of dedication to the Lord. The caste system is, indeed, a splendid thing. It is quite flawless. But the defect came in from somewhere else. The classes gradually neglected their duties. The test of ability and character slowly vanished. Birth became the chief consideration in determining castes. All castes fell from their ideals and forgot all about their duties."

Scriptures treated all the Varnas as same and none was higher than the other. And nobody belongs to any Varna by birth. Vajra Suchikopanishad clearly states that one cannot be a Brahmin either by its being, birth, physical equipment of body and colour or by wisdom and knowledge or by religious action even The basis of Varna was guna and not birth.

Vajra suchikopanishad of Sama Veda defines the word

Brahmin in most unambiguous terms thus: One is a Brahmin not because of his birth or caste or heredity or colour or profession or acquisition of worldly knowledge or mere observation of social and moral codes, but because of his spiritual knowledge, his abidance in the Supreme Reality, his state of self-realization.

This is the conclusion of all Veda, Srutis, Puranas, Itihasas and of all great men of India.

According to 'Guru Bala Prabodhika' a commentary on Amara Kosa, the ancient Sanskrit lexicon, a Brahmin is one who knows Brahman (Supreme God), not one who is borne into a caste. (Brahmin Parabrahmani nishtatwat Brahmana).

One of the main reasons for confusion about Varnas is that there is a vast amount of scriptures in the Hindu Dharma. People do not always know the order of the scriptures. Even when the order is known, the scriptures are not easily interpreted since all scriptures are written in Sanskrit. Even the people who can interpret the scriptures not necessarily understand them. The confusion is not what is written originally in Sanskrit but in the misunderstanding of the Sanskrit translations. The first issue in understanding of Varna Dharma is to understand the order of the scriptures. The Vedas are the ultimate authority in Hindu Dharma. The second issue is to understand that Varna Ashram is evolutionary in nature.

A key issue in understanding of Varna lies in knowledge of Sanskrit. There was and is no misunderstanding about Varnas as written in Sanskrit. The Varna Ashram started falling apart when the original Sanskrit work is translated in to English, especially by the people who do not have command over both languages (Sanskrit and English) and with limited knowledge about the scriptures. There are many words and terms in Sanskrit which have no equivalent in English language-Dharma and Varna are two examples. The closest meaning in English is a force fit and not necessarily the right choice. The right approach in understanding Vedic concepts starts with learning of Sanskrit. As Swami Sivananda said "Varnasrama pertains to body alone, but not to the pure, allpervading, immortal soul or Atman. Attain Knowledge of the Self and become an Ativarnasrami like Lord Dattatreya. Hear what he says:-

Mahadadi jagat sarvam

Na kinchit pratibhati me

Brahmaiva kevalam sarvam

Katham varnasramasthitih

"The whole world, from Mahat downwards, does not shine in Me. Everything is Brahman only. Where then is Varnasrama?"

Vedic Vocations

Rather coincidentally, at the dawn of civilization, as the people gathered and lived in clans or tribes (Visha), they collectively-irrespective of their undertakings within Visha (such as in agriculture, woodworking, trade and other vocations)-came to be known as the Vaishya (meaning-belonging to Visha).

To meet the liturgical needs of the society, the Vaishya-from among themselves-would select, on the basis of skills in elocution, the Brahmins (students or orators of the Vedas-compiled knowledge). Similarly, for administrative purposes, Vaishya with qualities of leadership would be selected as Kshatriya (sovereign, tribal chieftain, administrator of Kshatar-dominion or tribal area / town). Furthermore, a Visha (tribe)-in addition to having the Vaishyas (including Brahmins, Kshatriya, cowherders and woodworkers etc.)-also embodied people known as Shudra (meaning-not of tribe) representing all the newcomers (immigrants) to that particular tribe. They included persons from other tribes (such as the vanquished foes and the migrants) and the children born out of inter-tribal unions. Being somewhat new into that tribe and encountering unfamiliar rules, regulations and customs, a Shudra was limited in his vocational options and was generally relegated to providing service and assistance to members of the host tribe. But over time, like a modern day immigrant, he would surpass the tribal or social barriers so as to fully assimilate in that society and pursue other professions. Thus, all the responsibilities related to a Visha could be grouped into four sub-categories: Brahmin, Kshatriya, Vaishya and Shudra; the duties and skills involved with each of them are indicated in the following Sections.

Note also that, in old times, there was no concept of money or cash. People produced things and bartered (traded) them for other goods and services. A producer or trader belonging to Vaishya would include people such as farmer producing grains and milk etc., blacksmith (Lohar) making iron implements, leather-worker (Charmar or Chamar, charm meaning leather) manufacturing shoes, and so on.

Thus, for subsistence, a Brahmin would do worship (puja) in a 'Vaishya' farmer's house and get grains and milk in return. Similarly, a Chamar would exchange shoes for food items from a farmer, iron implements from a Lohar, and so on. Similarly, a 'Shudra' servant might work or help in a farmer's field for food in return. If he were to help a Lohar, then Lohar would provide him with food items. Moreover, all these people would give a share of their goods (produce) and services to the Kshatriya (tribal chief) for administration of Visha (tribe or society).

Society was basically managed through bartering system. As a part of God's creation (work), the four vocations are subgrouped according to people's guna (skills) and karma (assignments). Know that all work is for Him, even though He is beyond work, in Eternity. (Ch. 4-verse 13)

Ignorant men, but not the wise, say that Sankhya (variously as: Jnana Yoga, Sanyasa or Surrender, Path of Vision or Wisdom) and Yoga (variously as: Karma Yoga, Tyaga or Renunciation, Path of Action, Bhakti or devotional service, Japaa or Silence, Dhayana or Contemplation / Meditation, Brahamcharya or Austerity, Vaanprastha or Hermitlike) are different paths; but he who gives his self (soul) to one reaches the end of two. (Ch. 5-verse 4)

Even if the greatest sinner worships God with all his soul, he must be considered righteous because of his righteous will. (Ch. 9-verse 30)

And he shall soon become pure and reach everlasting peace. For this is His covenant that he who adores Him is not lost. (Ch. 9-verse 31)

God is one in all, but it seems as if he were many; He (as Vishnu / preserver) supports all beings: from Him (as Rudra / destroyer) ensues end, and from Him (as Brahma / creator) ensues beginning. (Ch. 13-verse 16)

The duties involving Brahmin, Kshatriya, Vaishya and Shudra are grouped according to people's abilities and skills. (Ch. 18-verse 41)

The skills for a Brahmin involve serenity, self-harmony, austerity and purity, loving-forgiveness and righteousness; vision, wisdom and faith. (Ch. 18-verse 42)

The qualities needed according to Kshatriya are: a heroic mind, splendor or inner fire, constancy, resourcefulness, courage in battle, generosity and noble leadership. (Ch. 18-verse 43)

Trade, agriculture and rearing of cattle may be tackled by Vaishya; and the background (tenure) of a Shudra is also suited to providing support (Ch. 18-verse 44)

People attain perfection when they find joy in their work. Hear how a person attains perfection and finds joy in his work. (Ch. 18-verse 45)

A person achieves perfection when his work is-performed with pure feeling of-worship of God, from whom all things come and who is in all. (Ch. 18-verse 46)

The words of vision and wisdom have been conveyed. Ponder them in the silence of your soul, and then in freedom do your will. (Ch. 18-verse 63)

Hindu Dharma (Hinduism): Hinduism is religion based on the Vedas, and also known as the Sanatan Dharma (eternal religion) or Vedic Dharma. In the Vedas, god Bhaga was the bestower of auspicious blessings. It soon became the power of goodness, and he who possessed this power was called Bhagvan. The religion associated with Bhagvan (or Bhagvat) was called Bhagvata Dharma.

Likewise, Indu (Soma-juice or nectar) used to be offered to God as libation in Vedic yajnas (worships), and consumed afterwards by people (Hindu) for health, life, prosperity and progeny. Hindu means as someone propitiated by Indu (the Vedic libation). Note, H—in Hindu, and pronounced as in hut—implies auspiciousness or delight.

Religion belonging to Hindu is called Hindu Dharma.

In response to the misconception that the word Hindu originated as some foreigners stepped into India, note that no one from outside could have come to India and started calling the locals Hindu suddenly if such a word (in Sanskrit—not those foreigners' language) had not already existed there. 'Hindu' also is not related to 'Sindhu'—a word with similar ending and meaning ocean or river, especially in the west of India.

The words Sindhu (ocean or river) and Hindu (expiated by Indu) are linguistically and phonetically different, and Hindu is not derived from Sindhu. Note that Vedic Sanskrit did use the letters (sounds) 's' and 'dh' and therefore would not replace them with 'h' and 'd', respectively, transforming Sindhu into Hindu. In addition, the ancient Greeks reaching India (circa Alexander the great) could have easily pronounced Sindhu without changing it to Hindu by dropping S in favour of H since they were used to pronounce Sigma (an alphabet in Greek, their mother-toungue) which is syllabically somewhat similar to Sindhu. Furthermore, Muslims entering India for the first time and speaking Arabic or Persian—languages having alphabets Sad and Sin etc. for 's' sounds—would not have to substitute H for S in Sindhu (and thus make it Hindu) to pronounce or use it in their own languages. The word Hindu—not specific to any particular region or area—was already in use when these foreigners arrived in India, and they did not invent it from Sindhu accidentally or due to necessity.

Women's Issues: It seems from the above that the ancient society was quite considerate and respectful to those (both men and women) engaged in various vocations, and people were free to make choices or changes in their careers or skills if the opportunity existed. Vedic prayers also indicate that the women had considerable say in selecting their marriage partners, and were espoused to live in monogamous relationships while enjoying same rights as their husbands. Furthermore, in the Vedas there is little evidence of child marriages, dowry system and the practice of suttee or sati (self-immolation of a woman upon her husband's death). Similarly, there is no indication of any stigma relating to widowhood or the remarriage of a widow. Note also that the well-educated, scholarly and charismatic women of yore, who also participated in many philosophical debates with men, included Gargi (the daughter of Vachaknu-from the Brihadaranyaka Upanishad) and Vidyottama (wife of the famed poet and writer, Kaalidasa, who started his life as a humble and menial worker in the woods). It is clear that the women or the lowly and humble in the society were neither ignored nor abandoned.

Listed below are a few examples of multi-vocational families and people changing their occupations and life styles.

(a) As indicated in the above, from the Rigveda, the mother of a bard (probably of the scriptures) was working in corn-grinding (an activity usually for a Shudra).

(b) Majority of the Rishis (sages) were both Brahmin and Kshatriya so as to manage their Aashramas (hermitages) effectively.

(c) In the Chandogya Upanishad, Satyakama (the illegitimate, varnasankra, son of a Shudra woman who did not even remember who her son's father was) went on to be accepted and educated for Brahmin work (the Gita: Ch. 18-verse 42). This shows that the people (including the Shudra and of unknown lineage) had the choice of pursuing any occupation (even that of a Brahmin).

(d) Valmiki (given to chanda-meaning impetuosity-in his early days) started life as a robber. But later in life, after performing penance, he studied to become a Brahmin. He went on to become a great Rishi (sage) and wrote the Ramayana in Sanskrit. Thus, going from being a chandaal (meaning-cruel and brutal person) to a great human being not only demonstrates his personal endeavour, but also that the society was quite accepting of such a process and its outcome. In general, as indicated here and in the Vedic passages, the concept of untouchability (with respect to the Shudra or any one else as a dalit / untouchable) did not exist. Any shunning or condemnation of a person was due mainly to his / her engaging in an activity not useful or acceptable to the society. Above all, it is also clear that any type of socially stigmatic situation could be easily improved through penance and by changing one's behaviour. Incidentally, this type of humane rehabilitation of criminals and sinners is a sign of civilized people long ago; and this humane practice exists even today in various countries claiming to be modern and civilized.

(e) In one of the stories from the Ramayana, Rishi Vishvamitra is said to have conducted Yajna (worship) at which the officiating priest was a once Kshatriya and the Yajamaan (worshipper) a Chandaal.

(f) In the Mahabharata, Satyavati (a Shudra-girl whose father was a fisherman), when presented with a marriage proposal from king Shantanu, married him only after he accepted her pre-nuptial agreement. Her own children, in stead of another older heir to the throne, went on to inherit the Kshatriya kingdom as was demanded in the pre-nuptial agreement. This indicates that the intercaste marriages and exchanges were quite prevalent; and that the women and Shudras could make free choices even when there was royalty involved.

(g) *Matrimonial and Vocational Choices:* The evolution of society and customs was mainly due to the individual and collective needs and choices (as indicated also in some of the above Vedic quotes on marriage, vocational activities etc.). In addition, the role and influence of various espoused or suggested proclamations such as involving the varnashrama dharma (casteo-monastic orders) etc.-based on non-scriptural (non-Vedic) writings (such as Manusmriti etc. accredited to Manu et al.)-on the development and progress of society at large (across-the-board) was rather insignificant.

The ancient society (generally modest and homogeneous economically) did not restrict the cross-caste matrimonial and occupational choices. In spite of the socially liberal conditions, though, the change in vocation did not always lead to significant economic gains. In addition, some vocations (e.g., Vaishya and Shudra) were inherently conducive for their young to quickly and easily engage in the family business / profession and settle down (socially and economically) early in life. Consequently, the children from these families found the other vocations (such as the Brahmins and, to some extent, the Kshatriya) to be less rewarding and not worth the preparatory effort, which included living and training (and paying the teacher through labour) for decades in hermitages in harsh and forest-like conditions where the knowledge exchange between the guru and the pupils was usually in the oral tradition since the written manuscripts (on papyrus etc.) were scarce. On the other hand, the children from the Brahmins and the Kshatriyas families were predisposed (through the natural and continuous exposure to the family business) and were readily inducted by their parents into their traditional professions. Over time, this type of selecting the professions inadvertently gave rise to the tradition of vocation based families all around even though the society had not sought such an outcome. Note that the society in this respect remained flexible and allowed people (including the Shudra, who also engaged in menial and ignoble pursuits) the freedom of choice in their undertakings.

In a similar and related context, it was deemed vocationally advantageous and convenient for a couple to marry if they both had the same background, because they would then be able to get involved in their family occupation quickly and easily without facing any uncertainty or requiring any additional apprenticeship. Moreover, the bride or the groom in this type of wedding arrangement would be less likely to encounter any unexpected, unfamiliar, inhospitable and unwanted post-marital social situations. Note also that, in addition to the weddings involving same type of families, the marriages among people from vastly different backgrounds also frequently took place (as in the case of Satyavati and Shantanu) and the society posed no restrictions.

Thus it was basically an arbitrary social custom which arose over time as a matter of convenience whereby the people stuck to their family professions and also married within same type of families (vocations). Note, the lack of relevant information available in print etc. probably also led to the guru-pupil based disciplic tradition for knowledge/spirituality which would otherwise be not as crucial. In any case, people (of any caste) desiring to not follow these customs or to break away from them simply should go on their own-without any fear of repercussions from the state, society or religion-to learn and pursue new vocations; and in the process they would also be able to find compatible and willing marriage partners for themselves within the society at large. Moreover (as regards to the Gita: Ch. 5-V. 18, Ch. 6-V. 9, Ch. 9-V. 32), the priests and temples that serve (cater to) and admit all (Brahmin, Kshatriya, Vaishya, Shudra including the disadvantaged or Dalit) should be accorded the greatest respect and support.

Illustration of the Rise of Sub-castes within Castes: As humans continued to create and adopt new occupations, move to new places and territories, or encounter unfamiliar surroundings and situations, the four primary vocations (castes: Brahmin, Kshatriya, Vaishya and Shudra) developed or transformed into several secondary sub-castes characterized by peoples' tasks etc. For example, vocationally speaking, if a person-while trying to become a Brahmin-learnt two Vedas, he would be called a Dwivedi, whereas the learner of three Vedas would be known as a Trivedi. It shows that titles (or sub-castes) as Dwivedi and Trivedi basically correspond to certain specific Brahminic pursuits.

Similarly, a Vaishya engaged in forming objects from loha (iron) would be called the Lohar, whereas, the maker of articles from sona (gold) would be called the Sonar. Moreover, if a Sonar's son pursued his father's occupation (business) and was followed by his son, and so on, it would give rise to a sub-caste (lineage) called Sonars within the Vaishya caste. Note that such preference or tradition for family business would occur for several reasons. First, the parents generally found it easy and safe to guide their young towards a familiar and time assured vocation. Second, the familiarity with parents' job made it easy for children to learn and practice that occupation. Third, it might probably help in attaining the familial stability and lead to an easy transfer of accumulated knowledge and expertise between generations.

The influence of migration on sub-castes can be similarly explored. Consider the following example. At some point in history, a certain inhabited area was to be inundated under a new dam and the people had to move and live elsewhere. As they settled in a new area, the locals there would address them as the Damiya (meaning-from the dam). Some of the newcomers might even prefer this new title to that they had before moving to the new place.

Moreover, when, for example, a newcomer (migrant or Shudra) started working as Mistree (mason), he would be called a Damiya-Mistree (a Vaishya-usually a person in non-priestly or non-administrative occupation). Similarly, if the person worked as a priest, he would be known as the Damiya-Brahmin. This indicates that the title 'Damiya' had suddenly acquired the status as a sub-caste. More importantly, note that two principal castes (Brahmin and Vaishya) had gained sub-castes with the same name (Damiya) with reference to totally different tasks (as priests and masons).

The above examples illustrate the manner in which the sub-castes are created and the way they relate to the principal castes. Note also that, depending on the circumstances, the newly created sub-castes may either co-exist with the original sub-castes, or replace some or all of the latter.

This surely can lead to drastic fluctuations in their numbers. As this process of creating and retaining of sub-castes occurs time and again over vast places and cultures, their numbers remain uncertain and alter frequently making it difficult to keep track of them. Nonetheless, the sub-castes are functional in character and subject to easy transformations.

Vedic/Hindu Tenets: The ancients were in favour of progressive ideas (e.g., about the environment, philosophy / religion and life style) and appear to have conducted their affairs reasonably and democratically. They either shunned or actively opposed the stagnant, blind and baseless practices (rituals) and the intolerant / autocratic persons and beliefs (faiths). The rituals for invocations of the physical, imagery (tales / myths) and the mundane were deemed less rewarding than the meditation of the spiritual, the source (truth / logic) and the divine; (meditation is explained in Ch. 6 of the Gita). Note that the reality expressed in terms of various physical (artistic) forms or through poetry can have different interpretations. For example, in some of the ancient texts, a viman may just be a cart or chariot and not necessarily an airplane or sky-craft.

While considering chatur as four (and bhuj meaning arm, and mukh meaning face or mouth), chatur-bhuj and chatur-mukh are shown as four-armed and four-faced idols. In stead, consider for example, chatur as the skilled one: chatur-bhuj and chatur-mukh will then represent, anthropomorphically (like a human with a face and two arms), a god (deva: friendly and blissful, superior being) who is skilled-armed (or ambidextrous: probably in all the occupations) and skilled-orator (i.e., a fine instructor).

Thus, chatur-bhuj and chatur-mukh are, respectively, symbols of the omnipotence and the omniscience of One God, or reflect His excellence in enterprise (as Vishnu) and instruction (as Brahma). God is One: Braham or BRAHMAN (not the Brahmin caste). When He (as Atman) enters the body (or as spirit unites with nature), life begins, and He is called Brahma. As long as He stays in the body, the life continues, and He is seen as preserving it and is called Vishnu.

Once He leaves the body, life ends (or body expires); and His departure is seen as if He has worked as Rudra in bringing an end to life. But, throughout, He remains One: Brahma, Vishnu and Rudra are only His aspects of creation, preservation and termination.

Thus, in regard to man-made symbols for displaying various Divine attributes for the purposes of worship and meditation etc., there should be some correspondence between the attribute and the symbol.

For example, if omnipotent God is to be represented 'as meaning Vishnu' in human form, it is sufficient and logical to interpret chatur (in chatur-bhuj) as skilled (even as ambidextrous) in all the tasks. Similarly, if omniscient God is to be represented 'as meaning Brahma' in human form, it is sufficient and logical to interpret chatur (in chatur-mukh) as skilled in oratory and knowledge. Thus, there is no need to interpret chatur as four in chatur-bhuj or chatur-mukh; and hence it is unnecessary to assume or create various four-headed and four-armed religious symbols for representing God anthropomorphically. Incidentally, note of the Gita, Arjun-after having realized vision of the Omnipresent encompassing all Creation-wishes (verse 46) to see the lord (mentor) in chatur-bhuj form (holding scepter and circle), which seems to refer only to latter's dexterity.

And Arjun's wish is soon fulfilled (Ch. 11-V. 50) as he is able to see Krishan as a regular (normal looking) person, and there is no suggestion anywhere that the former had an encounter with anyone bearing four arms.

Metaphorically speaking, Shiv-Linga (or Shiv-Lingam) refers only to Shiva-the remover of destruction, i.e., same as the preserver (Vishnu or God), and it necessarily is not a certain special symbol (e.g., shown often in pollex or index form); because in Linga (or Lingam), the word Li (which in second or Object case singular form becomes Lim or Lin with nasal sound ending) means loss or destruction, and ga (or gam) implies removing or going away. Thus, Shiv-Linga (or Shiv-Lingam) symbolizes God's power (attribute) to extricate from destruction or loss.

In this regard, the symbols dedicated to Agni (or Shiv, God) should also correspond to logic and not just to myth or fiction. The identification of Agni symbol (i.e., jwala, or Agni-ling: ling meaning symbol) as a phallus is perhaps due to the confusion that their shapes are similar. Note that the early humans were praying and worshipping for everything.

They also prayed to God for children (heroes, sons). In this regard, religiously and psychologically, the Agni symbol 'looking like phallus' became the favourite idol. Unfortunately, over time, people forgot about its association with Agni, and identified it only in terms of biology and procreation. (Note: Since Shiva refers also to the auspicious flame or Agni-jwala, Agni-ling or a similar looking object probably was referred to as Shiv-ling.)

SALVATION, KARMA, REINCARNATION AND METAMORPHOSIS

It was realized long ago that, irrespective of one's background, attaining the immortality or overcoming the death (or the fear of it) is in understanding oneself (individual life or being)-the union between soul (spirit-real, sat or eternal) and body (matter-unreal, asat or transient)-as part of the Supreme (stated also in Ch. 2, 6, 7 & 9 of the Bhagawad Gita). Symbolically, therefore (as stated in Ch. 8 of the Gita), following the path (or going in the time) of clarity (as in the light of day or the sun) about the self is liberating (Ch. 6); whereas, following the path (or going in the time) of confusion (as in the darkness of night or the moon) about the self brings nothing but fear (morbidity). It is worth noting (the Gita: Ch. 6-verse 45) that, whatever a person's social status or civic duty, the spiritual gains derived from all efforts for achieving the union of one with the One are imminent and cumulative.

In this context, the Karmic principle (i.e., a good or bad action leads to a good or bad outcome) is assumed to influence the course of events taking place during this life and, supposedly, afterwards. Accordingly, each experience or action by a person affects him in body* and soul in the next situation or future. Each experience itself is a life/Janma: its beginning and end symbolically being birth and death. Moreover, according to the Karmic principle, even when the body dies, the soul continues to live and may feel the residual effect of the preceding existence.

The reincarnation therefore symbolically represents the extension of this principle during the hereafter. It is, in other words, a new opportunity or promise to accrue spiritual gains on the basis of actions during previous life. Note also that reincarnation merely presents to a person a new possibility (opportunity) arising out of countless influences, and, depending upon the new surroundings (people, environment etc.) and the future actions by the individual himself, it may or may not fully materialize (the Gita: Ch. 18-verse 14). For example, as indicated above, even though Satyakama started as a Shudra (in a non-Brahmin vocation), he went on, through his own initiative and effort and with the help of his guru, to acquire new skills to become a Brahmin (the profession of choice for him). Thus, reincarnation-being associated with the soul-appears to be unimportant with regards to the worldly pursuits such as involving vocations (castes) etc. Similarly, salvation (Moksha)-which also relates to the soul-is achievable by all (irrespective of their background), and can be easily attained by uniting (elevating) one's soul with God by practicing good deeds and penance etc. The Gita, to this end, states in response to a query in regarding the rituals to ancestors-that God's grace and the good deeds by a person during his own lifetime are important to seek salvation.

The supposed metamorphoses of God as Ram and Krishan etc., heroes of the early civilizations (in epics Ramayana and Mahabharata etc.), should be taken in spiritual/moralistic/philosophical context. The reverence (mainly ritualistic or for a reward) to them-dedicated according to their physical eminence and existence, and based primarily on the stories which appear to be skewed over time into myths/tales (Pauranic etc.)-thus needs to reduce. Note that God alone is deemed worthy of all worships (the Gita: Ch. 9-V. 24, Chs. 10 & 4) since all the eminence and creation—including even all the gods and goddesses associated with various places, times or events—are ultimately due to Him. Incidentally, when Krishna speaks in the Gita, he is not only speaking as a friend (well-wisher) and charioteer (worker and assistant) of Arjuna, but he is also advising Arjuna in the capacity of a guru. Above all, in essence, Krishna also is both BRAHMAN (Iswara) and Atman in the Gita.

Note also in this regard that the notion of a personal God sometimes results in a very informal devotee-deity relationship. The devotee often uses various preferred salutations, representations and rituals (worships and offerings) to express his unique love and reverence towards the 'kind and caring' deity. But, when many people engaging in this manner-in their own special ways of worships, etc., are viewed collectively, their society is seen to be overly ritualistic and following many gods, even though, in reality the ultimate object of reverence remains One. (Note, the Gita: Ch. 9-V. 26).

CONCLUSION

The vocational choice long ago was mainly need-based (personal and tribal) and circumstantial (in terms of the availability of labour at a place or time, natural disasters and battles among tribes). It inspired that the societal tasks and responsibilities be dispensed solely in terms of a person's nature or qualification (Guna) and his active undertaking or assignment (Karma). It was a great vision at work that is referred to also in the Bhagawad Gita (as in the original Sanskrit verse 13 of Ch. 4, where the reference is made only to Guna-nature / qualification, and it does not mean born nature). Incidentally, the original vocations seem to have been similar to the present jobs that also require compatibility between the worker's qualifications and the potential assignment.

Inherently, the above system satisfied one and the all. The Gita (Ch. 18-verse 41) further elaborates that all occupations are important and correspond to various needs or segments of the society and are dispensed according to ability (svabhava) on the basis (prabhva) of qualification (guna; which does not mean born nature). The duties relating to each adopted vocation (as explained in the above Introduction: Brahmin, Kshatriya, Vaishya, Shudra) are also listed in the Gita (Ch. 18-verses 42, 43 & 44). It is also indicated in the Gita (Ch. 5-verse 4) that all spiritual paths are applicable and bring same results to people with different vocations. The Gita (Ch. 16 & 18) stresses that, while it is of utmost importance to recognize and adhere to one's own responsibility or the task at hand, there is no other special advantage or basis (in terms of ritualism or one's heredity) for pursuing a particular undertaking. A socially necessary and useful activity for the physical well-being of person is as important as any worship/puja for his/her salvation (The Gita: Ch. 3-verse 8). The Gita (Ch. 3-verse 35) further notes that taking care of one's own responsibility (purpose/ dharma) merits higher than venturing needlessly elsewhere, since keeping one's own obligation (even in a miniscule way) leads to satisfaction that outweighs the trappings, uncertainty and formidableness associated with another's task. It is also stated in the Gita (Ch. 12, Ch. 18-verses 45 & 46) that, no matter what a person's duty or task (whether shubh-appealing, or ashubh-unappealing), he attains perfection or heavenly bliss if he is fully dedicated to it and performs it with pleasure and interest as if it were a service to the Lord (Transcendent or the Manifest). Lord, God or Hari (Saviour) is expressed (Ch. 17) divinely (in accordance with tattva**) as OM TAT SAT (Creator, Master and the Righteous). (Creation seems to arise from OM during contemplation as the omniscient, TAT is what maintains it through omnipotence, and it has the noble and righteous end according to SAT.) Note also that God is one, yet He can manifest in more ways than one (Ch. 4 & 9); and He dwells in the heart of all (Ch. 18). He is One in all (stated above; the Gita: Ch. 13-verse 16). In addition, one need not be preoccupied about the hereafter (or the heaven and the hell) as long as he understands the good from the bad (Ch. 16 of the Gita) and the redemption (spiritual) through penance (monetarily free and as stated in the Gita.

BIBLIOGRAPHY

Atal, Yogesh: *The Changing Frontiers of Caste*, Delhi, National Publishing House, 1968.

Ayrookuzhiel, A. M. Abraham: *The Dalit Desiyata: The Kerala Experience in Development and Class Struggle*, Delhi, ISPCK, 1990.

Beteille, Andre.: *The Backward Classes and the New Social Order*, Oxford University Press, Delhi, 1981.

Bhagwat, Vidyut: *Dalit Women in India: Issues and Perspectives - Some Critical Reflections*, New Delhi, Gyan Publishing House, 1995.

Bhai, P. N.: *Harijan Women in Independent India,* B. R. Publishing, New Delhi, 1986.

Blunt, E. A. H. *Caste System of Northern India*, London, Oxford University Press, 1931.

Bondurant, J.: *Harijan: A Journal of Applied Journalism, 1933-35*, Garland, New York, 1973.

Bose, N. K.: *The Scheduled Castes and Tribes and Their Present Conditions*, Calcutta, University of Calcutta, 1969.

Busi, Subhamani N.: *Mahatma Gandhi and Babasaheb Ambedkar: Crusaders Against Caste and Untouchability*, Andhra Pradesh: Saroja Publications, Hyderabad, 1997.

Chatterjee, Partha: *Caste and Subaltern Consciousness*, Delhi, Oxford Unviersity Press, 1994.

Cohan, B. N.: *The Changing Status of a Depressed Class*, Chicago, The University of Chicago Press, 1955.

Dangle, Arjun: *Poisoned Bread: Translations from Modern Marathi Dalit Literature*, New Delhi, Orient Longman, 1992.

Deshpande, Vasant: *The Mhaisal Untouchables*, Pune, Dastane Ramchandra & Co., 1983.

Dumont, Louis: *The Caste System and Its Implications*, London, Granada Pub. Ltd., 1970.

Freeman, James M.: *Untouchable : An Indian Life History*, CA, Stanford University Press, 1979.

Ganesan, L.: *Relevance of Reservation*, Madras, Valentina Publications, 1991.

Gorringe, H.: *Untouchable Citizens : Dalit Movements and Democratization in Tamil Nadu*, Delhi, Sage Publications, 2005.

Gough, Kathleen: *Harijans in Thanjavur*, New York, Monthly Review Press, 1973.

Goyal, Bhagat Ram: *Educating Harijans*, Haryana, Academic Press, 1981.

Hutton, J. H.: *Caste in India: Its Nature, Function and Origins*, London, Cambridge University Press, 1946.

Jaffrelot, Christopher: *Dr. Ambedkar and Untouchability: Fighting the Indian Caste System*, New York, Columbia University Press, 2005.

Joshi, Barbara R.: *Untouchable! Voices of the Dalit Liberation Movement,* London, Zed Books, 1986.

Juergensmeyer, Mark: *Religion as Social Vision: The Movement Against Untouchability in 20th Century Punjab*, University of California Press, Berkeley, 1979.

Kamble, N. D.: *Deprived Castes and their Struggle for Equality*, Ashish Publishing House, New Delhi, 1983.

Kananaikil, Jose: *Constitutional Provisions for the Scheduled Castes*, New Delhi, Indian Social Institute, 1984.

Kavlekar, K.K.: *Non-Brahmin Movement in Southern India. 1873-1949,* Kolhapur, Shivaji University, 19790

Khan, Mumtaz Ali: *Identity Formation and Self Identity Among Harijan Elite*, New Delhi, Uppal Publishing House, 1994.

Kinsley, D.: *Hindu Goddesses. Vision of the Divine Feminine in the Hindu Religious Tradition*, Delhi, Motilal Banarsidass, 1987.

Kosambi, D. D.: *The Culture and Civilisation of Ancient India in Historical Outline*, London, Routledge and Kegan Paul, 1956.

Lakshmanna, C.: *Caste Dynamics in Village India*, Nachiketa Publications, Bombay, 1973.

Liddle, J., and Joshi, R. : *Daughters of Independence: Gender, Caste, and Class in India.* NJ, Rutgers University Press, 1986.

Luke, P.Y. & Carmen, J.B.: *Village Christians and Hindu Culture: Study of a Rural Church in Andhra Pradesh, South India*, London, Lutterworth Press, 1968.

Massey, James: *People: Dalits - Dalit Issues in Today's Theological Debate,* Delhi, Indian Society for Promoting Christian Knowledge (ISPCK), 1994.

Mayer, A.: *Caste in an Indian Village: Change and Continuity 1954-1992*, Delhi, OUP, 1996.

Mishra, J.: *Equality vs Justice. The Problem of Reservations for Backward Classes,* New Delhi, Deep & Deep, 1996.

Mitter, Sara S.: *Dharma's Daughters: Contemporary Indian Women and Hindu Culture,* NJ, Rutgers University Press, 1991.

Naidu, A. Nagaraja: *Caste and Land in Colonial South India*, Rawat Publications, New Delhi, 1994.

Narayan, K.: *Storytellers, Saints, and Scoundrels*, Philadelphia, University of Pennsylvania Press, 1989.

Nath, Trilok: *Politics of the Depressed Classes*, Delhi, Deputy Publications, 1987.

Nirmal, Arvind P.: *Towards A Common Dalit Ideology,* Madras, Gurukul Lutheran Theological College and Research Institute, 1990.

Oddie, G.A.: *Hindu and Christian in South-East India*, London, Curzon Press, 1991.

Omvedt, Gail: *Dalit Visions: The Anti-Caste Movement and the Construction of an Indian Identity*, New Hyderabad, Orient Longman Ltd., 1995.

Omvedt, Gail: *Land, Caste and Politics in Indian States,* Authors Guild Publications, Delhi, 1982.

Patnaik, Nitayananda: *Caste and Social Change: An Anthropological Study of Three Orissa Villages*, National Institute of Community Development, Hyderabad, 1969.

Patwardhan, Sunanda: *Change Among India's Harijans: Maharashtra a Case Study*, New Delhi, Orient Longmans, 1973.

Prabhavathi, M.: *Dalit Women in India: Issues and Perspectives,* New Delhi, Gyan Publishing House, 1995.

Punekar, S.M.: *Harijan Contribution to Medieval Thought*, Prasaranga, Bangalore University, Bangalore, 1991.

Quigley, D.: *The Interpretation of Caste*, Cambridge, CUP, 1993.

Raheja, G.G.: *The Poison in the Gift. Ritual, Prestation and the Dominant Caste in a North Indian Village*, Chicago, University of Chicago Press, 1988.

Rao, Hemlata and Babu, M. Devendra: *Scheduled Castes and Tribes: Socio-Economic Upliftment Programmes*, Ashish Publishing House, New Delhi, 1994.

Robb, Peter: *Dalit Movements and the Meanings of Labour in India*, New Delhi, Oxford University Press, 1993.

Satyamurthy, T.V.: *Region, Religion, Caste, Gender and Culture in Contemporary India*, Delhi, OUP, 1996.

Shukla, K. S. and Verma, B. M.: *Development of Scheduled Castes and Administration*, New Delhi, Uppal Publishing House, 1993.

Tripathi, R. S. and Tiwari, P. O.: *Dimensions of Scheduled Caste Development in India*, Uppal Publishing House, New Delhi, 1991.

Tripathy, R. B.: *Dalits: A Sub-Human Society*, New Delhi, Ashish Publishing House, 1994.

Venkateshwarlu, D.: *Harijan-Upper Class Conflicts*, Discovery, New Delhi, 1990.

Webster, John: *The Christian Dalits: A History,* Delhi, Indian Society for Promoting Christian Knowledge (ISPCK), 1994.

Zakaria, Rafiq: *Gandhi and the Break-up of India*, Bharatiya Vidya Bhavan, Mumbai, 1999.

INDEX

I

J

K

L

M

N

O

P

◆◆◆